HEATH DISCOVERING FRENCH

PREMIÈRE PARTIE

BLEU

Jean-Paul Valette
Rebecca M. Valette

McDougal Littell
Evanston, Illinois • Boston • Dallas

Teacher Consultants

Sue Arandjelovic, *Dobson High School, Arizona*
Kay Dagg, *Washburn Rural High School, Kansas*
Olga Davis, *G. H. Englesby Junior High School, Massachusetts*
Tina Dietrich, *Washington Junior High School, Ohio*
Rosine Gardner, *Newcomb Central School, New York*
Andrea Henderson, *First Colony Middle School, Texas*
Bill Price, *Day Junior High School, Massachusetts*
T. Jeffrey Richards, *Roosevelt High School, South Dakota*
Margie Ricks, *Dulles High School, Texas*
Valerie Sacks, *Britton Middle School, California*

McDougal Littell wishes to express its heartfelt appreciation to **Gail Smith**, Supervising Editor for *DISCOVERING FRENCH*. Her creativity, organizational skills, determination and sheer hard work have been invaluable in all aspects of the program, including the award winning *DISCOVERING FRENCH* CD-ROM.

Illustrations

Yves Calarnou
Jean-Pierre Foissy
Élisabeth Schlossberg

Printed in the United States of America
International Standard Book Number: 0-395-86655-3

2 3 4 5 6 7 8 9 0 – VHP – 02 01 00 99 98

Lycée Jean-Baptiste Corot

MERCI

Special thanks to the students and staff of
• **Collège Eugène Delacroix,** *Paris*
• **Lycée Jean-Baptiste Corot,** *Savigny-sur-Orge*
for their cooperation and assistance.

Collège Eugène Delacroix

Contents

Rentrée des classes
6^{em} → Lundi 10 Septembre à 9^H
(pas de cours l'après.midi)
5e-4e-3e → Lundi 10 Septembre
à 14^H

v

vi

xi

Parlons français!

Chers amis,

Welcome to DISCOVERING FRENCH and congratulations on your choice of French as a foreign language!

There are many reasons why people decide to learn French. Some people choose French because they plan to visit Canada or Europe or French-speaking Africa. Others want to learn to read articles or books written in French. Still others study French because in their work, they will come into contact with French speakers or because their own family is of French or French-American heritage. And there are many people who learn French for pleasure: They want to enjoy French films and French music, and they like French poetry and French art.

There is another reason for studying French that you have perhaps not thought about. As you learn another language, you develop a better understanding of your own language and how it works. You also develop a better appreciation of your own country and culture as you expand your world view and discover the various French-speaking areas of the globe. You will discover cultural similarities and differences, and you will realize how much French civilization has contributed to our life in the United States.

And, of course, everyone will agree that studying a foreign language also helps us get to know and communicate with people from other cultures. By speaking French, you will be in touch with the many millions of people who use that language in their daily lives. These French speakers **(les francophones)** represent a wide variety of ethnic and cultural backgrounds. As you will see, they live not only in France and other parts of Europe but also in Africa, in North and South America, in Asia . . . in fact, on all continents!

On the pages of this book and in the accompanying video and CD-ROM Discovering French Interactive, you will meet many young people who speak French. Listen carefully to what they say and how they express themselves. They will help you understand not only their language but also the way they live.

Bonne chance!

Jean-Paul Valette   Rebecca M. Valette

Bienvenue!

Je m'appelle Jean-Paul.

Je m'appelle Nathalie.

Je m'appelle François.

Bonjour!

Je m'appelle David.

Salut!

Je m'appelle Dominique.

Je m'appelle Marc.

Bonjour, les francophones!

The people portrayed on these pages represent many different backgrounds. Some live in France, some in the United States. They are from Europe, Africa, Asia, and North America. They do, however, have one thing in common. They all speak French. Let's meet them.

1

Sophie Lafont, 14, is from Toulouse, a city in southern France. She is a student at the Lycée Saint-Exupéry. (A **lycée** is the equivalent of an American high school.)

2

Philippe Martin, 15, lives in Paris and goes to the Collège Eugène Delacroix.

3

Stéphanie Malle, 14, also lives in Paris and attends the Collège Eugène Delacroix. Her family is from Martinique, a French island in the Caribbean.

4

Ahmed Belkacem, 14, lives in Lyon, France, and goes to the Lycée Jean Moulin. His parents are from Algeria and speak French and Arabic. Ahmed, who was born in France, speaks only French.

5

Fredy Vansattel, 20, lives near Lausanne, a city in French-speaking Switzerland. He is a student at the well-known École Hôtelière. In addition to French, Fredy also speaks English and German.

6

Prak Maph, 15, left Cambodia with his family when he was four. He lives in Paris and goes to the Lycée Claude Monet. Maph speaks French as well as Khmer, the national language of Cambodia.

7

Amélan Konan, 13, lives in Abidjan, a large city in Ivory Coast, a country of West Africa. Amélan goes to the Collège Moderne Voltaire, where many of the teachers are from France. Amélan is fluent in both French and Baoulé, the tribal language that she speaks with her relatives.

8

Pauline Lévêque, 14, is from Quebec City in the province of Quebec, in Canada. Pauline goes to the École Louis-Jolliet. She speaks both French and English, but she prefers to speak French with her friends and family.

9

Moustapha Badid is a French athlete of North African origin who lives in Paris. At age 23, he won the wheelchair title at the Boston Marathon and established a world record in the event. In that same year, he also won an Olympic gold medal. He speaks French, Arabic, and some English.

10

Dr. Michèle Klopner, a clinical psychologist, grew up in Haiti, where her family resides. She came to the United States to study at the University of Michigan and Rutgers University. Dr. Klopner speaks French, Haitian Creole, and English. She uses all these languages in her work at the Cambridge Hospital in Cambridge, Massachusetts.

11

Marie-Christine Mouis was born in Canada of a French father and a Canadian mother. At the age of 16, Marie-Christine joined the Paris Opera Ballet, becoming the youngest dancer in the world's oldest ballet company. She was the principal ballerina of the Boston Ballet for ten years.

12

Dr. Larry Phan was born in Vietnam. At the age of ten, he went to France, where he received his high school education. In 1976, he came to the United States to pursue a medical career. He attended the University of California and Tufts School of Dental Medicine. Dr. Phan is on the staff of the Children's Hospital in Boston.

ACTIVITÉS CULTURELLES

1. On a world map or globe, locate the cities and countries of origin for each of the people pictured.
2. Do you know any people in your community who have French names or people who speak French? Where are their families originally from?

Bonjour, le monde français!

*I*n today's world, French is an international language spoken daily by more than 100 million people. French is understood by another 100 million in many countries and regions of the globe.

IN NORTH AMERICA

■ In Canada, about one third of the population speaks French. These French speakers live mainly in the province of Quebec **(le Québec)**. They are descendants of French settlers who came to Canada in the 17th and 18th centuries.

■ In the United States, French is understood and spoken in many families whose French and French-Canadian ancestors came to Louisiana **(la Louisiane)** and New England **(la Nouvelle-Angleterre)** at various times in our history.

■ In the Caribbean, French and Creole are spoken in the Republic of Haiti **(Haïti)**. French is also spoken on the islands of Martinique **(la Martinique)** and Guadeloupe **(la Guadeloupe)**; the inhabitants of these two islands are French citizens.

IN OTHER PARTS OF THE WORLD

■ French is spoken as far away as Tahiti **(Tahiti)** and New Caledonia **(la Nouvelle-Calédonie)**, two French territories in the South Pacific.

■ In the Middle East, French is still taught and spoken in Lebanon **(le Liban)**.

■ French is also used and understood by many Vietnamese and Cambodian families who have left their countries **(le Viêt-nam, le Cambodge)** to settle in other parts of the world.

LE CANADA
LE QUÉBEC
AMÉRIQUE DU NORD
SAINT-PIERRE-ET-MIQUELON
LES ÉTATS-UNIS
LA NOUVELLE-ANGLETERRE
LA LOUISIANE
HAÏTI
OCÉAN ATLANTIQUE
AMÉRIQUE CENTRALE
LA GUADELOUPE
LA MARTINIQUE
LA GUYANE FRANÇAISE
OCÉAN PACIFIQUE
équateur
AMÉRIQUE DU SUD
TAHITI
LA POLYNÉSIE FRANÇAISE

French is the most important language

Some French is spoken

IN EUROPE

French is not only spoken in France **(la France)** but also in parts of Belgium **(la Belgique)**, Switzerland **(la Suisse)**, and Luxembourg **(le Luxembourg)**.

IN AFRICA

French is an important language in countries which have strong commercial and cultural ties to France.

■ In Western and Central Africa, about 20 countries have adopted French as their official language.

These countries include Senegal **(le Sénégal)**, the Ivory Coast **(la Côte d'Ivoire)**, and Zaire **(le Zaïre)**. French is also spoken on the large island of Madagascar **(Madagascar)**.

■ In North Africa, French is understood and spoken by many people of Algeria **(l'Algérie)**, Morocco **(le Maroc)**, and Tunisia **(la Tunisie)**. More than two million people from these countries have emigrated to France and have become French citizens.

ACTIVITÉS CULTURELLES

1. Name at least six African countries where French is spoken. Find out the capital of each country. (Source: atlas, encyclopedia)
2. Collect clippings from newspapers and magazines in which a French-speaking country is mentioned. Try to find one clipping for each of the areas on the map.

NOTE: You may also wish to refer to the reference map of the French-speaking world on pages R2–R3.

Bonjour, la France!

L'ANGLETERRE

LA BELGIQUE

Lille

la Manche

LE LUXEMBOURG

L'ALLEMAGNE

Rouen

LA NORMANDIE

Paris

la Seine

Strasbourg

L'ALSACE

LA BRETAGNE

l'océan Atlantique

Nantes

Tours

LA TOURAINE

la Loire

LA SUISSE

LA FRANCE

Lyon

Château d'Azay-le-Rideau, Touraine

Grenoble

L'ITALIE

Bordeaux

aerospatiale

le Rhône

les Alpes

la Garonne

LA PROVENCE

Nice

MONACO

Toulouse

Marseille

Toulon

les Pyrénées

la Méditerranée

LA CORS

L'ESPAGNE

Les Pyrénées

Eguisheim, Alsace

Les Alpes, Chamonix

Menton, Côte d'Azur

*B*efore starting your study of French, you may be interested in learning a few facts about France.

■ In area, France is the second-largest country in Western Europe.

■ Economically, France is one of the most developed countries of the world with a sophisticated high-tech industry.

■ France is the only European country with a space exploration program. French communication satellites provide 400 million Europeans with direct TV transmission.

■ France is a country with a strong cultural tradition. French philosophers, writers, and artists have influenced our ways of thinking and looking at the world.

■ France has a long history reaching back through Roman times into distant prehistory.

■ Geographically, France is a very diversified country with the highest mountains in Europe **(les Alpes et les Pyrénées)** and an extensive coastline along the Atlantic **(l'océan Atlantique)** and the Mediterranean **(la Méditerranée)**.

■ France consists of many different regions which have maintained their traditions, their culture, and—in some cases—their own language. Some of the traditional provinces are Normandy and Brittany **(la Normandie et la Bretagne)** in the west, Alsace **(l'Alsace)** in the east, Touraine **(la Touraine)** in the center, and Provence **(la Provence)** in the south.

ACTIVITÉS CULTURELLES

1. Find the countries which have a common border with France. What are their capitals? (Source: atlas, encyclopedia)
2. Imagine that you are spending a year in France. Where would you go if you wanted to ski in the winter? Which provinces would you want to visit in the summer if you wanted to swim in the Atlantic? in the Mediterranean? Are there any particular parts of France you would like to explore?

NOTE: You may also wish to refer to the reference map of France on page R4.

*B*onjour! Je m'appelle ...

Here is a list of some traditional French names. As you begin your study of the French language, you may want to "adopt" a French name from the list.

Alain	Geoffroy	Mathieu
Albert	Georges	Michel
André	Grégoire	Nicolas
Antoine	Guillaume	Olivier
Bernard	Henri	Patrick
Bertrand	Jacques	Paul
Charles	Jean	Philippe
Christophe	Jean-Claude	Pierre
Daniel	Jean-François	Raoul
David	Jean-Louis	Raymond
Denis	Jean-Paul	Richard
Dominique	Jérôme	Robert
Édouard	Joseph	Roger
Éric	Julien	Samuel
Étienne	Laurent	Simon
François	Marc	Thomas
Frédéric		

Sylvie

Alice

Alain

Jean-Paul

Éric

Laure

Olivier

Alice Éléonore Marthe
Andrée Élisabeth Michèle
Anne Émilie Monique
Anne-Marie Florence Nathalie
Barbara Françoise Nicole
Béatrice Hélène Patricia
Brigitte Isabelle Pauline
Caroline Jeanne Rachel
Catherine Judith Renée
Cécile Juliette Rose
Charlotte Karine Sophie
Christine Laure Stéphanie
Claire Lise Suzanne
Corinne Louise Sylvie
Delphine Lucie Thérèse
Denise Marguerite Véronique
Diane Marie Virginie
Dominique Marie-Christine

Jean? *Guillaume?* *Georges?*
Henri? *Philippe?* *François?*
Jacques? *Charles?* *Michel?*
Sébastien? *Gérard?* *Paul?*
Jean-Paul? *Pierre?* *Marc?*
Lucien? *Jean-Pierre?* *Luc?*
André?

Nathalie

Faisons

Bonjour et bienvenue!

Bonjour!

Hello and welcome, as you begin your study of French. The title of the first part of your French program is **Faisons connaissance!** *Let's get acquainted!*

What are some of the kinds of things you would like to learn to say in French? Well, when you meet new French friends, you will want to tell them about yourself: your name, your hometown, your family, your friends. And you will want to find out some of the same information about them.

So, as you begin your study of French, here are some of the things that you will be learning:

- how to greet people
- how to introduce yourself and say where you are from
- how to talk about yourself, your family, and your friends
- how to give your age and ask your friends how old they are

You will also learn expressions that will be useful when you travel to a French-speaking country, for example:

- how to count to 100
- how to ask about the weather
- how to tell time
- how to give the date
- how to order something to eat or drink in a café, and how to ask for the check

And now . . . **En avant!** *Let's begin!*

Jean-Paul Valette   Rebecca M. Valette

INTRODUCTION
culturelle

Salutations *(Greetings)*

How do you greet people in the United States? You may nod or smile. With adults, you may shake hands when you are introduced for the first time.

   In France, people shake hands with friends and acquaintances each time they see one another, and not only to say hello but also when they say good-bye. Among teenagers, boys shake hands with boys. Girls kiss each other on the cheeks two or three times. (This is called **une bise**). Boys and girls who are close friends also greet each other with **une bise.**

Getting acquainted

In this unit, you will be meeting French people.

You will learn . . .
- to say hello and good-bye
- to introduce yourself and say where you are from

You will also learn . . .
- to count to 60
- to tell time

La rentrée

This is the first day of school. Students are greeting their friends and meeting new classmates.

Bonjour! Je m'appelle Philippe.

Et moi, je m'appelle Stéphanie.

«
—Bonjour! Je m'appelle Philippe.
—Et moi, je m'appelle Stéphanie.
»

Je m'appelle Marc. Et toi?

Moi, je m'appelle Isabelle.

Comment t'appelles-tu?

Je m'appelle Nathalie.

«
—Je m'appelle Marc. Et toi?
—Moi, je m'appelle Isabelle.
»

«
—Comment t'appelles-tu?
—Je m'appelle Nathalie.
—Bonjour.
—Bonjour.
»

POUR *COMMUNIQUER*

Bonjour!

How to say hello:

| **Bonjour!** | *Hello!* | —**Bonjour,** Nathalie!
—**Bonjour,** Jean-Paul! |

How to ask a classmate's name:

| **Comment t'appelles-tu?** | *What's your name?* | — **Comment t'appelles-tu?** |
| **Je m'appelle . . .** | *My name is . . .* | — **Je m'appelle** Stéphanie. |

OTHER EXPRESSIONS

| **moi** | *me* | **Moi,** je m'appelle Marc. |
| **et toi?** | *and you?* | **Et toi,** comment t'appelles-tu? |

■ NOTES ■ CULTURELLES

Rentrée des classes

6^{em} → Lundi 10 Septembre à 9^H
(pas de cours l'après-midi)

5e- 4e- 3e → Lundi 10 Septembre
à 14^H

1 La rentrée *(Back to school)*

French and American students have about the same number of days of summer vacation. In France, summer vacation usually begins at the end of June and classes resume in early September. The first day back to school in fall is called **la rentrée.**

2 Les prénoms français
(French first names)

Many traditional French names have corresponding equivalents in English.

For boys:	For girls:
Jean *(John)*	**Marie** *(Mary)*
Pierre *(Peter)*	**Monique** *(Monica)*
Marc *(Mark)*	**Cécile** *(Cecilia)*
Philippe *(Philip)*	**Alice**
Nicolas *(Nicholas)*	**Caroline**

Often the names **Jean** and **Marie** are combined in double names such as **Jean-Paul** and **Marie-Christine.** In recent years, names of foreign origin, like **Dimitri** and **Karine,** have become quite popular.

Bonjour! Je m'appelle Astérix.

Petit commentaire

Astérix le Gaulois *is one of the best-loved cartoon characters in France. Small in size but extremely clever and courageous, he represents the "little man" defending his country Gaul (the ancient name of France) against the invading Roman legions led by Julius Caesar.*

1 Bonjour!

Say hello to the student nearest to you.

▶ Bonjour!

Bonjour!

2 Je m'appelle . . .

Introduce yourself to your classmates.

▶ Je m'appelle (Paul).

▶ Je m'appelle (Denise).

3 Et toi?

Ask a classmate his or her name.

▶ —Comment t'appelles-tu?
—Je m'appelle (Christine).

4 Bonjour, les amis! *(Hello everyone!)*

Say hello to the following students.

▶ Bonjour, Marc!

Jean-Paul

Isabelle

Juliette

Marc

Stéphanie

Nathalie

Philippe

François

L'alphabet

A	B	C	D	E	F	G	H	I	J	K	L
a	bé	cé	dé	e	effe	gé	hache	i	ji	ka	elle

Les signes orthographiques *(Spelling marks)*

French uses accents and spelling marks that do not exist in English. These marks are part of the spelling and cannot be left out.

In French, there are four accents that may appear on vowels.

´	**l'accent aigu** *(acute accent)*	Cécile, Stéphanie
`	**l'accent grave** *(grave accent)*	Michèle, Hélène
^	**l'accent circonflexe** *(circumflex)*	Jérôme
¨	**le tréma** *(diaeresis)*	Noël, Joëlle

There is only one spelling mark used with a consonant. It occurs under the letter "**c**."

¸	**la cédille** *(cedilla)*	François

5 La rentrée

It is the first day of class. The following students are introducing themselves. Act out the dialogues with your classmates.

▶ Hélène et Philippe

Moi, je m'appelle Philippe.

Je m'appelle Hélène. Et toi?

1. Stéphanie et Marc
2. Cécile et Frédéric
3. Michèle et François
4. Béatrice et Joël
5. Céline et Jérôme

Les nombres de 0 à 10

0	1	2	3
zéro	un	deux	trois

4	5	6	7
quatre	cinq	six	sept

8	9	10	
huit	neuf	dix	

6 Numéros de téléphone

Imagine you are visiting a family in Quebec. Give them your American phone number in French.

▶ 617-963-4028   six, un, sept — neuf, six, trois — quatre, zéro, deux, huit

M	N	O	P	Q	R	S	T	U	V	W	X	Y	Z
emme	enne	o	pé	ku	erre	esse	té	u	vé	double vé	ixe	i grec	zède

2

Tu es français?

It is the opening day of school and several of the students meet in the cafeteria (**la cantine**) at lunchtime. Marc discovers that not everyone is French.

> Tu es français?

> Oui, je suis français.

MARC: Tu es français?
JEAN-PAUL: Oui, je suis français.

MARC: Et toi, Patrick, tu es français aussi?
PATRICK: Non! Je suis américain. Je suis de Boston.

> Non! Je suis américain.

MARC: Et toi, Stéphanie, tu es française ou américaine?
STÉPHANIE: Je suis française.
MARC: Tu es de Paris?
STÉPHANIE: Non, je suis de Fort-de-France.
MARC: Tu as de la chance!

> Je suis française.

MARC: Are you French?
JEAN-PAUL: Yes, I'm French.

MARC: And you, Patrick, are you French too?
PATRICK: No! I'm American. I'm from Boston.

MARC: And you, Stéphanie, are you French or American?
STÉPHANIE: I'm French.
MARC: Are you from Paris?
STÉPHANIE: No, I'm from Fort-de-France.
MARC: You're lucky!

POUR COMMUNIQUER

Tu es de Denver?

How to talk about where people are from:

Tu es de ...?	*Are you from . . . ?*	—**Tu es de** Denver?
Je suis de ...	*I'm from . . .*	—Non, **je suis de** Dallas.

How to talk about one's nationality:

Tu es ...?	*Are you . . . ?*	—Pierre, **tu es** français?
Je suis ...	*I am . . .*	—Oui, **je suis** français.

Les nationalités

🇫🇷	**français**	**française**
🇬🇧	**anglais**	**anglaise**
🇺🇸	**américain**	**américaine**
🇨🇦	**canadien**	**canadienne**

OTHER EXPRESSIONS

oui	*yes*	Tu es français? **Oui,** je suis français.
non	*no*	Tu es canadien? **Non,** je suis américain.
et	*and*	Je suis de Paris. **Et** toi?
ou	*or*	Tu es français **ou** canadien?
aussi	*also, too*	Moi **aussi,** je suis française.

LA MARTINIQUE

BALATA
jardin botanique

NOTE CULTURELLE

Fort-de-France et la Martinique

Fort-de-France is the capital of Martinique, a small French island in the Caribbean. Because Martinique is part of the French national territory, its inhabitants are French citizens. Most of them are of African origin. They speak French as well as a dialect called **créole.**

Martinique is also known as the Island of the Flowers (**l'Île aux Fleurs**) because of its warm tropical climate and magnificent vegetation. In the winter months, it attracts thousands of European and American tourists.

Petit commentaire

The Statue of Liberty (**la statue de la Liberté**) was a gift to the United States from the French people on the occasion of the 100th anniversary of American independence. The Eiffel Tower (**la tour Eiffel**) was built to celebrate the 100th anniversary of the French Revolution.

français, française

Names of nationalities may have two different forms, depending on whom they refer to:

	MASCULINE	FEMININE
Je suis ... **Tu es ...?**	français américain	française américaine

➡ Note that in written French the feminine forms always end in **-e**.

1 Et toi?

Give your name, your nationality, and your city of origin.

Bonjour!
Je m'appelle Bob Jones.
Je suis américain.
Je suis de Providence.

Bonjour!
Je m'appelle Linda Carlson.
Je suis américaine.
Je suis de Boston.

2 Français ou française?

You meet the following young people. Ask them if they are French. A classmate will answer you, as in the model. (Be sure to use **français** with boys and **française** with girls.)

▶ —Sophie, tu es française?
—Oui, je suis française. Je suis de Strasbourg.

Paris

Sophie

Strasbourg

1. Jean-Pierre

2. Paul

3. Éric

Lyon

5. Nicole

Bordeaux

Nice

4. Michèle

Marseille

3 **Quelle nationalité?** *(Which nationality?)*
Greet the following young people and find out each one's nationality. A classmate will answer you, according to the model.

▶ —Bonjour, Marc. Tu es canadien?
—Oui, je suis canadien. Je suis de Montréal.

| Marc |
| Montréal |

| 1. Claire | 2. Patrick |
| Québec | Boston |

| 3. Denise | 4. Donna | 5. Paul |
| Liverpool | Memphis | Cambridge |

Les nombres de 10 à 20

10 dix	11 onze	12 douze
13 treize	14 quatorze	15 quinze
16 seize	17 dix-sept	18 dix-huit
19 dix-neuf	20 vingt	

4 **La fusée Ariane**
(The Ariane rocket)

Give the countdown for the lift-off of the French rocket Ariane, from 20 to 0.

Prononciation

Les lettres muettes *(Silent letters)*

In French, the last letter of a word is often not pronounced.

Paris

- Final "**e**" is always silent.
  Répétez: **Sophie Philippe Stéphanie anglaise française onze douze treize quatorze quinze seize**

- Final "**s**" is almost always silent.
  Répétez: **Paris Nicolas Jacques anglais français trois**

- The letter "**h**" is always silent.
  Répétez: **Hélène Henri Thomas Nathalie Catherine**

Salut! Ça va?

On the way to school, François meets his friends.

François also meets his teachers.

Monsieur Masson   **Madame Chollet**   **Mademoiselle Lacour**

After class, François says good-bye to his teacher and his friends.

POUR
COMMUNIQUER

Salut!

How to greet a friend or classmate:

Salut! *Hi!*

How to greet a teacher or another adult:

Bonjour! *Hello!*

Bonjour, monsieur.
Bonjour, madame.
Bonjour, mademoiselle.

How to say good-bye:

Au revoir! *Good-bye!*

Au revoir, Philippe.
Au revoir, monsieur.

➡ In written French, the following abbreviations are commonly used:

M. Masson Monsieur Masson
Mme Chollet Madame Chollet
Mlle Lacour Mademoiselle Lacour

➡ Young people often use **Salut!** to say good-bye to each other.

■NOTE■
CULTURELLE

Bonjour ou Salut?

French young people may greet one another with **Bonjour,** but they often prefer the less formal **Salut.** When they meet their teachers, however, they always use **Bonjour.** French young people are generally much more formal with adults than with their friends. This is especially true in their relationships with teachers, whom they treat with great respect.

Have you noticed that in France adults are addressed as **monsieur, madame,** or **mademoiselle?** The last name is almost never used in greeting people.

1 Bonjour ou salut?

You are enrolled in a French school.
Greet your friends and teachers.

Sophie

Mademoiselle Pinot

▶ **Salut, Sophie!**

▶ **Bonjour, mademoiselle!**

1. Anne

2. Monsieur Masson

3. Nathalie

4. Marc

5. Madame Albert

6. Mademoiselle Boucher

POUR *COMMUNIQUER*

How to ask people how they feel:

—Ça va?	*How are you? How are things going? How's everything?*
—Ça va!	*(I'm) fine. (I'm) okay. Everything's all right.*

Ça va . . .   très bien   bien   comme ci, comme ça   mal   très mal

How to express one's feelings of frustration and appreciation:

Zut! *Darn!*   **Zut!** Ça va mal!   **Merci!** *Thanks!*   Ça va, **merci.**

➡ **Ça va?** *(How are you?)* is an informal greeting that corresponds to the following
expressions:

   Comment vas-tu? (when addressing a friend)
       Bonjour, Paul. Comment vas-tu?
   Comment allez-vous? (when addressing an adult)
       Bonjour, madame. Comment allez-vous?

2 Dialogue

Exchange greetings with your classmates and ask how they are doing.

▶ —Salut, (Thomas)! Ça va?
   —Ça va! Et toi?
   —Ça va bien. Merci.

ÇA VA?   OUI, ÇA VA TRÈS BIEN!

ÇA VA?   AH NON! ÇA VA MAL!

3 Situations

Sometimes we feel good and sometimes we don't. How would you respond in the following situations?

▶ You have the flu.
—Ça va?
—Ça va mal!

1. You just received an "A" in French.
2. You lost your wallet.
3. Your uncle gave you five dollars.
4. Your grandparents sent you a check for 100 dollars.
5. You bent the front wheel of your bicycle.
6. Your parents bought you a new bicycle.
7. Your little brother broke your walkman.
8. It's your birthday.
9. You have a headache.
10. You just had an argument with your best friend.
11. Your favorite baseball team has just lost a game.
12. Your French teacher has just canceled a quiz.

4 Ça va?

How would the following people answer the question **Ça va?**

Les nombres de 20 à 60

20 vingt	**30** trente	**40** quarante
vingt et un	trente et un	quarante et un
vingt-deux	trente-deux	quarante-deux
vingt-trois	trente-trois	quarante-trois
. . .	. . .	. . .
vingt-neuf	trente-neuf	quarante-neuf

50 cinquante   **60** soixante

cinquante et un
cinquante-deux
cinquante-trois
. . .
cinquante-neuf

➡ Note the use of **et** in numbers with **un**:
vingt et un.

5 Loto

Read out loud the numbers on the French Loto tickets.

Prononciation

Les consonnes finales
(Final consonants)

1 2 3
un deux trois

In French, the last consonant of a word is often not pronounced.

- Remember: Final "**s**" is usually silent.
  Répétez: **trois français anglais**

- Most other final consonants are usually silent.
  Répétez: **Richard Albert Robert salut américain canadien bien deux**

EXCEPTION: The following final consonants are usually pronounced: "**c**," "**f**," "**l**," and sometimes "**r**."
Répétez: **Éric Daniel Lebeuf Pascal Victor**

However, the ending **-er** is usually pronounced /e/.
Répétez: **Roger Olivier**

▶ ▶

LE FRANÇAIS
PRATIQUE

L'heure

LEÇON

A. Un rendez-vous

Jean-Paul and Stéphanie are sitting in a café.
Stéphanie seems to be in a hurry to leave.

STÉPHANIE:	Quelle heure est-il?
JEAN-PAUL:	Il est trois heures.
STÉPHANIE:	Trois heures?
JEAN-PAUL:	Oui, trois heures.
STÉPHANIE:	Oh là là. J'ai un rendez-vous avec David dans vingt minutes. Au revoir, Jean-Paul.
JEAN-PAUL:	Au revoir, Stéphanie. À bientôt!

STÉPHANIE:	*What time is it?*
JEAN-PAUL:	*It's three o'clock.*
STÉPHANIE:	*Three o'clock?*
JEAN-PAUL:	*Yes, three o'clock.*
STÉPHANIE:	*Uh, oh! I have a date with David in twenty minutes. Good-bye, Jean-Paul.*
JEAN-PAUL:	*Good-bye, Stéphanie. See you soon!*

POUR
COMMUNIQUER

Il est huit heures!

How to talk about the time:

Quelle heure est-il?	*What time is it?*
Il est . . .	*It's . . .*

une heure	deux heures	trois heures	quatre heures	cinq heures	six heures

sept heures	huit heures	neuf heures	dix heures	onze heures	midi	minuit

1 **Quelle heure est-il?**

Ask your classmates what time it is.

Quelle heure est–il?

Il est quatre heures.

2 **L'heure d'été** *(Daylight savings time)*

Philippe forgot to set his watch ahead for daylight savings time, so he is an hour off. Isabelle gives him the correct time.

▶ PHILIPPE: **Il est sept heures.**
ISABELLE: **Mais non, il est huit heures!**

➡ Although *o'clock* may be left out in English, the expression **heure(s)** must be used in French when giving the time.

It's ten. (It's ten o'clock.) **Il est dix heures.**

➡ To distinguish between A.M. and P.M., the French use the following expressions:

du matin	*in the morning*	Il est dix heures **du matin.**
de l'après-midi	*in the afternoon*	Il est deux heures **de l'après-midi.**
du soir	*in the evening*	Il est huit heures **du soir.**

NOTE DE PRONONCIATION: In telling time, the NUMBER and the word **heure(s)** are linked together. Remember, in French the letter "**h**" is always silent.

une heure   deux heures   trois heures   quatre heures   cinq heures   six heures

sept heures   huit heures   neuf heures   dix heures   onze heures

B. À quelle heure est le film?

Stéphanie and David have decided to go to a movie.

STÉPHANIE: Quelle heure est-il?
DAVID: Il est trois heures et demie.
STÉPHANIE: Et à quelle heure est le film?
DAVID: À quatre heures et quart.
STÉPHANIE: Ça va. Nous avons le temps.

STÉPHANIE: *What time is it?*
DAVID: *It's three-thirty (half past three).*
STÉPHANIE: *And at what time is the movie?*
DAVID: *At four-fifteen (quarter past four).*
STÉPHANIE: *That's okay. We have time.*

POUR COMMUNIQUER

À quelle heure est le dîner?

How to ask at what time something is scheduled:

À quelle heure est ...?   *At what time is . . . ?*
—**À quelle heure est le concert?**   *At what time is the concert?*
—**Le concert est à huit heures.**   *The concert is at eight.*

How to say that you have an appointment or a date:

J'ai un rendez-vous à ...   *I have an appointment (a date) at . . .*   **J'ai un rendez-vous à** deux heures.

How to indicate the minutes:

Il est ...	dix heures dix	six heures vingt-cinq	sept heures trente-cinq	deux heures cinquante-deux

How to indicate the half hour and the quarter hours:

et quart   **et demie**   **moins le quart**

Il est une heure **et quart.**   Il est deux heures **et demie.**   Il est trois heures **moins le quart.**

3 L'heure

Give the times according to the clocks.

▶ **Il est une heure et quart.**

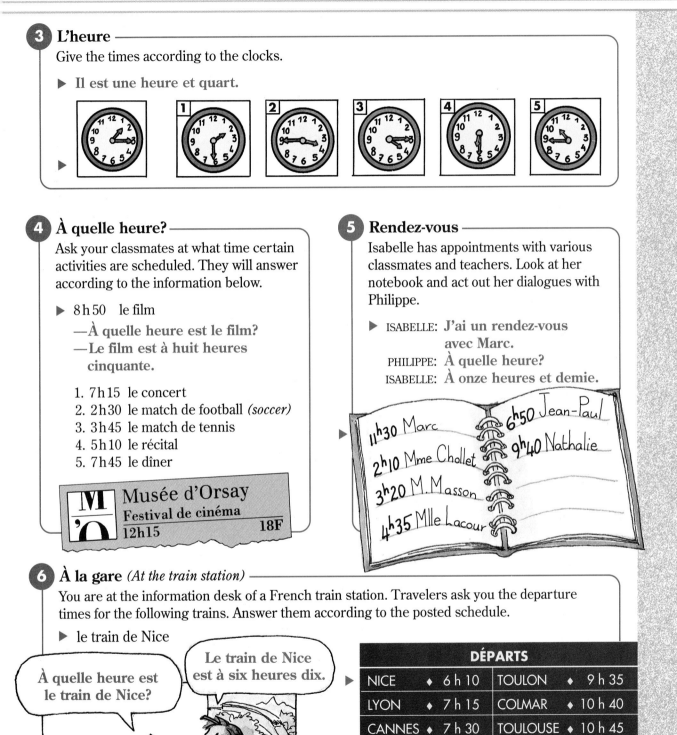

4 À quelle heure?

Ask your classmates at what time certain activities are scheduled. They will answer according to the information below.

▶ 8 h 50   le film
   —À quelle heure est le film?
   —Le film est à huit heures cinquante.

1. 7 h 15   le concert
2. 2 h 30   le match de football *(soccer)*
3. 3 h 45   le match de tennis
4. 5 h 10   le récital
5. 7 h 45   le dîner

Musée d'Orsay
Festival de cinéma
12h15   18F

5 Rendez-vous

Isabelle has appointments with various classmates and teachers. Look at her notebook and act out her dialogues with Philippe.

▶ ISABELLE: **J'ai un rendez-vous avec Marc.**
   PHILIPPE: **À quelle heure?**
   ISABELLE: **À onze heures et demie.**

11h30 Marc
2h10 Mme Chollet
3h20 M. Masson
4h35 Mlle Lacour
6h50 Jean-Paul
9h40 Nathalie

6 À la gare *(At the train station)*

You are at the information desk of a French train station. Travelers ask you the departure times for the following trains. Answer them according to the posted schedule.

▶ le train de Nice

À quelle heure est le train de Nice?

Le train de Nice est à six heures dix.

DÉPARTS			
NICE	♦ 6 h 10	TOULON	♦ 9 h 35
LYON	♦ 7 h 15	COLMAR	♦ 10 h 40
CANNES	♦ 7 h 30	TOULOUSE	♦ 10 h 45
TOURS	♦ 8 h 12	MARSEILLE	♦ 10 h 50
DIJON	♦ 8 h 25	BORDEAUX	♦ 10 h 55

À votre tour!

1 Nathalie et Marc

It is the first day of school. Nathalie is talking to Marc and you hear parts of their conversation. For each of Nathalie's greetings or questions, select Marc's reply from the suggested responses on the right.

1 Salut!

2 Ça va?

3 Comment t'appelles-tu?

4 Tu es français?

5 Quelle heure est-il?

6 Au revoir!

a. Bonjour!
b. Au revoir!
c. Non, je suis canadien.
d. Il est deux heures moins le quart.
e. Marc Boutin.
f. Oui, ça va bien! Merci!

2 Et toi?

You and Nathalie meet at a sidewalk café. Respond to her greetings and questions.

1. Salut! Ça va?
2. Comment t'appelles-tu?
3. Tu es canadien (canadienne)?
4. Quelle heure est-il?
5. Oh là là. J'ai un rendez-vous dans *(in)* dix minutes. Au revoir.

3 Conversation dirigée

Two students, Jean-Pierre and Janet, meet on the Paris-Lyon train. With a partner, compose and act out their dialogue according to the suggested script.

Jean-Pierre			**Janet**
	says hello	→	responds and asks how things are
	says things are fine	→	asks him what his name is
	says his name is Jean-Pierre . . . asks her name	→	says her name is Janet
	asks her if she is English	→	says no and responds that she is American
	asks her if she is from New York	→	replies that she is from San Francisco

4 Minidialogues

Create original dialogues on the basis of the pictures below.

1. David et Nicole

2. Monsieur Bertin et Mademoiselle Laval

3. Florence et Alain

4. Jean-Pierre et Sylvie

5. Thomas et Nicole

5 En scène

With a classmate, act out the following scene.

CHARACTERS:
You and a French exchange student

SITUATION:
You are at a party and meet a French exchange student who is happy to respond to your greetings and questions.

- Greet the student.
- Ask how things are going.
- Introduce yourself and ask his/her name.
- Ask if he/she is French.
- Ask if he/she is from Paris.
- Say good-bye.

6 Les nombres

1. Select any number between 0 and 15 and give the next five numbers in sequence.

2. Select a number between 1 and 9. Use that number as a starting point and count by tens to 60.

▶ deux

  douze, vingt-deux, trente-deux, etc.

Oui, vous parlez français!

Yes, you speak French! If you were visiting a French city, you would be able to understand many of the signs around you.

Look at the words on the following signs and compare them to their English equivalents. Which ones are spelled exactly the same? Which ones are spelled a little differently? What are the differences?

Office de Tourisme

AVENUE DE L'OPÉRA

Hôpital ·SILENCE·

AÉROPORT ORLY

DÉPARTS

ARRIVÉES

TAXI

musée

AVENUE FRANKLIN ROOSEVELT

cathédrale

THÉÂTRE

Station-service

AUTOBUS

DIRECTION BORDEAUX

HÔTEL

PARKING MUNICIPAL

téléphone

Restaurant

GARAGE

ATTENTION! DANGER!

TOILETTES

La présence FRANÇAISE en Amérique

Between 1600 and 1750, the French explored large parts of Canada and the United States, which they called **La Nouvelle France** *(New France)*. Today many American towns have French names, as you will see on the map below.

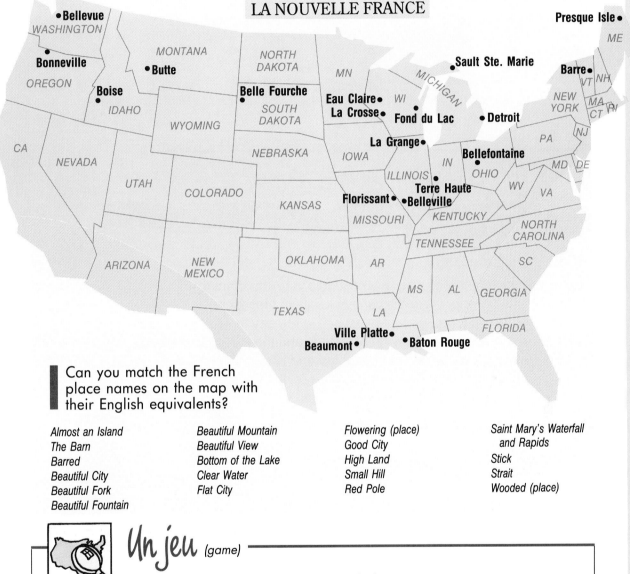

LA NOUVELLE FRANCE

Can you match the French place names on the map with their English equivalents?

Almost an Island	Beautiful Mountain	Flowering (place)	Saint Mary's Waterfall and Rapids
The Barn	Beautiful View	Good City	Stick
Barred	Bottom of the Lake	High Land	Strait
Beautiful City	Clear Water	Small Hill	Wooded (place)
Beautiful Fork	Flat City	Red Pole	
Beautiful Fountain			

Un jeu *(game)*

Many American cities were also named after:

- French people (such as King Louis XIV and his patron Saint Louis, General La Fayette, Napoleon, and of course, explorers like Champlain, Jolliet, Marquette, La Salle, Duluth, Dubuque)
- French cities (such as Paris, Montpellier, La Rochelle, Orléans)

In teams of three or four, see how many cities with French names you can locate on a map of the United States.

2 Les copains et la famille

INTRODUCTION
culturelle

L'amitié *(Friendship)*

Is friendship important to you? Friendship is very important to French teenagers. Of course, there are various levels of friendship and different types of friends: classmates whom we see every day in school, friends with whom we spend time outside of school, and the few special friends who are always there when we need them and who will remain our friends for the rest of our lives. As you will see, the French have different words to describe these various relationships.

THÈME ET OBJECTIFS

Talking about people

In this unit, you will be talking about people you know. You will learn . . .
- to identify friends, family, and relatives
- to say how old you are and find out someone's age
- to talk about birthdays and holidays

You will also learn . . .
- to count from 60 to 100
- to give the date and the day of the week

Copain ou copine?

In French, there are certain girls' and boys' names that sound the same. Occasionally this can be confusing.

Dominique? Qui est-ce? Un copain ou une copine?

Scène 1. Philippe et Jean-Paul

Philippe is at home with his friend Jean-Paul. He seems to be expecting someone. Who could it be . . . ? The doorbell rings.

PHILIPPE: Tiens! Voilà Dominique!
JEAN-PAUL: Dominique? Qui est-ce? Un copain ou une copine?
PHILIPPE: C'est une copine.

Scène 2. Philippe, Jean-Paul, Dominique

PHILIPPE: Salut, Dominique! Ça va?
DOMINIQUE: Oui, ça va! Et toi?
JEAN-PAUL: *(thinking)* C'est vrai! C'est une copine!

Salut, Dominique! Ça va?

Scene 1. Philippe and Jean-Paul

PHILIPPE: *Hey! There's Dominique!*
JEAN-PAUL: *Dominique? Who's that? A boy(friend) or a girl(friend)?*
PHILIPPE: *A girl(friend).*

Scene 2. Philippe, Jean-Paul, Dominique

PHILIPPE: *Hi, Dominique! How's everything?*
DOMINIQUE: *Fine! And you?*
JEAN-PAUL: *(thinking) It's true! She is a girlfriend!*

POUR
COMMUNIQUER

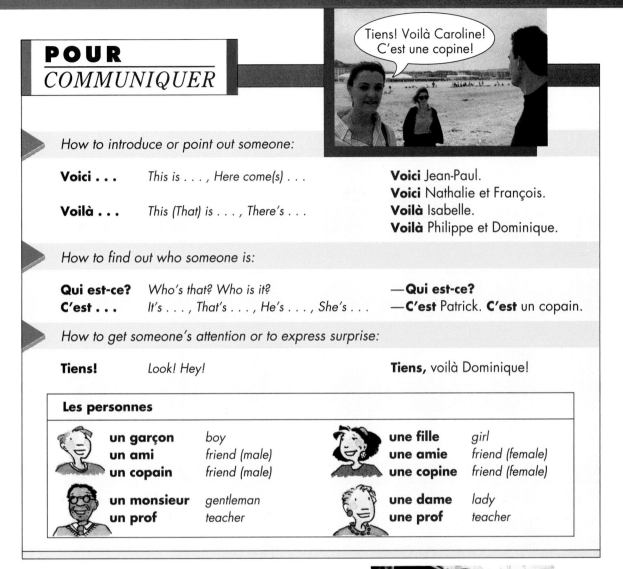

Tiens! Voilà Caroline! C'est une copine!

How to introduce or point out someone:

Voici . . .	*This is . . . , Here come(s) . . .*	**Voici** Jean-Paul. **Voici** Nathalie et François.
Voilà . . .	*This (That) is . . . , There's . . .*	**Voilà** Isabelle. **Voilà** Philippe et Dominique.

How to find out who someone is:

Qui est-ce?	*Who's that? Who is it?*	—**Qui est-ce?**
C'est . . .	*It's . . . , That's . . . , He's . . . , She's . . .*	—**C'est** Patrick. **C'est** un copain.

How to get someone's attention or to express surprise:

Tiens!	*Look! Hey!*	**Tiens,** voilà Dominique!

Les personnes

	un garçon	*boy*		**une fille**	*girl*
	un ami	*friend (male)*		**une amie**	*friend (female)*
	un copain	*friend (male)*		**une copine**	*friend (female)*
	un monsieur	*gentleman*		**une dame**	*lady*
	un prof	*teacher*		**une prof**	*teacher*

■ NOTE ■
CULTURELLE

Amis et copains

French young people, like their American counterparts, enjoy spending time with their friends. They refer to their friends as **un ami** (for a boy) and **une amie** (for a girl) or — more commonly — as **un copain** or **une copine.** Note that the words **copain, copine** can also have special meanings. When a boy talks about **une copine,** he is referring to a friend who is a girl. However, when he says **ma** *(my)* **copine,** he may be referring to his girlfriend. Similarly, a girl would call her boyfriend **mon copain.**

C'EST UN CHAMPION!

MAIS NON! C'EST UNE CHAMPIONNE.

un garçon, une fille

In French, all NOUNS are either MASCULINE or FEMININE.
Nouns referring to boys or men are almost always MASCULINE.
  They are introduced by **un** *(a, an).*
Nouns referring to girls or women are almost always FEMININE.
  They are introduced by **une** *(a, an).*

MASCULINE		FEMININE	
un garçon	*a boy*	**une** fille	*a girl*
un ami	*a friend (male)*	**une** amie	*a friend (female)*

UN

UNE

1 Copain ou copine?

Say that the following people are your friends. Use **un copain** or **une copine,** as appropriate.

▶ **Christine est une copine.**

Christine

1. Alice

2. Marie-Jeanne

3. Éric

4. David

5. Sylvie

2 Les amis

The same young people are visiting your school. Point them out to your classmates, using **un ami** or **une amie,** as appropriate.

▶ —**Tiens, voilà Christine!**
   —**Qui est-ce?**
   —**C'est une amie.**

3 Un ou une?

Identify the people below by completing the sentences with **un** or **une.**

1. Voici . . . fille.
2. Voilà . . . garçon.
3. Voici . . . dame.
4. C'est . . . amie.
5. Olivier est . . . ami.
6. Jean-Paul est . . . copain.
7. Cécile est . . . copine.
8. Voici Mlle Lacour. C'est . . . prof.
9. Voici M. Masson. C'est . . . prof.
10. Voici Mme Chollet. C'est . . . prof.

4 À la fenêtre *(At the window)*

You and a friend are walking down the street and you see the following people at their windows. Identify them in short dialogues.

▶ —Tiens, voilà un monsieur!
—Qui est-ce?
—C'est Monsieur Mercier. ▶

Monsieur Mercier

1. Nicole
2. Mademoiselle Lasalle
3. Éric
4. Madame Albert
5. Monsieur Lavie
6. Alain

Les nombres de 60 à 79

60 soixante

61 soixante et un	66 soixante-six
62 soixante-deux	67 soixante-sept
63 soixante-trois	68 soixante-huit
64 soixante-quatre	69 soixante-neuf
65 soixante-cinq	

70 soixante-dix

71 soixante et onze	76 soixante-seize
72 soixante-douze	77 soixante-dix-sept
73 soixante-treize	78 soixante-dix-huit
74 soixante-quatorze	79 soixante-dix-neuf
75 soixante-quinze	

➡ Note that in counting from 70 to 79, the French continue adding numbers to 60:
70 = 60 + 10   71 = 60 + 11   72 = 60 + 12, etc.

---

5 Numéros de téléphone

Read aloud the phone numbers of Jean-Paul's friends in Paris.

▶ Philippe   zéro un, quarante-deux, soixante et un, dix-neuf, soixante-quinze

Philippe   01.42.61.19.75
Martine   01.41.33.64.79
Michèle   01.42.56.76.62
Stéphanie 01.45.68.77.35
François   01.49.78.13.62

Prononciation

La liaison

Pronounce the following words:

un ami

un‿ami   un‿Américain   un‿Anglais   un‿artiste

In general, the "**n**" of **un** is silent. However, in the above words, the "**n**" of **un** is pronounced as if it were the *first* letter of the next word. The two words are *linked* together in LIAISON.

Liaison occurs between two words when the second one begins with a VOWEL SOUND, that is, with "**a**", "**e**", "**i**", "**o**", "**u**", and sometimes "**h**" and "**y**".

➡ Although liaison is not marked in written French, it will be indicated in your book by the symbol ‿ where appropriate.

Contrastez et répétez:

LIAISON: **un‿ami   un‿Américain   un‿Italien   un‿artiste**

NO LIAISON: **un copain   un Français   un Canadien   un prof**

LEÇON 6

Une coïncidence

Isabelle is at a party with her new Canadian friend Marc.
She wants him to meet some of the other guests.

Tu connais la fille là-bas?

Non. Qui est-ce?

C'est une copine. Elle s'appelle Juliette Savard.

Elle est française?

Non, elle est canadienne. Elle est de Montréal.

Moi aussi!

Quelle coïncidence!

ISABELLE:	Do you know the girl over there?
MARC:	No. Who is she?
ISABELLE:	She's a friend. Her name is Juliette Savard.

MARC:	Is she French?
ISABELLE:	No, she's Canadian. She is from Montreal.
MARC:	Me too!
ISABELLE:	What a coincidence!

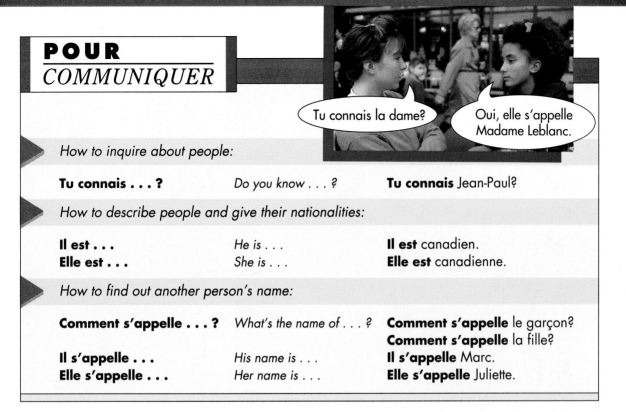

POUR
COMMUNIQUER

> **Tu connais la dame?**
>
> **Oui, elle s'appelle Madame Leblanc.**

How to inquire about people:

| **Tu connais . . . ?** | *Do you know . . . ?* | **Tu connais** Jean-Paul? |

How to describe people and give their nationalities:

| **Il est . . .** | *He is . . .* | **Il est** canadien. |
| **Elle est . . .** | *She is . . .* | **Elle est** canadienne. |

How to find out another person's name:

Comment s'appelle . . . ?	*What's the name of . . . ?*	**Comment s'appelle** le garçon?
		Comment s'appelle la fille?
Il s'appelle . . .	*His name is . . .*	**Il s'appelle** Marc.
Elle s'appelle . . .	*Her name is . . .*	**Elle s'appelle** Juliette.

■ NOTE ■
CULTURELLE

Montréal et la province de Québec

In population, metropolitan Montreal is the second-largest city in Canada. After Paris, it is also the second-largest French-speaking city in the world.

Montreal is located in the province of Quebec, where French is the official language. In fact, French speakers represent over 90% of the population. These people are the descendants of French settlers who came to Canada in the 17th and 18th centuries. If you visit Montreal, you will discover that the people of Quebec (**les Québécois**) are very proud of their heritage and dedicated to maintaining French as their language.

Petit commentaire

French teenagers are very much interested in the United States. They love American music and American movies. Every year, more and more French high school students come to visit our country either through exchange programs or summer homestays.

BONJOUR!

TU CONNAIS LE MONSIEUR?

OUI, IL S'APPELLE ONCLE SAM. IL EST AMÉRICAIN.

le garçon, la fille

The French equivalent of *the* has two basic forms: **le** and **la.**

MASCULINE		FEMININE	
le garçon	*the boy*	**la** fille	*the girl*
le copain	*the friend*	**la** copine	*the friend*

NOTE: Both **le** and **la** become **l'** before a vowel sound.

un copain → le copain   une copine → la copine
un ami → **l'**ami   une amie → **l'**amie

1 **Qui est-ce?**

Ask who the following people are, using **le, la,** or **l'.**

▶ une prof
  Qui est la prof?

1. un monsieur
2. une dame

3. une fille
4. un garçon

5. un prof
6. un ami

7. une amie

2 **Tu connais . . . ?**

Ask your classmates if they know the following people. They will answer that they do.

▶ une dame / Madame Vallée

Tu connais la dame?

Oui, c'est Madame Vallée.

1. un prof / Monsieur Simon
2. un garçon / Christophe
3. une fille / Sophie
4. une dame / Mademoiselle Lenoir
5. une prof / Madame Boucher
6. un monsieur / Monsieur Duval

3 **Comment s'appelle . . . ?**

Ask the names of the following people, using the words **le garçon, la fille.** A classmate will respond.

▶ —Comment s'appelle la fille?
  —Elle s'appelle Stéphanie.

▶ **Stéphanie** | **1. Marc** | **2. Juliette** | **3. François**

4. Jean-Paul | **5. Nathalie** | **6. Philippe** | **7. Isabelle**

4 **Français, anglais ou américain?**

Give the nationalities of the following people.

▶ Jane Fonda?
   Elle est américaine.

1. le prince Charles?
2. la princesse Diana?
3. Catherine Deneuve?
4. Vanna White?
5. Pierre Cardin?
6. Bill Cosby?
7. Oprah Winfrey?
8. Tom Cruise?
9. Paul McCartney?

Les nombres de 80 à 100

80 quatre-vingts

81 quatre-vingt-un
82 quatre-vingt-deux
83 quatre-vingt-trois
84 quatre-vingt-quatre
85 quatre-vingt-cinq
86 quatre-vingt-six
87 quatre-vingt-sept
88 quatre-vingt-huit
89 quatre-vingt-neuf

90 quatre-vingt-dix

91 quatre-vingt-onze
92 quatre-vingt-douze
93 quatre-vingt-treize
94 quatre-vingt-quatorze
95 quatre-vingt-quinze
96 quatre-vingt-seize
97 quatre-vingt-dix-sept
98 quatre-vingt-dix-huit
99 quatre-vingt-dix-neuf

100 cent

➡ Note that in counting from 80 to 99, the French add numbers to the base of **quatre-vingts** *(fourscore):*

$$80 = 4 \times 20 \qquad 90 = 4 \times 20 + 10$$
$$85 = 4 \times 20 + 5 \qquad 99 = 4 \times 20 + 19$$

5 **Au téléphone**

In France, the telephone area code (**l'indicatif**) is always a four-digit number. Your teacher will name a city (**une ville**) from the chart. Give the corresponding area code.

▶ Nice? *C'est le zéro quatre quatre-vingt-treize.*

VILLE	INDICATIF
Albi	0563
Avignon	0490
Cannes	0493
Dijon	0380
Marseille	0491
Montpellier	0467
Nancy	0383
Nice	0493
Nîmes	0466
Rennes	0299
Saint-Tropez	0494
Strasbourg	0388
Vichy	0470

Prononciation   /ɛ̃/

La voyelle nasale /ɛ̃/

In French, there are three nasal vowel sounds:

/ɛ̃/ **cinq** (5)   /ɔ̃/ **onze** (11)   /ɑ̃/ **trente** (30)

Practice the sound /ɛ̃/ in the following words. Note that this vowel sound can have several different spellings.

➡ Be sure not to pronounce an "**n**" or "**m**" after the nasal vowel.

Répétez: "in"   ci**n**q qui**n**ze vi**ng**t vi**ng**t-cinq quatre-vi**ng**t-qui**n**ze
          "ain"   américai**n** Alai**n** copai**n**
          "(i)en"   bie**n** canadie**n** tie**n**s!
          "un"   u**n**
          Tie**n**s! Voilà Alai**n**. Il est américai**n**.   E**t** Julie**n**? Il est canadie**n**.

5
ci̲n̲q̲

Les photos d'Isabelle

Isabelle is showing her family photo album to her friend Jean-Paul.

ISABELLE: Voici ma mère.

JEAN-PAUL: Et le monsieur, c'est ton père?

ISABELLE: Non, c'est mon oncle Thomas.

JEAN-PAUL: Et la fille, c'est ta cousine?

ISABELLE: Oui, c'est ma cousine Béatrice. Elle a seize ans.

JEAN-PAUL: Et le garçon, c'est ton cousin?

ISABELLE: Non, c'est un copain.

JEAN-PAUL: Un copain ou ton copain?

ISABELLE: Dis donc, Jean-Paul, tu es vraiment trop curieux!

ma mère

mon oncle Thomas

ma cousine Béatrice

??

ISABELLE: *This is my mother.*

JEAN-PAUL: *And the man, is he your father?*

ISABELLE: *No, that's my uncle Thomas.*

JEAN-PAUL: *And the girl, is she your cousin?*

ISABELLE: *Yes, that's my cousin Béatrice. She's sixteen.*

JEAN-PAUL: *And the boy, is he your cousin?*

ISABELLE: *No, that's a friend.*

JEAN-PAUL: *A friend or a boyfriend?*

ISABELLE: *Hey there, Jean-Paul, you are really too curious!*

POUR
COMMUNIQUER

How to introduce your family:

Voici mon père.	*This is my father.*
Et voici ma mère.	*And this is my mother.*

Voici mon chien Malice.

La famille *(Family)*

un frère	*brother*	**une soeur**	*sister*
un cousin	*cousin*	**une cousine**	*cousin*
un père	*father*	**une mère**	*mother*
un oncle	*uncle*	**une tante**	*aunt*
un grand-père	*grandfather*	**une grand-mère**	*grandmother*

Les animaux domestiques *(Pets)*

MIAOU

OUAF OUAF

un chat   **un chien**

■ NOTE ■
CULTURELLE

La famille française

When you and your friends talk about your families, you usually are referring to your brothers, sisters, and parents. In French, however, **la famille** refers not only to parents and children but also to grandparents, aunts, uncles, cousins, as well as a whole array of more distant relatives related by blood and marriage.

Since the various members of a family often live in the same region, French teenagers see their grandparents and cousins fairly frequently. Even when relatives do not live close by, the family finds many occasions to get together: for weekend visits, during school and summer vacations, on holidays, as well as on special occasions such as weddings and anniversaries.

Petit commentaire

The French people love pets, especially cats and dogs. What is important is the animal's personality and friendliness rather than its pedigree. Some common names given to animals are:

Minou, Pompon, Fifi *(cats)*
Titus, Milou, Médor *(dogs)*

mon cousin, ma cousine

The French equivalents of *my* and *your* have the following forms:

 MASCULINE

mon cousin	*my cousin (male)*
mon frère	*my brother*
ton cousin	*your cousin (male)*
ton frère	*your brother*

 FEMININE

ma cousine	*my cousin (female)*
ma soeur	*my sister*
ta cousine	*your cousin (female)*
ta soeur	*your sister*

➡ Note that the feminine **ma** becomes **mon** and the feminine **ta** becomes **ton** before a vowel sound. Liaison is required.

une amie → **mon** amie **ton** amie

---

1 L'album de photos

You are showing a friend your photo album. Identify the following people, using **mon** and **ma,** as appropriate.

▶ cousine Jacqueline   **Voici ma cousine Jacqueline.**

1. frère
2. soeur
3. tante Monique
4. oncle Pierre
5. père
6. mère
7. copain Nicolas
8. ami Jérôme
9. copine Pauline
10. amie Florence
11. grand-mère Michèle
12. grand-père Robert
13. chien Toto
14. chat Minou
15. cousine Sophie

2 Comment s'appelle . . . ?

Ask your classmates to name some of their friends, relatives, and pets. They can invent names if they wish.

▶ le copain

1. l'oncle
2. la tante
3. le cousin
4. la cousine
5. la copine
6. le grand-père
7. la grand-mère
8. le chien
9. le chat

Comment s'appelle ton copain?

Mon copain s'appelle Bob.

Quel âge as-tu?

J'ai treize ans.

POUR
COMMUNIQUER

How to find out how old a friend is:

Quel âge as-tu?	*How old are you?*	**—Quel âge as-tu?**
J'ai . . . ans.	*I'm . . . (years old).*	**—J'ai treize ans.**

How to ask about how old others are:

—Quel âge a ton père?	*How old is your father?*
—Il a quarante-deux ans.	*He is 42 (years old).*
—Quel âge a ta mère?	*How old is your mother?*
—Elle a trente-neuf ans.	*She is 39 (years old).*

➡ Although *years old* may be left out in English, the word **ans** must be used in French when talking about someone's age.

   Il a vingt ans.   *He's twenty. (He's twenty years old.)*

---

3 **Quel âge as-tu?**

Ask your classmates how old they are.

▶ —Quel âge as-tu?
   —J'ai (treize) ans.

4 **Joyeux anniversaire!**
(Happy birthday!)

Ask your classmates how old the following people are.

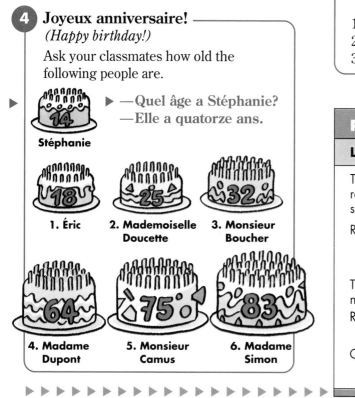

▶ —Quel âge a Stéphanie?
   —Elle a quatorze ans.

Stéphanie

1. **Éric**
2. **Mademoiselle Doucette**
3. **Monsieur Boucher**
4. **Madame Dupont**
5. **Monsieur Camus**
6. **Madame Simon**

5 **Curiosité**

Find out the ages of your classmates' friends and relatives. If they are not sure, they can guess or invent an answer.

▶ la copine —Quel âge a ta copine?
            —Ma copine a (treize) ans.

1. le père	4. la tante	7. le grand-père
2. la mère	5. le cousin	8. la grand-mère
3. l'oncle	6. la cousine	

Prononciation   /ɑ̃/   /ɔ̃/

Les voyelles nasales /ɑ̃/ et /ɔ̃/

    tante oncle

The letters "**an**" and "**en**" usually represent the nasal vowel /ɑ̃/. Be sure not to pronounce an "**n**" after the nasal vowel.

Répétez: a**n**s ta**n**te gra**n**d-père françai**s**
         a**n**glai**s** quara**n**te cinqua**n**te
         tre**n**te comme**n**t He**n**ri Laure**n**t

The letters "**on**" represent the nasal vowel /ɔ̃/. Be sure not to pronounce an "**n**" after the nasal vowel.

Répétez: no**n** mo**n** to**n** bo**n**jour o**n**cle
         garço**n** o**n**ze

Contrastez: a**n**—o**n** ta**n**te—to**n** o**n**ze—a**n**s
       Mon o**n**cle Françoi**s** a tre**n**te a**n**s.

LE FRANÇAIS
PRATIQUE

Le jour et la date

Super! Demain, c'est samedi!

A. Quel jour est-ce?

For many people, the days of the week are not all alike.

Dialogue 1. Vendredi

PHILIPPE: Quel jour est-ce?
STÉPHANIE: C'est vendredi.
PHILIPPE: Super! Demain, c'est samedi!

Dialogue 2. Mercredi

NATHALIE: Ça va?
MARC: Pas très bien.
NATHALIE: Pourquoi?
MARC: Aujourd'hui, c'est mercredi.
NATHALIE: Et alors?
MARC: Demain, c'est jeudi! Le jour de l'examen.
NATHALIE: Zut! C'est vrai! Au revoir, Marc.
MARC: Au revoir, Nathalie. À demain!

Demain, c'est jeudi! Le jour de l'examen.

Dialogue 1. *Friday*

PHILIPPE: *What day is it?*
STÉPHANIE: *It's Friday.*
PHILIPPE: *Great! Tomorrow is Saturday!*

Dialogue 2. *Wednesday*

NATHALIE: *How are things?*
MARC: *Not very good.*
NATHALIE: *Why?*
MARC: *Today is Wednesday.*

NATHALIE: *So?*
MARC: *Tomorrow is Thursday! The day of the exam.*
NATHALIE: *Darn! That's right! Good-bye, Marc.*
MARC: *Good-bye, Nathalie. See you tomorrow!*

POUR COMMUNIQUER

How to talk about days of the week:

Quel jour est-ce?　　　*What day is it?*
　Aujourd'hui, c'est mercredi.　　*Today is Wednesday.*
　Demain, c'est jeudi.　　*Tomorrow is Thursday.*

How to tell people when you will see them again:

À samedi!　　*See you Saturday!*
À demain!　　*See you tomorrow!*

> **À samedi!**

Les jours de la semaine *(Days of the week)*					
lundi	*Monday*	**vendredi**	*Friday*	**aujourd'hui**	*today*
mardi	*Tuesday*	**samedi**	*Saturday*	**demain**	*tomorrow*
mercredi	*Wednesday*	**dimanche**	*Sunday*		
jeudi	*Thursday*				

1 **Questions**

1. Quel jour est-ce aujourd'hui?
2. Et demain, quel jour est-ce?

2 **Un jour de retard** *(One day behind)*

Georges has trouble keeping track of the date. He is always one day behind. Monique corrects him.

▶ samedi

> Aujourd'hui, c'est samedi?

> Non, aujourd'hui, c'est dimanche!

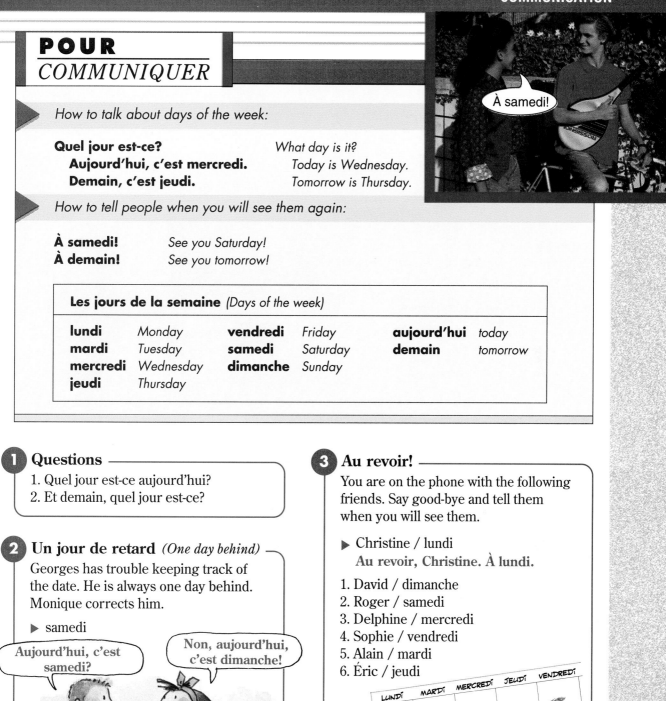

1. lundi	3. jeudi	5. dimanche
2. mardi	4. vendredi	6. mercredi

3 **Au revoir!**

You are on the phone with the following friends. Say good-bye and tell them when you will see them.

▶ Christine / lundi
　Au revoir, Christine. À lundi.

1. David / dimanche
2. Roger / samedi
3. Delphine / mercredi
4. Sophie / vendredi
5. Alain / mardi
6. Éric / jeudi

LUNDI　MARDI　MERCREDI　JEUDI　VENDREDI

Astérix

B. Anniversaire

François and Isabelle are on their way to Nathalie's birthday party. As they are talking, François wants to know when Isabelle's birthday is.

FRANÇOIS: C'est quand, ton anniversaire?
ISABELLE: C'est le 18 mars!
FRANÇOIS: Le 18 mars? Pas possible!
ISABELLE: Si! Pourquoi?
FRANÇOIS: C'est aussi mon anniversaire.
ISABELLE: Quelle coïncidence!

FRANÇOIS: When is your birthday?
ISABELLE: It's March 18!
FRANÇOIS: March 18? That's not possible!
ISABELLE: Yes, it is! Why?
FRANÇOIS: It's my birthday too.
ISABELLE: What a coincidence!

POUR COMMUNIQUER

Quelle est la date?

How to talk about the date:

Quelle est la date? | *What's the date?*
   C'est le 12 (douze) octobre. | *It's October 12.*
   C'est le premier juin. | *It's June first.*

How to talk about birthdays:

—C'est quand, ton anniversaire? | *When is your birthday?*
—Mon anniversaire est le 2 (deux) mars. | *My birthday is March 2.*

Les mois de l'année (Months of the year)			
janvier	**avril**	**juillet**	**octobre**
février	**mai**	**août**	**novembre**
mars	**juin**	**septembre**	**décembre**

La date

To express a date in French, the pattern is:

le	+	NUMBER	+	MONTH
le		11 (onze)		novembre
le		20 (vingt)		mai

EXCEPTION: The first of the month is **le premier.**

➡ In front of numbers, the French use **le** (and never **l'**): **le onze, le huit.**

➡ Note that when dates are abbreviated in French, the day always comes first.

   2/8   **le deux** août   **1/11**   **le premier** novembre

Les Rolling Stones
à Paris
Au Parc des Princes
le 23 juin

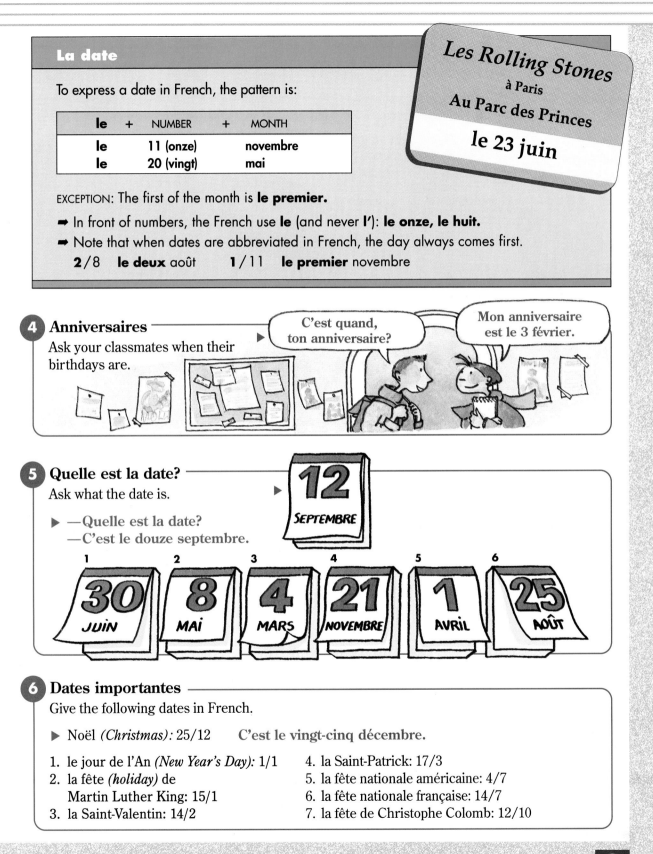

4 **Anniversaires**

Ask your classmates when their birthdays are.

C'est quand, ton anniversaire?

Mon anniversaire est le 3 février.

5 **Quelle est la date?**

Ask what the date is.

12 SEPTEMBRE

▶ —**Quelle est la date?**
—**C'est le douze septembre.**

1. **30** JUIN
2. **8** MAI
3. **4** MARS
4. **21** NOVEMBRE
5. **1** AVRIL
6. **25** AOÛT

6 **Dates importantes**

Give the following dates in French.

▶ Noël *(Christmas):* 25/12   **C'est le vingt-cinq décembre.**

1. le jour de l'An *(New Year's Day):* 1/1
2. la fête *(holiday)* de Martin Luther King: 15/1
3. la Saint-Valentin: 14/2
4. la Saint-Patrick: 17/3
5. la fête nationale américaine: 4/7
6. la fête nationale française: 14/7
7. la fête de Christophe Colomb: 12/10

À votre tour!

1 Nathalie et Philippe

Nathalie is talking to Philippe and you hear parts of their conversation. For each of Nathalie's questions, select Philippe's response from the suggested answers.

1. Qui est-ce?
2. C'est ta soeur?
3. Quel âge as-tu?
4. C'est quand, ton anniversaire?
5. Quel âge a ton oncle?
6. Tu connais Stéphanie?
7. Comment s'appelle ta prof de français?
8. Quel jour est-ce aujourd'hui?

a. Vendredi.
b. Oui, c'est une copine.
c. Quinze ans.
d. Non, c'est ma cousine.
e. Quarante-cinq ans.
f. Elle s'appelle Madame Doucette.
g. Le dix-huit décembre.
h. C'est mon cousin Christophe.

2 Et toi?

You have just met Nathalie at a party. Answer her questions.

1. Quel âge as-tu?
2. Quel âge a ton copain (ta copine)?
3. C'est quand, ton anniversaire?
4. C'est quand, l'anniversaire de ton copain (ta copine)?
5. Comment s'appelle le (la) prof de français?

3 Conversation dirigée

Nathalie and Christophe are in a café. Christophe sees another girl that Nathalie seems to know. He wonders who she is.

Christophe			Nathalie
asks Nathalie if she knows the girl	→ ↙	says she does and that she is a friend	
asks Nathalie the name of her friend	→ ↙	says that her name is Michèle Lafontaine	
asks if she is Canadian	→ ↙	says yes and adds that she is from Quebec City (de Québec)	
says what a coincidence (Quelle coïncidence!) and adds that he is also from Quebec City			

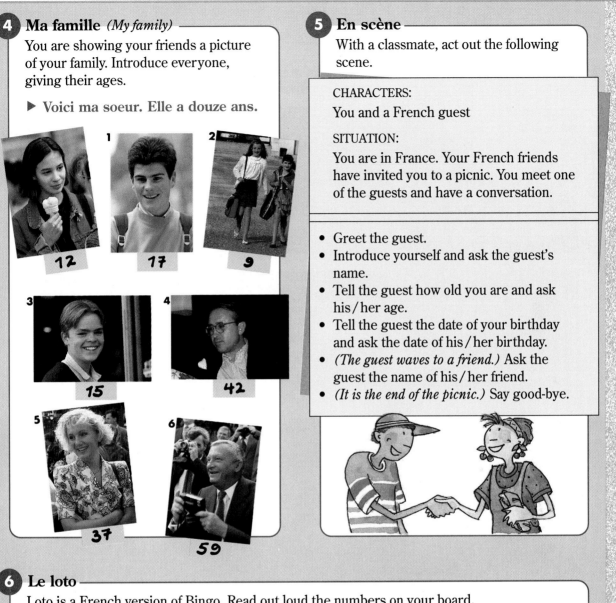

4 **Ma famille** *(My family)*

You are showing your friends a picture of your family. Introduce everyone, giving their ages.

▶ **Voici ma soeur. Elle a douze ans.**

1

2

12   17   9

3

4

15   42

5

6

37

59

5 **En scène**

With a classmate, act out the following scene.

CHARACTERS:
You and a French guest

SITUATION:
You are in France. Your French friends have invited you to a picnic. You meet one of the guests and have a conversation.

- Greet the guest.
- Introduce yourself and ask the guest's name.
- Tell the guest how old you are and ask his/her age.
- Tell the guest the date of your birthday and ask the date of his/her birthday.
- *(The guest waves to a friend.)* Ask the guest the name of his/her friend.
- *(It is the end of the picnic.)* Say good-bye.

6 **Le loto**

Loto is a French version of Bingo. Read out loud the numbers on your board.

	13	24		42			75	89
8		25	31		53	68		
	16		36		57		79	90

LES *BRUITS* FRANÇAIS *(French sounds)*

People in various countries can hear the same noises and interpret them differently. Notice how the French express certain common sounds.

TIC-TAC

TOC! TOC!

DRING DRING

PLOC... PLOC...

BOUM!

DING DONG

What sounds do animals make in France? They make French sounds, of course!

HI-HAN
l'âne

MEUH
la vache

OUAF OUAF
le chien

MIAOU
le chat

COT... COT... CODÈT
la poule

COIN COIN
le canard

ASTÉRIX
en action

Astérix and his friends lead an action-packed life. Can you match the sounds with the corresponding cartoon frames?

a **CRAAAC!**

b **POM POM! POM!**

c **RRROAAOOO!**

GRRRAOOR!

d GLOU! GLOU! GLOU! GLOU! GLOU!

e **TATARARA TATA!**

f **PAFF!**

1 From ASTÉRIX LE GAULOIS

2 From ASTÉRIX GLADIATEUR

3 From ASTÉRIX CHEZ LES BRETONS

AU NOM DE CÉSAR, OUVREZ!

4 From ASTÉRIX CHEZ LES BRETONS

5 From ASTÉRIX GLADIATEUR

6 From ASTÉRIX LE GAULOIS

3 Bon appétit!

INTRODUCTION

culturelle

Bon appétit!

Where do you go when you want something to eat or drink? Maybe to a fast-food restaurant or an ice cream place?

French teenagers also have a large choice of places to go when they are hungry or thirsty. Some go to a bakery **(une boulangerie)** or a pastry shop **(une pâtisserie)** to buy croissants, éclairs, or other small pastries. Some may buy pizzas, crepes, hot dogs, or ice-cream cones from street vendors. Still others may go to a fast-food restaurant **(un fast-food).** But the favorite place to get something to eat or drink is the café. There are cafés practically everywhere in France. As you will see, the café plays an important role in the social life of all French people.

THÈME ET OBJECTIFS

Having a snack in France

When in France, you will often want to buy something to eat or drink. In this unit, you will learn . . .
- to order some common foods and beverages in a café
- to ask about prices and pay the check
- to ask friends to give or lend you something

You will also learn . . .
- to identify French money
- to talk about the weather
- to name the seasons

9 LEÇON

Tu as faim?

Pierre, Philippe, and Nathalie are on their way home from school. They stop by a street vendor who sells sandwiches and pizza. Today it is Pierre's turn to treat his friends.

Scène 1. Pierre et Nathalie

PIERRE: Tu as faim?
NATHALIE: Oui, j'ai faim.
PIERRE: Tu veux un sandwich ou une pizza?
NATHALIE: Donne-moi une pizza, s'il te plaît.
PIERRE: Voilà.
NATHALIE: Merci.

Scène 2. Pierre et Philippe

PIERRE: Et toi, Philippe, tu as faim?
PHILIPPE: Oh là là, oui, j'ai faim.
PIERRE: Qu'est-ce que tu veux? Un sandwich ou une pizza?
PHILIPPE: Je voudrais un sandwich . . . euh . . . et donne-moi aussi une pizza.
PIERRE: C'est vrai! Tu as vraiment faim!

Scene 1. Pierre and Nathalie

PIERRE: *Are you hungry?*
NATHALIE: *Yes, I'm hungry.*
PIERRE: *Do you want a sandwich or a pizza?*
NATHALIE: *Give me a pizza, please.*
PIERRE: *Here you are.*
NATHALIE: *Thanks.*

Scene 2. Pierre and Philippe

PIERRE: *And you, Philippe, are you hungry?*
PHILIPPE: *Oh yes, I'm hungry.*
PIERRE: *What do you want? A sandwich or a pizza?*
PHILIPPE: *I would like a sandwich . . . er . . . and give me a pizza too.*
PIERRE: *It's true! You are really hungry!*

POUR COMMUNIQUER

How to say that you are hungry:

| **J'ai faim.** | *I'm hungry.* |
| **Tu as faim?** | *Are you hungry?* |

How to offer a friend something:

| **Tu veux . . . ?** | *Do you want . . .?* | **Tu veux** un sandwich? |
| **Qu'est-ce que tu veux?** | *What do you want?* | **Qu'est-ce que tu veux?** Un sandwich ou une pizza? |

How to ask a friend for something:

Je voudrais . . .	*I would like . . .*	**Je voudrais** un sandwich.
Donne-moi . . .	*Give me . . .*	**Donne-moi** une pizza.
S'il te plaît . . .	*Please . . .*	**S'il te plaît,** François, donne-moi une pizza.

J'ai faim! Tu as faim?

Les nourritures *(Foods)*

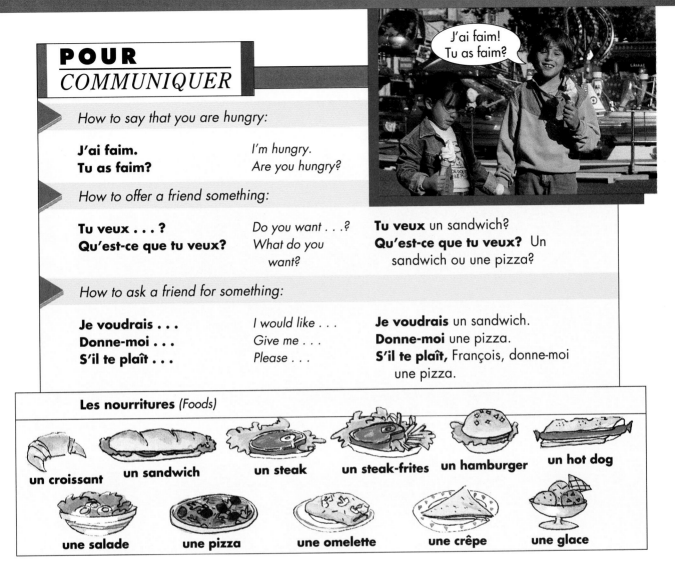

un croissant   un sandwich   un steak   un steak-frites   un hamburger   un hot dog

une salade   une pizza   une omelette   une crêpe   une glace

NOTE CULTURELLE

Les jeunes et la nourriture

In general, French teenagers eat their main meals at home with their families. On weekends or after school, however, when they are with friends, they often stop at a fast-food restaurant or a café for something to eat.

At fast-food restaurants, French teenagers order pretty much the same types of foods as Americans: hamburgers, hot dogs, and pizza.

At a café, teenagers may order a croissant, a sandwich, or a dish of ice cream. Some favorite sandwiches are ham **(un sandwich au jambon),** Swiss cheese **(un sandwich au fromage),** or salami **(un sandwich au saucisson).** And, of course, they are made with French bread, which has a crunchy crust. Another traditional quick café meal is a small steak with French fries **(un steak-frites).**

Petit commentaire

In France, sandwiches are tradition-ally very simple: a piece of French bread with a slice of ham or cheese. Usually sandwiches are not made with mayonnaise or lettuce.

un sandwich, une pizza

You may have noted that the names of some foods are masculine and others are feminine. In French, ALL NOUNS, whether they designate people or things, are either MASCULINE or FEMININE.

MASCULINE NOUNS	FEMININE NOUNS
un sandwich **le** sandwich **un** croissant **le** croissant	**une** pizza **la** pizza **une** salade **la** salade

---

1 **Au choix** *(Your choice)*

Offer your classmates a choice between the following items. They will decide which one they would like.

▶ une pizza ou un sandwich?

1. un hamburger ou un steak?
2. un hot dog ou un sandwich?
3. une salade ou une omelette?
4. un steak-frites ou une pizza?
5. une crêpe ou un croissant?
6. une glace à la vanille ou une glace au chocolat?

---

2 **Au café**

You are in a French café. Ask for the following dishes.

▶ **Je voudrais un croissant.**

3 **Tu as faim?**

You have invited French friends to your home. Ask if they are hungry and offer them the following foods.

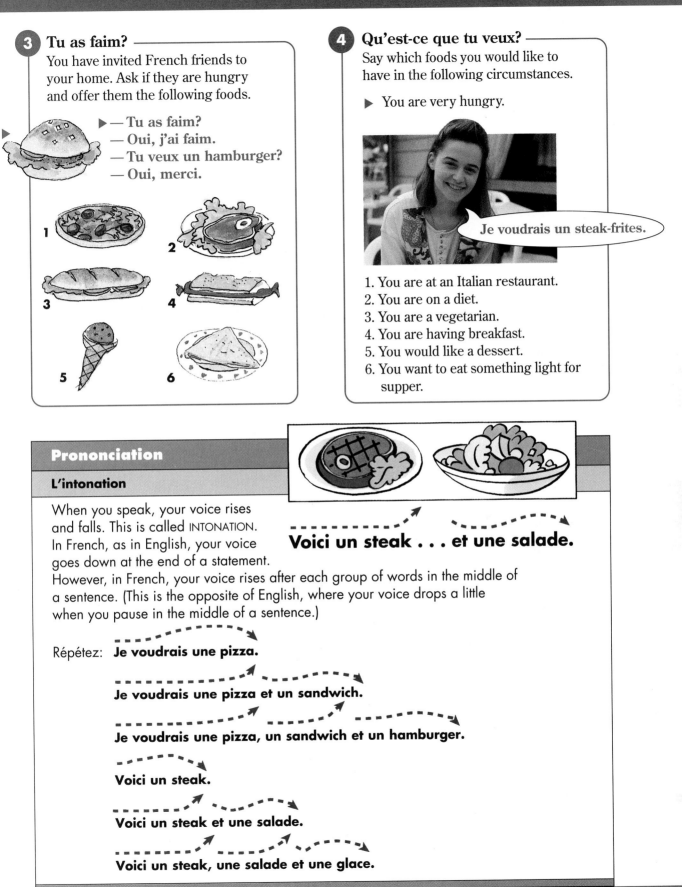

▶ — Tu as faim?
— Oui, j'ai faim.
— Tu veux un hamburger?
— Oui, merci.

1

2

3

4

5

6

4 **Qu'est-ce que tu veux?**

Say which foods you would like to have in the following circumstances.

▶ You are very hungry.

Je voudrais un steak-frites.

1. You are at an Italian restaurant.
2. You are on a diet.
3. You are a vegetarian.
4. You are having breakfast.
5. You would like a dessert.
6. You want to eat something light for supper.

Prononciation

L'intonation

When you speak, your voice rises and falls. This is called INTONATION. In French, as in English, your voice goes down at the end of a statement.

Voici un steak . . . et une salade.

However, in French, your voice rises after each group of words in the middle of a sentence. (This is the opposite of English, where your voice drops a little when you pause in the middle of a sentence.)

Répétez: **Je voudrais une pizza.**

Je voudrais une pizza et un sandwich.

Je voudrais une pizza, un sandwich et un hamburger.

Voici un steak.

Voici un steak et une salade.

Voici un steak, une salade et une glace.

Au café

This afternoon Jean-Paul and Isabelle went shopping. They are now tired and thirsty. Jean-Paul invites Isabelle to a café.

Tu as soif?

Vous désirez, mademoiselle?

Scène 1. Jean-Paul, Isabelle

JEAN-PAUL: Tu as soif?
ISABELLE: Oui, j'ai soif.
JEAN-PAUL: On va dans un café? Je t'invite.
ISABELLE: D'accord!

Scène 2. Le garçon, Isabelle, Jean-Paul

LE GARÇON: Vous désirez, mademoiselle?
ISABELLE: Un jus d'orange, s'il vous plaît.
LE GARÇON: Et pour vous, monsieur?
JEAN-PAUL: Donnez-moi une limonade,* s'il vous plaît.

C'est pour vous, mademoiselle?

Scène 3. Le garçon, Isabelle, Jean-Paul

LE GARÇON: *(à Isabelle)* La limonade, c'est pour vous, mademoiselle?
JEAN-PAUL: Non, c'est pour moi.
LE GARÇON: Ah, excusez-moi. Voici le jus d'orange, mademoiselle.
ISABELLE: Merci.

Scene 2. *The waiter, Isabelle, Jean-Paul*

WAITER: May I help you, Miss?
ISABELLE: An orange juice, please.
WAITER: And for you, Sir?
JEAN-PAUL: Give me a "limonade," please.

Scene 3. *The waiter, Isabelle, Jean-Paul*

WAITER: The "limonade" is for you, Miss?
JEAN-PAUL: No, it's for me.
WAITER: Oh, excuse me. Here is the orange juice, Miss.
ISABELLE: Thank you.

Scene 1. *Jean-Paul, Isabelle*

JEAN-PAUL: Are you thirsty?
ISABELLE: Yes, I'm thirsty.
JEAN-PAUL: Shall we go to a café? I'm treating (inviting) you.
ISABELLE: Okay!

*Une limonade is a popular inexpensive soft drink with a slight lemon flavor.

POUR *COMMUNIQUER*

Donnez-moi une limonade, s'il vous plaît!

How to say that you are thirsty:

J'ai soif.	*I'm thirsty.*
Tu as soif?	*Are you thirsty?*

How to order in a café:

Vous désirez?	*May I help you?*	**—Vous désirez?**
Je voudrais . . .	*I would like . . .*	**—Je voudrais** un Perrier.

How to request something . . .

from a friend:	*from an adult:*	
S'il te plaît, donne-moi . . .	**S'il vous plaît, donnez-moi . . .**	*Please, give me . . .*

➡ Note that French people have two ways of saying *please*. They use
s'il te plaît with friends, and
s'il vous plaît with adults.

As we will see later, young people address their friends as **tu** and adults that they do not know very well as **vous.**

Les boissons *(Beverages)*

| un soda | un jus d'orange | un jus de pomme | un jus de tomate | un jus de raisin* | une limonade | un café | un thé | un chocolat |

■ NOTE ■ CULTURELLE

Le café

The café is a favorite gathering place for French young people. They go there not only when they are hungry or thirsty but also to meet their friends. They can sit at a table and talk for hours over a cup of coffee or a glass of juice. French young people also enjoy mineral water and soft drinks, which they order by brand name **(un Coca, un Orangina, un Pepsi, un Schweppes, un Perrier).** In a French café, a 15% service charge is included in the check. However, most people also leave some small change as an added tip.

*****Jus de raisin** is a golden-colored juice made from grapes.

Petit commentaire

On the whole, French young people prefer natural beverages, such as flavored mineral water or juices, to carbonated soft drinks. In the larger cities, one can find inviting juice bars that offer a wide selection of freshly blended fruit drinks.

1 Tu as soif?

You have invited a French friend to your house. You offer a choice of beverages and your friend (played by a classmate) responds.

▶ un thé ou un chocolat?
—**Tu veux un thé ou un chocolat?**
—**Donne-moi un chocolat, s'il te plaît.**

1. un thé ou un café?
2. une limonade ou un soda?
3. un jus de pomme ou un jus d'orange?   4. un jus de raisin ou un jus de tomate?

2 Au café

You are in a French café. Get the attention of the waiter (**Monsieur**) or the waitress (**Mademoiselle**) and place your order. Act out the dialogue with a classmate.

3 Que choisir? *(What to choose?)*

You are in a French café. Decide what beverage you are going to order in each of the following circumstances.

▶ You are very thirsty.
S'il vous plaît, une limonade (un jus de pomme) . . .

1. It is very cold outside.
2. You do not want to spend much money.
3. You like juice but are allergic to citrus fruits.
4. It is breakfast time.
5. You have a sore throat.

4 La faim et la soif *(Hungry and thirsty)*

You are having a meal in a French café. Order the food suggested in the picture. Then order something to drink with that dish. A classmate will play the part of the waiter.
Note: **Et avec ça?** means *And with that?*

Vous désirez?

Je voudrais un steak-frites.

Et avec ça?

Un Orangina, s'il vous plaît.

1   2   3   4

Prononciation

L'accent final

In French, the rhythm is very even and the accent always falls on the *last* syllable of a word or group of words.

ŭn chŏcŏlāt

Répétez: **Philippe   Thomas   Alice   Sophie   Dominique**

un café	**Je voudrais un café.**
une salade	**Donnez-moi une salade.**
un chocolat	**Donne-moi un chocolat.**

If you want French people to understand you, the most important thing is to speak with an even rhythm and to stress the last syllable in each group of words. (Try speaking English this way: people will think you have a French accent!)

Ça fait combien?

At the café, Jean-Paul and Isabelle have talked about many things. It is now time to go. Jean-Paul calls the waiter so he can pay the check.

JEAN-PAUL: S'il vous plaît?
LE GARÇON: Oui, monsieur.
JEAN-PAUL: Ça fait combien?
LE GARÇON: Voyons, un jus d'orange, 12 francs, et une limonade, 10 francs. Ça fait 22 francs.
JEAN-PAUL: 22 francs . . . Très bien . . . Mais, euh . . . Zut! Où est mon porte-monnaie . . . ? Dis, Isabelle, prête-moi 30 francs, s'il te plaît.

Dis, Isabelle, prête-moi 30 francs, s'il te plaît.

JEAN-PAUL: *Excuse me? (Please?)*
WAITER: *Yes, Sir.*
JEAN-PAUL: *What do I owe you? (How much does that make?)*
WAITER: *Let's see, one orange juice, 12 francs, and one "limonade" 10 francs. That comes to (makes) 22 francs.*

JEAN-PAUL: *22 francs . . . Very well . . . But, uh . . . Darn! Where is my wallet . . . ? Hey, Isabelle, loan me 30 francs, please.*

■ NOTE ■
CULTURELLE

L'argent français *(French money)*

The monetary unit of France is the **franc,** which is divided into 100 **centimes.** French currency consists of bills and coins. French bills are of different sizes— the greater the value, the larger the bill: **500 francs, 200 francs, 100 francs, 50 francs,** and **20 francs.** The people represented on the bills are famous French writers, painters, scientists, and musicians.

POUR *COMMUNIQUER*

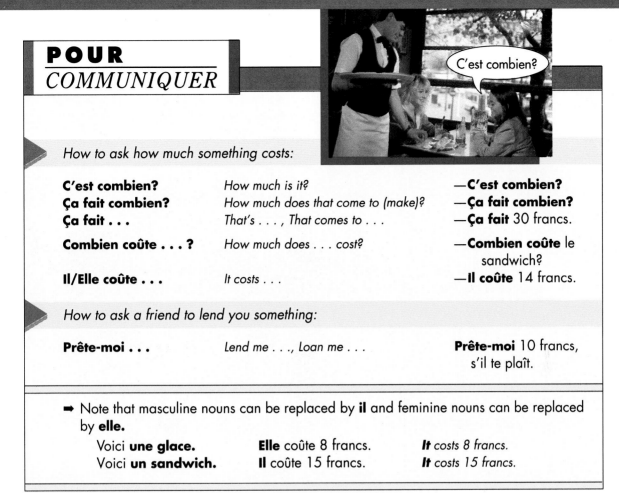

C'est combien?

How to ask how much something costs:

C'est combien?	*How much is it?*	**—C'est combien?**
Ça fait combien?	*How much does that come to (make)?*	**—Ça fait combien?**
Ça fait . . .	*That's . . . , That comes to . . .*	**—Ça fait** 30 francs.
Combien coûte . . . ?	*How much does . . . cost?*	**—Combien coûte** le sandwich?
Il/Elle coûte . . .	*It costs . . .*	**—Il coûte** 14 francs.

How to ask a friend to lend you something:

Prête-moi . . .	*Lend me . . ., Loan me . . .*	**Prête-moi** 10 francs, s'il te plaît.

➡ Note that masculine nouns can be replaced by **il** and feminine nouns can be replaced by **elle.**

Voici **une glace.**	**Elle** coûte 8 francs.	*It costs 8 francs.*
Voici **un sandwich.**	**Il** coûte 15 francs.	*It costs 15 francs.*

ÇA FAIT COMBIEN?

Petit commentaire

*French people of all ages love to eat out, and French restaurants have the reputation of offering the best cuisine in the world. Of course, there are all kinds of restaurants for all kinds of budgets, ranging from the simple country inn (**l'auberge de campagne**) with its hearty regional food to the elegant three-star restaurant (**restaurant trois étoiles**) with its exquisite—and expensive—menu.*

1   S'il te plaît . . .

You have been shopping in Paris and discover that you did not exchange enough money. Ask a friend to loan you the following sums.

▶ 10 francs
   S'il te plaît, prête-moi dix francs.

1. 20 francs	4. 60 francs	7. 85 francs
2. 30 francs	5. 75 francs	8. 90 francs
3. 45 francs	6. 80 francs	9. 95 francs

2   Décision

Before ordering at a café, Stéphanie and Émilie are checking the prices. Act out the dialogues.

▶ le chocolat

Combien coûte le chocolat?

Il coûte douze francs.

1. le thé
2. le jus d'orange
3. la salade de tomates
4. la glace à la vanille
5. le café
6. le steak-frites
7. le hot dog
8. l'omelette
9. la salade mixte
10. le jus de raisin

LE SELECT

BOISSONS

café 8F
chocolat..............................12F
thé 8F
limonade 10F
jus d'orange 12F
jus de raisin 12F

GLACES

glace au chocolat 8F
glace à la vanille 8F

SANDWICHS

sandwich au jambon 15F
sandwich au fromage 15F

ET AUSSI . . .

steak-frites 35F
salade mixte 7F
salade de tomates.............10F
omelette 15F
hot dog 15F
croissant..............................8F
pizza..................................12F

LE SELECT
P. SOULIE
CAFÉ RESTAURANT *
Tél. 01.45.22.46.29
30, boulevard des Batignolles 75017 Paris

3 Ça fait combien?

You have gone to Le Select with your friends and have ordered the following items. Now you are ready to leave the café, and each one wants to pay. Check the prices on the menu for Le Select, and act out the dialogue.

▶ —Ça fait combien, s'il vous plaît?
—Ça fait 12 francs.
—Voici 12 francs.
—Merci.

4 Au «Select»

You are at Le Select. Order something to eat and drink. Since you are in a hurry, ask for the check right away. Act out the dialogue with a classmate who will play the part of the waiter/waitress.

Prononciation

La consonne «r» /r/

The French consonant "**r**" is not at all like the English "**r**." It is pronounced at the back of the throat. In fact, it is similar to the Spanish "jota" sound of José.

Répétez:
Ma̲rie   Pa̲ris   o̲range   Henri̲
f̲ranc   t̲rès   c̲roissant   f̲romage
bonjou̲r   pou̲r   Pie̲rre   qua̲rt
Robe̲rt   Richa̲rd   Re̲née   Raoul

Ma̲rie, p̲rête-moi t̲rente f̲rancs.

Ma̲rie

LEÇON 12

Le temps

It is nine o'clock Sunday morning. Cécile and her brother
Philippe have planned a picnic for the whole family.
Cécile is asking about the weather.

> Quel temps fait-il?

> Il fait mauvais.

> Zut, zut et zut!

> Papa va nous inviter au restaurant.

CÉCILE:	Quel temps fait-il?
PHILIPPE:	Il fait mauvais!
CÉCILE:	Il fait mauvais?
PHILIPPE:	Oui, il fait mauvais! Regarde! Il pleut!
CÉCILE:	Zut, zut et zut!
PHILIPPE:	!!!???
CÉCILE:	Et le pique-nique?
PHILIPPE:	Le pique-nique? Ah oui, le pique-nique! . . . Écoute, ça n'a pas d'importance.
CÉCILE:	Pourquoi?
PHILIPPE:	Pourquoi? Parce que Papa va nous inviter au restaurant.
CÉCILE:	Super!

CÉCILE:	How's the weather?
PHILIPPE:	It's bad!
CÉCILE:	It's bad?
PHILIPPE:	Yes, it's bad! Look! It's raining!
CÉCILE:	Darn, darn, darn!
PHILIPPE:	!!!???
CÉCILE:	And the picnic?
PHILIPPE:	The picnic? Oh yes, the picnic! . . . Listen, it's not important (that has no importance).
CÉCILE:	Why?
PHILIPPE:	Why? Because Dad is going to take us out (invite us) to a restaurant.
CÉCILE:	Great!

Quel temps fait-il?

POUR
COMMUNIQUER

How to talk about the weather:

Quel temps fait-il?   *How's the weather?*

Il fait beau.	**Il fait bon.**	**Il fait chaud.**	**Il fait frais.**
Il fait froid.	**Il fait mauvais.**	**Il pleut.**	**Il neige.**

Les saisons *(Seasons)*

le printemps	*spring*	**au printemps**	*in (the) spring*
l'été	*summer*	**en été**	*in (the) summer*
l'automne	*fall, autumn*	**en automne**	*in (the) fall*
l'hiver	*winter*	**en hiver**	*in (the) winter*

1 Ta région

Tell Cécile what the weather is like in your part of the country.

▶ en juillet

En juillet, il fait chaud.

1. en août
2. en septembre
3. en novembre
4. en janvier
5. en mars
6. en mai

2 Les quatre saisons

Describe what the weather is like in each of the four seasons in the following cities.

▶ à Miami

En été, il fait chaud. En automne, il fait chaud aussi. En hiver, il fait frais. Au printemps, il fait bon.

Miami

1. à Chicago
2. à San Francisco
3. à Denver
4. à Boston
5. à Seattle
6. à Dallas

À votre tour!

1 Isabelle et Jean-Paul

Isabelle is talking to Jean-Paul. You hear parts of their conversation. For each of Isabelle's questions, select Jean-Paul's response from the suggested answers.

1 Tu as faim?

2 Tu veux un jus de pomme?

3 Combien coûte le café au Café Français?

4 Quel temps fait-il?

5 Quelle est ta saison favorite?

a. Il fait chaud.
b. Huit francs.
c. Oui, merci, j'ai soif.
d. C'est le printemps.
e. Oui, je voudrais un sandwich.

2 Et toi?

Now Isabelle is phoning you. Answer her questions.

1. Quel temps fait-il aujourd'hui?

2. Quel temps fait-il en hiver?

3. Quelle est ta saison favorite?

3 Conversation dirigée

Stéphanie is in a café called Le Petit Bistrot. The waiter is taking her order. With a partner, compose and act out a dialogue according to the script suggested below.

le garçon			Stéphanie
greets client and asks if he may help her	→ ↙	says that she would like a croissant and asks how much an orange juice costs	
answers 15 francs	→ ↙	asks for an orange juice . . . calls the waiter and asks how much she owes	
says 22 francs	→ ↙	gives waiter 25 francs (Voici . . .)	
says thank you			

4 Au café

You are in a French café. Call the waiter/waitress and order the following items. A classmate will play the part of the waiter/waitress.

▶ —Monsieur (Mademoiselle), s'il vous plaît!
—Vous désirez?
—Un croissant, s'il vous plaît!
(Donnez-moi un croissant, s'il vous plaît!)
(Je voudrais un croissant, s'il vous plaît!).

5 En scène

With two classmates, act out the following scene.

CHARACTERS:

You, a French friend, and the waiter in the café

SITUATION:

A French friend has been showing you around Paris. You invite your friend to a café and discover too late that you have not changed enough money. Your friend will respond to your questions.

- Ask your friend if he/she is thirsty.
- Ask if he/she wants a soft drink.
- Ask if he/she is hungry.
- Ask if he/she wants a sandwich.
- When the waiter comes, your friend orders and you ask for a croissant and a cup of hot chocolate.
- Ask the waiter how much everything is.
- Ask your friend to please lend you 20 francs.

6 La date, la saison et le temps

Look at the calendar days. For each one, give the date, the season, and the weather.

▶ C'est le dix avril.
C'est le printemps.
Il pleut.

Une chanson: Alouette

Alouette *(The Lark)* is a popular folksong of French-Canadian origin. As the song leader names the various parts of the bird's anatomy, he points to his own body. The chorus repeats the refrain with enthusiasm.

bonjour QUÉBEC

1. Alouette, gentille alouette,
   Alouette, je te plumerai.

   Je te plumerai la tête,
   Je te plumerai la tête.

   Et la tête—et la tête
   Alouette—Alouette
   Oh oh oh oh

2. Alouette, gentille alouette
   Alouette, je te plumerai.

   Je te plumerai le bec,
   Je te plumerai le bec.

   Et le bec—et le bec
   Et la tête—et la tête
   Alouette—Alouette
   Oh oh oh oh

3. Je te plumerai le cou . . .

4. Je te plumerai les ailes . . .

5. Je te plumerai le dos . . .

6. Je te plumerai les pattes . . .

7. Je te plumerai la queue . . .

le bec
la tête
le cou
le dos
les ailes
la queue
les pattes

Québec

Les parties du corps

(Parts of the body)

l'oeil (les yeux)
le nez
la bouche
le bras
le ventre
la jambe

les cheveux
la tête
l'oreille
le cou
le dos
la main
le pied

Un jeu   Jacques a dit

The French sometimes play a game called **Jacques a dit** *(Jim said)*. The rules are the same as the English game of Simon Says. Everyone stands up to play.

The game leader says: **Jacques a dit: Les mains sur la tête!** placing her hands on her head. The other players also place their hands on their head.

Then the game leader may say: **Les mains sur le dos!** placing her hands on her back. This time, however, the other players should not move, because the game leader did not first say **Jacques a dit.** Any player that did move must sit down.

The game continues until only one player is left standing.

À l'école en France

BONJOUR, Nathalie!

Bonjour!

Je m'appelle Nathalie Aubin.

J'ai 15 ans et j'habite° à Savigny-sur-Orge avec ma famille. (Savigny est une petite° ville° à 20 kilomètres au sud° de Paris.)

J'ai un frère, Christophe, 17 ans, et deux soeurs, Céline, 13 ans, et Florence, 7 ans.

Mon père est programmeur. (Il travaille° à Paris.)

Ma mère est dentiste. (Elle travaille à Savigny.)

Je vais au lycée Jean-Baptiste Corot.

Je suis élève° de seconde°. Et vous?

Nathalie

j'habite *I live*   **petite** *small*   **ville** *city*   **sud** *south*
travaille *works*   **élève** *student*   **seconde** *tenth grade*

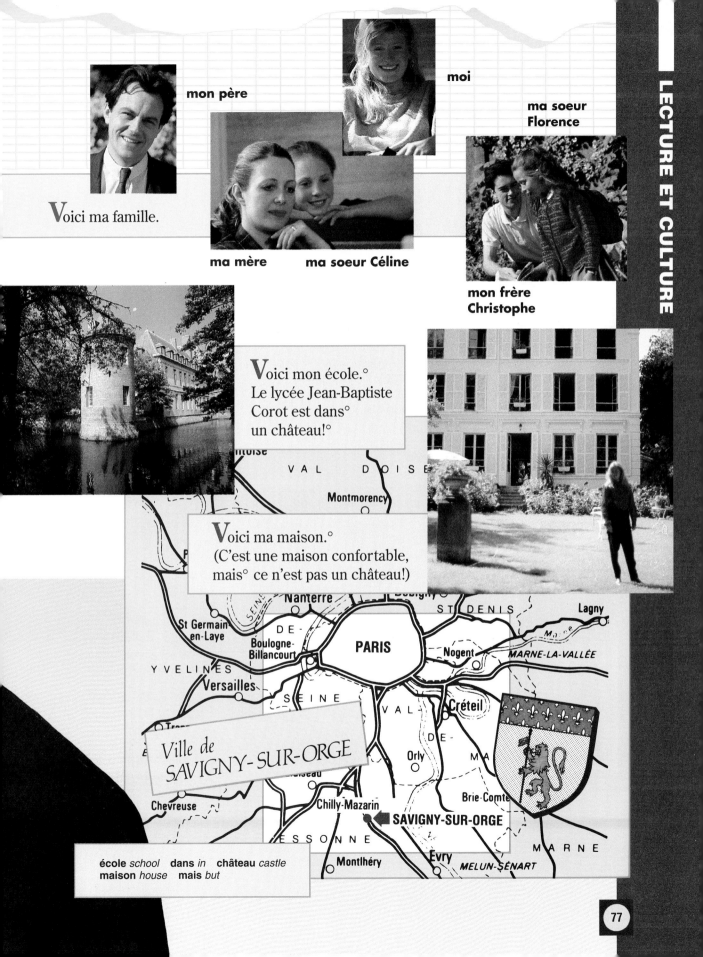

mon père

moi

ma soeur Florence

Voici ma famille.

ma mère   **ma soeur Céline**

mon frère Christophe

Voici mon école.°
Le lycée Jean-Baptiste
Corot est dans°
un château!°

Voici ma maison.°
(C'est une maison confortable,
mais° ce n'est pas un château!)

Ville de
SAVIGNY-SUR-ORGE

SAVIGNY-SUR-ORGE

école *school* **dans** *in* **château** *castle*
maison *house* **mais** *but*

Un jour de classe

Le matin

À la maison

Nathalie gets up every morning at seven. After a light breakfast (toasted bread with butter and jam, hot chocolate), she leaves for school.

Nathalie sur sa mobylette

Since she does not live too far from her lycée, she goes there on her moped **(sa mobylette).** Students who live farther away take the school bus.

La classe de sciences-éco

Nathalie arrives at school at about 8:25, five minutes before her first class. Today, Thursday, her first class is economics **(les sciences économiques),** which is her favorite subject.

L'après-midi

À la cantine

At 12:30, Nathalie goes to the school cafeteria **(la cantine)** for lunch. As in American schools, the food is served cafeteria-style. During lunch break, Nathalie meets with her friends from other classes.

La classe d'anglais

Classes start again at two o'clock. Today they finish at four.

Après les classes

Depending on when her last class ends, Nathalie either goes home right after school or participates in one of the many school clubs.

Le soir

Dans la salle à manger

The Aubins have dinner around 7:30. Everyone helps with the kitchen chores. Today it is Christophe's turn.

Nathalie does her homework after dinner. She usually has about one or two hours of homework every night. When she is finished, she reads or listens to cassettes for a while, then goes to bed around 11 P.M.

Nathalie dans sa chambre

L'emploi du temps

LYCÉE JEAN-BAPTISTE COROT

Étudiante: AUBIN, Nathalie

	LUNDI	MARDI	MERCREDI	JEUDI	VENDREDI	SAMEDI
8h30 à 9h30	Histoire	Allemand				
9h30 à 10h30	Anglais	Français	Anglais	Sciences économiques		Français
10h30 à 11h30	Sport	Français	Sciences économiques	Sciences physiques (13h30)	Allemand	Français
11h30 à 12h30	Français	Latin	Maths	Maths (13h30)	Latin	Latin
13h00 à 14h00					Sciences physiques	Histoire ou Civilisation
14h00 à 15h00	Sciences physiques	Maths				
15h00 à 16h00	Géographie	Maths		Allemand		
16h00 à 17h00	Civilisation	Anglais		Histoire		

NOTE CULTURELLE

Le programme scolaire

At the lycée, all students take a certain number of required subjects. These include French, math, one foreign language, history and geography, physical sciences, natural sciences, and physical education. Depending on their career plans, French students also have to choose among certain electives: a second foreign language, economics, computer science, biology, music.

Here are some of the subjects taught in French secondary schools. How many can you identify?

le français
l'anglais
l'espagnol
l'allemand
le latin

l'histoire
la géographie
les sciences
   économiques
l'éducation civique *(civics)*
la musique
le dessin
l'éducation physique

les maths
la biologie
la physique
la chimie
l'informatique *(computer science)*
les sciences naturelles
la philosophie

ACTIVITÉS CULTURELLES

1. Look carefully at Nathalie's class schedule. You may have noted certain differences between the French and the American school systems.
   - French students have more class hours than American students. How many hours of classes does Nathalie have each week?
   - French students learn more foreign languages than American students. In France, the study of foreign languages is compulsory. What languages is Nathalie learning?
   - French students usually have Wednesday afternoon free. Does Nathalie have school on Saturday morning? on Saturday afternoon?
2. Write out your own class schedule in French.

*L*e lycée *J*ean-*B*aptiste *C*orot

un pastel de Corot

Jean-Baptiste Corot

*L*ike many French schools, the lycée Jean-Baptiste Corot of Savigny-sur-Orge is named after a famous French person. Jean-Baptiste Corot is a 19th century painter, remembered especially for his landscapes.

The lycée Jean-Baptiste Corot is both very old and very modern. It was created in the 1950's on the grounds of a historical castle dating from the 12th century. The castle, which serves as the administrative center, is still surrounded by a moat. The lycée itself has many modern facilities which include:

- **les salles de classe** *(classrooms)*
- **la cantine** *(cafeteria)*
- **le stade** *(stadium)* **et le terrain de sport** *(playing field)*

Plan du lycée Jean-Baptiste Corot

une salle de classe

la cantine

le terrain de sport

■ NOTES ■ CULTURELLES

1 L'école secondaire

There are two types of secondary schools in France:
- **le collège,** which corresponds to the U.S. middle school (grades 6 to 9)
- **le lycée,** which corresponds to the U.S. high school (grades 10 to 12)

On the following chart, you will notice that each grade **(une classe)** is designated by a number (as in the United States): **sixième (6e), cinquième (5e), quatrième (4e),** etc. However, the progression from grade to grade is the opposite in France. The secondary school begins in France with **sixième** and ends with **terminale.**

École	Classe	Âge des élèves	Équivalent américain
Le collège	sixième (6e)	11–12 ans	*sixth grade*
	cinquième (5e)	12–13 ans	*seventh grade*
	quatrième (4e)	13–14 ans	*eighth grade*
	troisième (3e)	14–15 ans	*ninth grade*
Le lycée	seconde (2e)	15–16 ans	*tenth grade*
	première (1re)	16–17 ans	*eleventh grade*
	terminale	17–18 ans	*twelfth grade*

2 Le bulletin de notes

At the end of each term, French students receive a report card **(le bulletin de notes),** which must be signed by their parents. Most schools assign grades on a scale of 0 (low) to 20 (high). Most teachers also write a brief evaluation of the student's progress in each subject.

Here is a report card for the first semester.

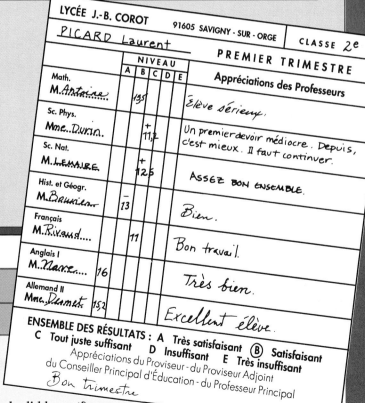

LYCÉE J.-B. COROT — 91605 SAVIGNY - SUR - ORGE — CLASSE 2e

PICARD Laurent

PREMIER TRIMESTRE

	NIVEAU A B C D E	Appréciations des Professeurs
Math. M. Antoine	13,5	Élève sérieux.
Sc. Phys. Mme Durin	+11,2	Un premier devoir médiocre. Depuis, c'est mieux. Il faut continuer.
Sc. Nat. M. Lemaire	+12,5	ASSEZ BON ENSEMBLE.
Hist. et Géogr. M. Brunier	−13	Bien.
Français M. Rivaud	11	Bon travail.
Anglais I M. Narre	16	Très bien.
Allemand II Mme Dumet	15,2	Excellent élève.

ENSEMBLE DES RÉSULTATS : **A** Très satisfaisant **B** Satisfaisant **C** Tout juste suffisant **D** Insuffisant **E** Très insuffisant

Appréciations du Proviseur - du Proviseur Adjoint du Conseiller Principal d'Éducation - du Professeur Principal

Bon trimestre

ACTIVITÉ CULTURELLE

1. What is the name of the student?
2. What is the name of his school?
3. What grade is he in?
4. What is his best subject? What grade did he get?
5. What is his weakest subject? What grade did he get?
6. How many foreign languages is he studying? Which ones?

Expressions pour la classe

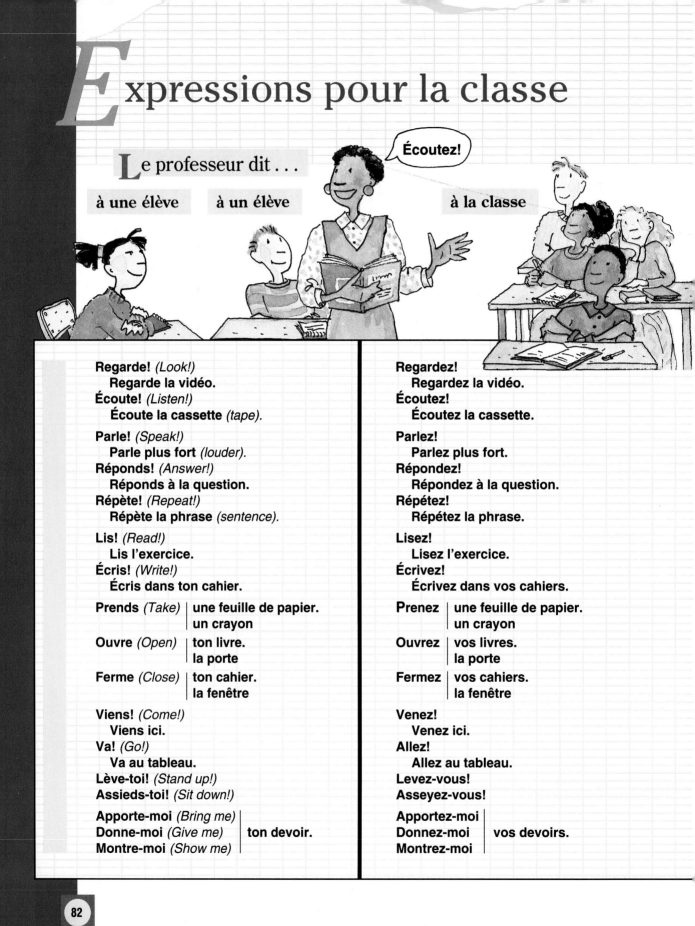

Le professeur dit . . .

à une élève   à un élève   à la classe

Écoutez!

Regarde! *(Look!)*	**Regardez!**
Regarde la vidéo.	**Regardez la vidéo.**
Écoute! *(Listen!)*	**Écoutez!**
Écoute la cassette *(tape).*	**Écoutez la cassette.**
Parle! *(Speak!)*	**Parlez!**
Parle plus fort *(louder).*	**Parlez plus fort.**
Réponds! *(Answer!)*	**Répondez!**
Réponds à la question.	**Répondez à la question.**
Répète! *(Repeat!)*	**Répétez!**
Répète la phrase *(sentence).*	**Répétez la phrase.**
Lis! *(Read!)*	**Lisez!**
Lis l'exercice.	**Lisez l'exercice.**
Écris! *(Write!)*	**Écrivez!**
Écris dans ton cahier.	**Écrivez dans vos cahiers.**

Prends *(Take)*	une feuille de papier. un crayon	**Prenez**	une feuille de papier. un crayon
Ouvre *(Open)*	ton livre. la porte	**Ouvrez**	vos livres. la porte
Ferme *(Close)*	ton cahier. la fenêtre	**Fermez**	vos cahiers. la fenêtre

Viens! *(Come!)*	**Venez!**
Viens ici.	**Venez ici.**
Va! *(Go!)*	**Allez!**
Va au tableau.	**Allez au tableau.**
Lève-toi! *(Stand up!)*	**Levez-vous!**
Assieds-toi! *(Sit down!)*	**Asseyez-vous!**

Apporte-moi *(Bring me)*		**Apportez-moi**	
Donne-moi *(Give me)*	ton devoir.	**Donnez-moi**	vos devoirs.
Montre-moi *(Show me)*		**Montrez-moi**	

Quelques objets

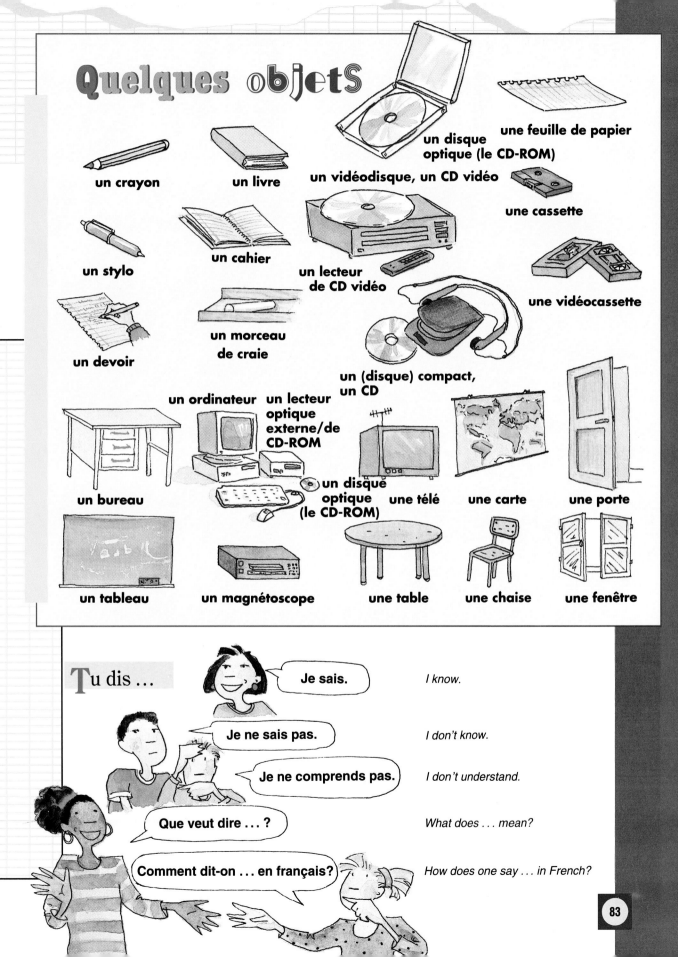

un crayon

un livre

un disque optique (le CD-ROM)

une feuille de papier

un vidéodisque, un CD vidéo

une cassette

un stylo

un cahier

un lecteur de CD vidéo

une vidéocassette

un devoir

un morceau de craie

un (disque) compact, un CD

un ordinateur

un lecteur optique externe/de CD-ROM

un bureau

un disque optique (le CD-ROM)

une télé

une carte

une porte

un tableau

un magnétoscope

une table

une chaise

une fenêtre

Tu dis ...

Français	English
Je sais.	*I know.*
Je ne sais pas.	*I don't know.*
Je ne comprends pas.	*I don't understand.*
Que veut dire ... ?	*What does ... mean?*
Comment dit-on ... en français?	*How does one say ... in French?*

83

La vie de

Félicitations!

Congratulations! Now that you have learned how to meet and greet people in French, you are going to discover more about everyday life in France: **La vie de tous les jours.**

What are some of the aspects of daily life that you and your friends often talk about? You probably discuss home and family, things you own, and people you know. You talk about what you like to do, where you like to go, and what your weekend plans are. If you were going to France, you would discover that French young people are interested in the same topics.

In this second part of your book, you will learn . . .
- how to talk about your daily activities (both in school and out of school)
- how to make future plans: what you are going to do
- how to describe people you know
- how to describe objects you own
- how to talk about your home and your family
- how to express your opinions

You will also learn . . .
- how to ask your way around in a French city
- how to extend and accept invitations

In order to express yourself accurately, you will also begin to learn how the French language works: how to ask and answer questions, how to describe people, places, and things.

En avant et bon courage!

Jean-Paul Valette   Rebecca M. Valette

tous les jours

85

UNITÉ 4

Qu'est-ce qu'on fait?

THÈME ET OBJECTIFS

Daily activities

In this unit, you will be talking about the things you do every day, such as working and studying, as well as watching TV and listening to the radio.

You will learn . . .
- to describe some of your daily activities
- to say what you like and do not like to do
- to ask and answer questions about where others are and what they are doing

You will also learn . . .
- to invite friends to do things with you
- to politely accept or turn down an invitation

LEÇON 13 Mes activités

Accent sur ... Les activités de la semaine

French teenagers, as well as their parents, put a lot of emphasis on doing well in school. On the whole, French students spend a great deal of time on their studies. French schools have a longer class day than American schools, and teachers tend to assign quite a lot of homework.

However, French teenagers do not study all the time. They also watch TV and listen to music. Many participate in various sports activities, but to a lesser extent than young Americans. On weekends, French teenagers like to go out with their friends. Some go shopping. Others go to the movies. Many enjoy dancing and going to parties. Sunday is usually a family day for visiting relatives or going for a drive in the country.

Au cinéma
Des copains sont au cinéma.

Au café
Stéphanie est au café.

Une boum
Dominique et Stéphanie
sont à une boum.

**Le terrain de foot
au lycée Corot**
Des jeunes jouent au foot.

En classe
Marc et Patrick sont en classe.

A. Préférences

Est-ce que tu aimes parler français?

How to talk about what you like and don't like to do:

Est-ce que tu aimes . . .?	*Do you like . . .?*	**Est-ce que tu aimes** parler *(to speak)* français?
J'aime . . .	*I like . . .*	Oui, **j'aime** parler français.
Je n'aime pas . . .	*I don't like . . .*	Non, **je n'aime pas** parler français.
Je préfère . . .	*I prefer . . .*	**Je préfère** parler anglais.

J'aime . . .

téléphoner
to phone

parler français
to talk, speak French

parler anglais
to speak English

parler espagnol
to speak Spanish

manger
to eat

chanter
to sing

danser
to dance

nager
to swim

1 **Et toi?**

Indicate what you like to do in the following situations by completing the sentences.

1. En classe,
   j'aime . . .
   mais je préfère . . .
   - étudier
   - écouter le professeur
   - parler avec *(with)* un copain
   - parler avec une copine

2. En été,
   j'aime . . .
   mais je préfère . . .
   - travailler
   - nager
   - voyager
   - jouer au volley

J'aime aussi (also) . . .

jouer au tennis
to play tennis

jouer au volley
to play volleyball

jouer au basket
to play basketball

jouer au foot
to play soccer

Mais (but) **je préfère** . . .

regarder la télé
to watch TV

écouter la radio
to listen to the radio

dîner au restaurant
to have dinner at the restaurant; to eat out

voyager
to travel

Je n'aime pas toujours (always) . . .

étudier
to study

travailler
to work

HAVE YOU NOTED?
1. French people like to shorten words. For example, the words **volleyball, basketball, football,** and **télévision** are often shortened to **volley, basket, foot,** and **télé.**
2. In French, **foot** (or **football**) refers to *soccer*.

3. Avec mes (*my*) copains,
   j'aime . . .
   mais je préfère . . .

   • chanter
   • manger

   • écouter la radio
   • jouer au basket

4. Avec ma famille,
   j'aime . . .
   mais je préfère . . .

   • voyager
   • regarder la télé

   • jouer à «Trivial Pursuit»
   • dîner au restaurant

5. À la maison (*At home*),
   j'aime . . .
   mais je préfère . . .

   • étudier
   • téléphoner

   • manger
   • écouter mon walkman

2 Tu aimes ou tu n'aimes pas?

Say whether or not you like to do the following things.

▶ parler français?

J'aime parler français.

Je n'aime pas parler français.

1. parler anglais?
2. étudier?
3. danser?
4. chanter?
5. jouer au basket?
6. jouer au tennis?

7. regarder la télé?
8. dîner au restaurant?
9. manger?
10. travailler?
11. écouter la radio?
12. téléphoner?

3 Préférences

Ask your classmates if they like to do the following things.

▶ —Est-ce que tu aimes téléphoner?
—Oui, j'aime téléphoner. (Non, je n'aime pas téléphoner.)

4 Dialogue

Philippe is asking Hélène if she likes to do certain things. She replies that she prefers to do other things. Play both roles. Note: "??" means you can invent an answer.

▶ PHILIPPE: **Est-ce que tu aimes nager?**

HÉLÈNE: **Oui, mais je préfère jouer au tennis.**

B. Souhaits (Wishes)

Je voudrais voyager en France.

How to talk about what you want, would like, and do not want to do:

Je veux . . .	*I want . . .*	**Je veux** parler français.
Je voudrais . . .	*I would like . . .*	**Je voudrais** voyager en France.
Je ne veux pas . . .	*I don't want . . .*	**Je ne veux pas** étudier aujourd'hui.

5 Ce soir *(Tonight)*

Say whether or not you want to do the following things tonight.

▶ étudier?
   Oui, je veux étudier.
   (Non, je ne veux pas étudier.)

1. parler français?
2. travailler?
3. jouer au ping-pong?
4. chanter?
5. danser?
6. regarder la télé?
7. écouter la radio?
8. dîner avec une copine?
9. parler à *(to)* mon frère?
10. téléphoner à mon cousin?

6 Weekend

Caroline and her friends are discussing their weekend plans. What do they say they would like to do?

▶ CAROLINE: **Je voudrais jouer au tennis.**

7 Trois souhaits *(Three wishes)*

Read the list of suggested activities and select the three that you would like to do most.

parler français
parler espagnol
parler avec *(with)* Oprah Winfrey
dîner avec le Président
dîner avec Tom Cruise

voyager avec ma cousine
voyager en France
chanter comme *(like)* Stevie Wonder
jouer au tennis avec Steffi Graf
jouer au basket comme Michael Jordan

▶ **Je voudrais parler espagnol.**
  Je voudrais chanter comme Stevie Wonder.
  Je voudrais voyager en France.

Est-ce que tu veux jouer au tennis?

C. Invitations

▶ *How to invite a friend:*

Est-ce que tu veux …?	*Do you want to . . . ?*	**Est-ce que tu veux** jouer au tennis?
Est-ce que tu peux …?	*Can you . . . ?*	**Est-ce que tu peux** parler à mon copain?
avec moi/toi	*with me/you*	Est-ce que tu veux dîner **avec moi?**

▶ *How to accept an invitation:*

Oui, bien sûr …	*Yes, of course . . .*	
Oui, merci …	*Yes, thanks . . .*	
Oui, d'accord …	*Yes, all right, okay . . .*	
je veux bien.	*I'd love to.*	**Oui, bien sûr, je veux bien.**
je veux bien …	*I'd love to . . .*	**Oui, merci, je veux bien** dîner avec toi.

▶ *How to turn down an invitation:*

Je regrette, mais	*I'm sorry, but*	**Je regrette, mais je ne peux pas**
je ne peux pas …	*I can't . . .*	dîner avec toi.
Je dois …	*I have to, I must . . .*	**Je dois** étudier.

---

8 Invitations ───────

Imagine a French exchange group is visiting your school. Invite the following French students to do things with you. They will accept. (Your classmates will play the parts of the students.)

▶ Monique / dîner

Monique, est-ce que tu veux dîner avec moi?

Oui, d'accord, je veux bien dîner avec toi.

1. Éric / parler français
2. Philippe / étudier
3. Céline / jouer au tennis
4. Anne / manger une pizza
5. Jean-Claude / chanter
6. Caroline / danser

9 Conversation ───────

Ask your classmates if they want to do the following things. They will answer that they cannot and explain what they have to do.

▶ jouer au basket? (étudier)
 —**Est-ce que tu veux jouer au basket?**
 —**Non, je ne peux pas. Je dois étudier.**

1. jouer au volley? (travailler)
2. jouer au ping-pong? (téléphoner à ma cousine)
3. étudier avec moi? (étudier avec ma copine)
4. dîner avec moi? (dîner avec ma famille)
5. nager? (jouer au foot à deux heures)

À votre tour!

1 Créa-dialogue

Ask your classmates if they want to do the following things with you. They will answer that they cannot and will give one of the excuses in the box.

> Est-ce que tu veux jouer au tennis avec moi?

> Non, je ne peux pas. Je dois travailler.

▶ jouer au tennis

1. jouer au basket
2. manger une pizza
3. regarder la télé
4. jouer au ping-pong
5. dîner au restaurant

Excuses:
étudier
travailler
téléphoner à une copine

dîner avec ma cousine
parler avec ma mère
chanter avec la chorale *(choir)*

2 Conversation dirigée

Philippe is phoning Stéphanie. Write out their conversation according to the directions. You may want to act out the dialogue with a classmate.

Philippe				Stéphanie
asks Stéphanie how she is	➚	answers that she is fine		
asks her if she wants to eat out	➚	asks at what time		
says at 8 o'clock	➘	says that she is sorry but that she has to study		
says it is too bad (**Dommage!**)				

3 Expression personnelle

What we like to do often depends on the circumstances. Complete the sentences below saying what you like and don't like to do in the following situations.

▶ En hiver . . .
En hiver, j'aime regarder la télé.
J'aime aussi jouer au basket.
Je n'aime pas nager.

1. En été . . .
2. En automne . . .
3. Le samedi *(On Saturdays)* . . .
4. Le dimanche . . .
5. Le soir *(In the evening)* . . .
6. En classe . . .
7. Avec mes *(my)* amis . . .
8. Avec ma famille . . .

4 Composition

Write three things that you like to do and three things that you do not like to do.

▶ J'aime jouer au volley. Je n'aime pas jouer au foot.

5 Correspondance

This summer, you are going to spend two weeks in France. Your pen pal Philippe has written, asking what you like and don't like to do on vacation (**en vacances**). Write a postcard answering his questions.

▶

Cher Philippe,
En vacances,
j'aime . . .

PHILIPPE RAYMOND
12 AV. VICTOR HUGO
PARIS 75116
FRANCE

Qui est là?

It is Wednesday afternoon. Pierre is looking for his friends but cannot find anyone. Finally he sees Hélène at the Café Bellevue and asks her where everyone is.

PIERRE:	<u>Où</u> est Jacqueline?	*Where*
HÉLÈNE:	Elle est <u>à la maison</u>.	*at home*
PIERRE:	Et Jean-Claude? Il est <u>là</u>?	*here*
HÉLÈNE:	Non, il n'est pas là.	
PIERRE:	Où est-il?	
HÉLÈNE:	Il est <u>en ville</u> avec une copine.	*in town*
PIERRE:	Et Nicole et Sandrine? Est-ce qu'elles sont <u>ici</u>?	*here*
HÉLÈNE:	Non, elles sont au restaurant.	
PIERRE:	<u>Alors</u>, qui est là?	*So*
HÉLÈNE:	Moi, je suis ici.	
PIERRE:	C'est <u>vrai</u>, tu es ici! Eh bien, <u>puisque</u> tu es là,	*true / since*
	<u>je t'invite au cinéma</u>. D'accord?	*I'll invite you to the movies*
HÉLÈNE:	Super! Pierre, tu es un <u>vrai</u> copain!	*real*

● Compréhension

Indicate where the following people are by selecting the appropriate completions.

1. Jacqueline est . . .   a) au café
2. Jean-Claude est . . .   b) à la maison
3. Nicole et Sandrine sont . . .   c) en ville
4. Hélène et Pierre sont . . .   d) au restaurant

■ NOTE ■
CULTURELLE

Le mercredi après-midi

French high school students do not have classes on Wednesday afternoons. They use this free time to go out with their friends or to catch up on their homework. For some students, Wednesday afternoon is also the time for music and dance lessons as well as sports club activities. However, in contrast to the United States, many French schools have classes on Saturday mornings.

A. Le verbe *être* et les pronoms sujets

Être *(to be)* is the most frequently used verb in French. Note the forms of **être** in the chart below.

	être	*to be*	
SINGULAR	je **suis** tu **es** il/elle **est**	*I am* *you are* *he/she is*	Je **suis** américain. Tu **es** canadienne. Il **est** anglais.
PLURAL	nous **sommes** vous **êtes** ils/elles **sont**	*we are* *you are* *they are*	Nous **sommes** à Paris. Vous **êtes** à San Francisco. Ils **sont** à Genève.

➡ Note the liaison in the **vous** form:

  Vous êtes français?

➡ Note the expression **être d'accord** *(to agree)*:

  —Tu **es** d'accord   *Do you agree*
    avec moi?   *with me?*
  —Oui, je **suis** d'accord!   *Yes, I agree.*

TU or VOUS?

When talking to ONE person, the French have two ways of saying *you:*

- **tu** ("familiar *you*") is used to talk to someone your own age (or younger) or to a member of your family
- **vous** ("formal *you*") is used when talking to anyone else

When talking to TWO or more people, the French use **vous.**

> **Learning about language**
> The words **je** *(I)*, **tu** *(you)*, **il** *(he)*, **elle** *(she)*, etc. are called SUBJECT PRONOUNS.
> - SINGULAR pronouns refer to one person (or object).
> - PLURAL pronouns refer to two or more people (or objects).
>
> The VERB **être** *(to be)* is IRREGULAR because its forms do not follow a predictable pattern.
>
> A chart showing the subject pronouns and their corresponding verb forms is called a CONJUGATION.

REMINDER: You should use . . .
- **vous** to address your teacher
- **tu** to address a classmate

Tu es français? Vous êtes français? Vous êtes français?

ILS or ELLES?

The French have two ways of saying *they:*

- **ils** refers to two or more males or to a
  mixed group of males and females
- **elles** refers to two or more females

Ils sont à Paris.   Ils sont à Bordeaux.

Ils sont à Lyon.   Elles sont à Nice.

1 En France

The following students are on vacation in France.
Which cities are they in?

▶ Alice . . . à Nice.   **Alice est à Nice.**

1. Philippe . . . à Toulon.
2. Nous . . . à Paris.
3. Vous . . . à Marseille.
4. Je . . . à Lyon.
5. Tu . . . à Tours.
6. Michèle et Francine . . . à Lille.
7. Éric et Vincent . . . à Strasbourg.
8. Ma cousine . . . à Toulouse.
9. Mon copain . . . à Bordeaux.

Vocabulaire: *Où?*

Où est Cécile?   *Where is Cécile?*

Elle est . . .

ici *(here)*	**là** *(here, there)*	**là-bas** *(over there)*
à Paris *(in Paris)*	**à** Boston	**à** Québec
en classe *(in class)*	**en ville** *(downtown, in town, in the city)*	
en vacances *(on vacation)*	**en** France *(in France)*	
au café *(at the café)*	**au restaurant**	**au cinéma** *(at the movies)*
à la maison *(at home)*		

---

2 À Nice

Catherine is spending her summer
vacation in Nice at the home of her pen
pal Stéphanie Lambert. Catherine has
met many different people and is asking
them various questions. Complete her
questions with **Tu es** or **Vous êtes,** as
appropriate.

▶ *(Stéphanie's brother)* . . . en vacances?
Tu es en vacances?

▶ *(Monsieur Lambert)* . . . de *(from)* Tours?
Vous êtes de Tours?

1. *(Mélanie, a friend of Stéphanie's)* . . . canadienne?
2. *(Olivier, Stéphanie's boyfriend)* . . . souvent *(often)* avec Stéphanie?
3. *(Monsieur Tardif, the neighbor)* . . . en vacances?
4. *(the mailman)* . . . de Nice?
5. *(Frédéric, Stéphanie's young cousin)* . . . souvent à Nice?
6. *(a woman in the park)* . . . française?
7. *(a little girl at the beach)* . . . en vacances?
8. *(a man reading* Time *magazine)* . . . américain?

3 Où sont-ils?

Corinne is wondering if some of the people she knows are in certain places. Tell her she is right, using **il, elle, ils,** or **elles** in your answers.

▶ —Ta cousine est à Chicago?
—Oui, elle est à Chicago.

▶ —Pierre et Vincent sont au café?
—Oui, ils sont au café.

1. Stéphanie est à Lyon?
2. Monsieur Thomas est à San Francisco?
3. Suzanne et Monique sont à Genève?
4. Cécile et Charlotte sont au café?

5. Ta soeur est en ville?
6. Ton cousin est en vacances?
7. Claire, Alice et Éric sont au cinéma?
8. Monsieur et Madame Joli sont à Montréal?

4 Où?

You want to know where certain people are. A classmate will answer you on the basis of the illustrations.

▶ —Où est Céline?
—Elle est à New York.

Céline

1. Daniel
2. Caroline
3. Jean-Louis
4. Robert
5. Florence
6. Hélène
7. Julien

B. Les questions à réponse affirmative ou négative

The sentences on the left are statements. The sentences on the right are questions. These questions are called YES/NO QUESTIONS because they can be answered by *yes* or *no*. Note how the French questions begin with **est-ce que.**

STATEMENTS	YES/NO QUESTIONS	
Stéphanie est ici.	**Est-ce que** Stéphanie est ici?	*Is Stéphanie here?*
Tu es français.	**Est-ce que** tu es français?	*Are you French?*
Paul et Marc sont au café.	**Est-ce que** Paul et Marc sont au café?	*Are Paul and Marc at the café?*
Tu veux dîner avec moi.	**Est-ce que** tu veux dîner avec moi?	*Do you want to have dinner with me?*

Yes/no questions can be formed according to the pattern:

est-ce que + STATEMENT?	**Est-ce que** Pierre est ici?
est-ce qu' (+ VOWEL SOUND)	**Est-ce qu'**il est en ville?

⇒ In yes/no questions, the voice goes up at the end of the sentence.

Est-ce que Paul et Florence sont au café?

⇒ In casual conversation, yes/no questions can be formed without **est-ce que** simply by letting your voice rise at the end of the sentence.

Tu es français?   Cécile est en ville?

OBSERVATION: When you expect someone to agree with you, another way to form a yes/no question is to add the tag **n'est-ce pas** at the end of the sentence.

Tu es américain, **n'est-ce pas?**   *You are American, **aren't you?***
Tu aimes parler français, **n'est-ce pas?**   *You like to speak French, **don't you?***
Vous êtes d'accord, **n'est-ce pas?**   *You agree, **don't you?***

5 Nationalités

You are attending an international music camp. Ask about the nationalities of the other participants.

▶ Marc/canadien?   **Est-ce que Marc est canadien?**

1. Jim/américain?
2. Luisa/mexicaine?
3. Paul et Philippe/français?
4. tu/canadien?
5. vous/anglais?
6. Anne/française?
7. Ellen et Carol/ américaines?

Expressions pour la conversation

How to answer a yes/no question:

Oui!	*Yes!*	**Non!**	*No!*
Mais oui!	*Sure!*	**Mais non!**	*Of course not!*
Bien sûr!	*Of course!*		
Peut-être . . .	*Maybe . . .*		

---

6 Conversation

Ask your classmates the following questions. They will answer, using an expression from **Expressions pour la conversation.**

▶ Ton cousin est français?

1. Ta mère est à la maison?
2. Ta cousine est en France?
3. Ton copain est en classe?
4. Tu veux dîner avec moi?
5. Tu veux jouer au tennis avec moi?

Mais oui!   (Mais non!)

Alice, est-ce que ton cousin est français?

C. La négation

Compare the affirmative and negative sentences below:

AFFIRMATIVE	NEGATIVE	
Je **suis** américain.	Je **ne suis pas** français.	*I'm not French.*
Nous **sommes** en classe.	Nous **ne sommes pas** en vacances.	*We are not on vacation.*
Claire **est** là-bas.	Elle **n'est pas** ici.	*She is not here.*
Vous **êtes** à Paris.	Vous **n'êtes pas** à Lyon.	*You are not in Lyon.*
Tu **es** d'accord avec moi.	Tu **n'es pas** d'accord avec Marc.	*You do not agree with Marc.*

Negative sentences are formed as follows:

SUBJECT + **ne** + VERB + **pas** . . . ↓ **n'** (+ VOWEL SOUND)	Éric et Anne **ne** sont **pas** là. Michèle **n'**est **pas** avec moi.

Je suis en classe.
Je **ne** suis **pas** à la maison.

7 Non!

Answer the following questions negatively.

▶ —Est-ce que tu es français (française)?
—**Non, je ne suis pas français (française).**

1. Est-ce que tu es canadien (canadienne)?
2. Est-ce que tu es à Québec?
3. Est-ce que tu es à la maison?
4. Est-ce que tu es au café?
5. Est-ce que tu es en vacances?
6. Est-ce que tu es au cinéma?

8 D'accord

It is raining. François suggests to his friends that they go to the movies. Say who agrees and who does not, using the expression **être d'accord.**

▶ ☹ Philippe — Philippe n'est pas d'accord.

▶ ☺ Hélène — Hélène est d'accord.

1. ☺ nous
2. ☺ je
3. ☹ tu
4. ☺ Patrick et Marc
5. ☹ Claire et Stéphanie
6. ☹ vous
7. ☺ ma copine
8. ☹ mon frère

Vocabulaire: Mots utiles *(Useful words)*

à	*at*	Je suis **à** la maison **à** dix heures.
	in	Nous sommes **à** Paris.
de	*from*	Vous êtes **de** San Francisco.
	of	Voici une photo **de** Paris.
et	*and*	Anne **et** Sophie sont en vacances.
ou	*or*	Qui est-ce? Juliette **ou** Sophie?
avec	*with*	Philippe est **avec** Pauline.
pour	*for*	Je veux travailler **pour** Monsieur Martin.
mais	*but*	Je ne suis pas français, **mais** j'aime parler français.

Fête Nationale
mardi 14 juillet
à 22h
PARIS

➡ **De** becomes **d'** before a vowel sound:
Patrick est **de** Lyon.   François est **d'**Annecy.

9 **Le mot juste** *(The right word)*

Complete the sentences below with the word in parentheses that fits logically.

1. Monsieur Moreau est en France. Aujourd'hui, il est . . . Lyon. (à/de)
2. Martine est canadienne. Elle est . . . Montréal. (de/et)
3. Florence n'est pas ici. Elle est . . . Jean-Claude. (et/avec)
4. Alice . . . Paul sont au restaurant. (avec/et)
5. Jean-Pierre n'est pas à la maison. Il est au café . . . au cinéma. (ou/et)
6. J'aime jouer au tennis . . . je ne veux pas jouer avec toi. (ou/mais)
7. Je dois travailler . . . mon père. (pour/à)

10 **Être ou ne pas être** *(To be or not to be)*

We cannot be in different places at the same time. Express this according to the model.

▶ Aline est en ville. (ici)
Aline n'est pas ici.

1. Frédéric est là-bas. (à la maison)
2. Nous sommes en classe. (au restaurant)
3. Tu es à Nice. (à Toulon)
4. Vous êtes au café. (au cinéma)
5. Jérôme est avec Sylvie. (avec Catherine)
6. Juliette et Sophie sont avec Éric. (avec Marc)

Prononciation   /a/

La voyelle /a/

The letter "**a**" alone always represents the sound /a/ as in the English word *ah*. It never has the sound of "*a*" as in English words like *class, date,* or *cinema*.

chat

Répétez: **ch**a**t ç**a **v**a **à l**a **l**à-**b**a**s **a**vec **a**mi voil**à
cla**sse c**a**fé s**a**l**a**de d**a**me d**a**te M**a**d**a**me C**a**n**a**d**a

Anne est au C**a**n**a**d**a **a**vec M**a**d**a**me L**a**v**a**l.

À votre tour!

1 Allô!

Jacques is phoning some friends. Match his questions on the left with his friends' answers on the right.

1. Où es-tu?
2. Où est ta soeur?
3. Est-ce que ton frère est à la maison?
4. Tes parents sont en vacances, n'est-ce pas?
5. Ta soeur est avec une copine?

a. Non, il est au cinéma.
b. Oui, elles sont au restaurant.
c. Je suis à la maison.
d. Elle est en classe.
e. Oui! Ils sont à Paris.

2 Où sont-ils?

Read what the following people are saying and decide where they are.

▶ **Anne et Éric sont au café.**

Une limonade, s'il vous plaît.

▶ **Anne et Éric**

Le film est excellent.

1. nous

Où est le musée *(museum)*?

2. les touristes

Une pizza, s'il vous plaît.

3. vous

Bonjour, Maman.

4. tu

Stéphanie, est-ce que tu veux nager?

5. Paul

3 Créa-dialogue

You are working for a student magazine in France. Your assignment is to interview tourists who are visiting Paris. Ask them where they are from. (Make sure to address the people appropriately as **tu** or **vous.**) Remember: The symbol "??" means you may invent your own responses.

Nationalité	Villes (Cities)	
▶ anglaise	Londres? *(London)* Liverpool	

▶ — Bonjour. <u>Vous êtes anglaise</u>?
— Oui, je suis <u>anglaise</u>.
— Est-ce que <u>vous êtes</u> de <u>Londres</u>?
— Mais non, je ne suis pas de <u>Londres</u>. Je suis de <u>Liverpool</u>.

Nationalité	Villes	
1 américaine	New York? Washington	
2 canadien	Québec? Montréal	
3 française	Paris? Nice	
4 mexicain	Mexico? Puebla	
5 ??	?? ??	
6 ??	?? ??	

4 Composition: Et toi?

Write a short paragraph about yourself and your friends.

1. Say what city you are from. **(Je suis de . . .)**
2. Say what city your father or your mother is from. **(Mon père / ma mère est de . . .)**
3. Say where one of your friends is from. **(Mon copain / ma copine . . .)**
4. Name an activity you like to do with a friend. **(J'aime . . . avec . . .)**
5. Name an activity you want to do with two friends. **(Je veux . . .)**
6. Name an activity you would like to do with one of your relatives. **(Je voudrais . . .)**

5 Composition: Personnellement

On a separate piece of paper, or on a computer, write where you are and where you are not at each of the following times.

▶ à 9 heures du matin
  • à 4 heures
  • à 7 heures du soir
  • samedi
  • dimanche
  • en juillet

À neuf heures du matin, je suis en classe. Je ne suis pas à la maison.

Une boum

Jean-Marc has been invited to a party. He is trying to decide whether to bring Béatrice or Valérie. First he talks to Béatrice.

JEAN-MARC:	<u>Dis</u>, Béatrice, tu aimes danser?	*Hey*
BÉATRICE:	Bien sûr, j'aime danser!	
JEAN-MARC:	Est-ce que tu danses bien?	
BÉATRICE:	Oui, je danse très, <u>très bien</u>.	*very well*
JEAN-MARC:	Et ta cousine Valérie? Est-ce qu'elle danse bien?	
BÉATRICE:	Non, elle ne danse pas très bien.	
JEAN-MARC:	<u>Alors</u>, c'est Valérie <u>que</u> j'invite à la <u>boum</u>.	*So / that / party*
BÉATRICE:	Mais <u>pourquoi</u> elle? Pourquoi pas moi?	*why*
JEAN-MARC:	Écoute, Béatrice, <u>je ne sais pas</u> danser! <u>Alors</u>, je préfère inviter une fille qui ne danse pas très bien. C'est normal, non?	*don't know how / So*

Compréhension: Vrai ou faux?

Read the following statements and say whether they are true (**C'est vrai!**) or false (**C'est faux!**).

1. Béatrice aime danser.
2. Elle danse bien.
3. Valérie danse très bien.
4. Jean-Marc invite Béatrice.
5. Il invite Valérie.

NOTE CULTURELLE

Une boum

On weekends, French teenagers like to go to parties that are organized at a friend's home. Often the guests contribute something to the buffet: sandwiches or soft drinks. There is also a lot of music and dancing. (French teenagers love to dance!)

These informal parties have different names according to the age group of the participants. For students at a **collège** (or junior high), a party is sometimes known as **une boum** or **une fête.** For older students at a **lycée** (or high school), it is called **une soirée** or **une fête.**

A. Les verbes en *-er*: le singulier

Many French verbs end in **-er** in the infinitive. Most of these verbs are conjugated like **parler** *(to speak)* and **habiter** *(to live)*.
Note the forms of the present tense of these verbs in the singular. Pay attention to their endings.

INFINITIVE	parler		habiter		ENDINGS
STEM	parl-		habit-		
PRESENT TENSE (SINGULAR)	Je **parle** français. Tu **parles** anglais. Il / Elle **parle** espagnol.		J' **habite** à Paris. Tu **habites** à Boston. Il / Elle **habite** à Madrid.		-e -es -e

The present tense forms of -er verbs consist of two parts:

STEM + ENDING

- The STEM does not change. It is the infinitive minus **-er:**

  parler   parl-   **habiter**   habit-

- The ENDINGS change with the subject:

  je → -e   **tu →** -es   **il / elle →** -e

➡ The above endings are silent.

➡ **Je** becomes **j'** before a vowel sound.

  je parle   **j'**habite

1 Curiosité

At the party, Olivier wants to learn more about Isabelle.
She answers his questions affirmatively. Play both roles.

Tu parles anglais?

Oui, je parle anglais.

▶ parler anglais?

1. parler espagnol?
2. habiter à Paris?
3. étudier ici?
4. jouer au volley?
5. jouer au basket?
6. chanter?

Vocabulaire: Les verbes en -er

Verbs you already know:

chanter	to sing	**nager**	to swim
danser	to dance	**parler**	to speak, talk
dîner	to have dinner	**regarder**	to watch, look at
écouter	to listen (to)	**téléphoner**	to phone, call
étudier	to study	**travailler**	to work
jouer	to play	**voyager**	to travel
manger	to eat		

New verbs:

aimer	to like	Tu **aimes** Paris?
habiter	to live	Philippe **habite** à Toulouse?
inviter	to invite	J'**invite** un copain.
organiser	to organize	Sophie **organise** une **boum**/une **soirée**/une **fête** *(party)*.
visiter	to visit (places)	Hélène **visite** Québec.

➡ **Regarder** has two meanings:
   to look (at)   Paul **regarde** Cécile.
   to watch   Cécile **regarde** la télé.

➡ Note the construction **téléphoner à:**

Hélène **téléphone**	à	Marc.
Hélène calls	. . .	*Marc.*

➡ Note the constructions with **regarder** and **écouter:**

Philippe **regarde**	. . .	Alice.
Philippe looks	*at*	*Alice.*

Alice **écoute**	. . .	le professeur.
Alice listens	*to*	*the teacher.*

---

2 **Quelle activité?**

Describe what the following people are doing by completing the sentences with one of the verbs below. Be logical in your choice of activity.

chanter   écouter   parler   travailler   manger   voyager   regarder   inviter

1. Je . . . un sandwich. Tu . . . une pizza.
2. Tu . . . anglais. Je . . . français.
3. Éric . . . la radio. Claire . . . un compact (un CD).
4. Jean-Paul . . . la télé. Tu . . . un match de tennis.
5. M. Simon . . . en *(by)* bus. Mme Dupont . . . en train.
6. Nicolas . . . Marie à la boum. Tu . . . Alain.
7. Mlle Thomas . . . dans *(in)* un hôpital. Je . . . dans un supermarché *(supermarket)*.
8. Mick Jagger . . . bien. Est-ce que tu . . . bien?

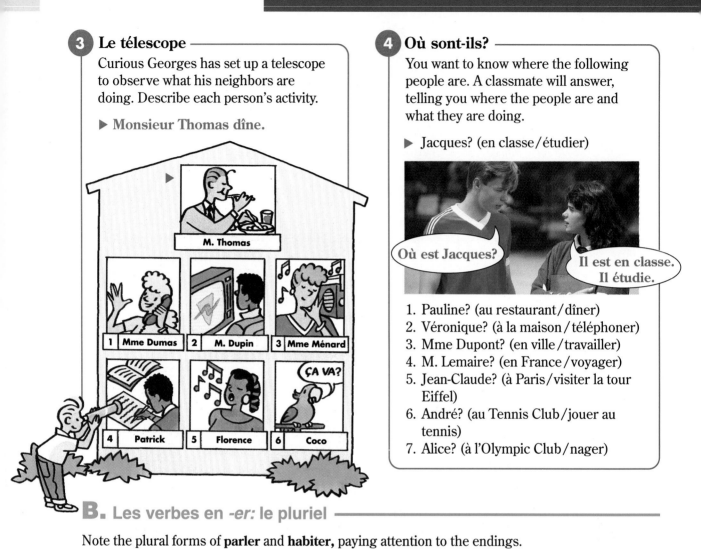

3 Le télescope

Curious Georges has set up a telescope to observe what his neighbors are doing. Describe each person's activity.

▶ **Monsieur Thomas dîne.**

M. Thomas

1 Mme Dumas 2 M. Dupin 3 Mme Ménard

4 Patrick 5 Florence 6 Coco

ÇA VA?

4 Où sont-ils?

You want to know where the following people are. A classmate will answer, telling you where the people are and what they are doing.

▶ Jacques? (en classe / étudier)

Où est Jacques?

Il est en classe. Il étudie.

1. Pauline? (au restaurant / dîner)
2. Véronique? (à la maison / téléphoner)
3. Mme Dupont? (en ville / travailler)
4. M. Lemaire? (en France / voyager)
5. Jean-Claude? (à Paris / visiter la tour Eiffel)
6. André? (au Tennis Club / jouer au tennis)
7. Alice? (à l'Olympic Club / nager)

B. Les verbes en -er: le pluriel

Note the plural forms of **parler** and **habiter,** paying attention to the endings.

INFINITIVE	parler	habiter	ENDINGS
STEM	parl-	habit-	
PRESENT TENSE (PLURAL)	Nous **parlons** français. Vous **parlez** anglais. Ils / Elles **parlent** espagnol.	Nous **habitons** à Québec. Vous **habitez** à Chicago. Ils / Elles **habitent** à Caracas.	-ons -ez -ent

➡ In the present tense, the plural endings of **-er** verbs are:

nous → **-ons**   vous → **-ez**   ils / elles → **-ent**

➡ The **-ent** ending is silent.

➡ Note the liaison when the verb begins with a vowel sound:

Nous étudions.   Vous invitez Thomas.   Ils habitent en France.   Elles aiment Paris.

OBSERVATION: When the infinitive of the verb ends in **-ger,** the **nous**-form ends in **-geons.**

nager: nous na**geons**   manger: nous man**geons**   voyager: nous voya**geons**

5 Qui?

Stéphanie is speaking to or about her friends. Complete her sentences with **tu, elle, vous,** or **ils.**

▶ ... étudient à Toulouse.
   Ils étudient à Toulouse.

1. ... habitez à Tours.
2. ... aime Paris.
3. ... étudiez à Tours.
4. ... aiment danser.
5. ... organisent une boum.
6. ... parlez espagnol.
7. ... téléphone à Jean-Pierre.
8. ... invites un copain.
9. ... dîne avec Cécile.
10. ... invitent Monique.

6 À la boum

At a party, Olivier is talking to two Canadian students, Monique and her friend. Monique answers yes to his questions.

▶ parler français?

> Oui, nous parlons français.

> Vous parlez français, n'est-ce pas?

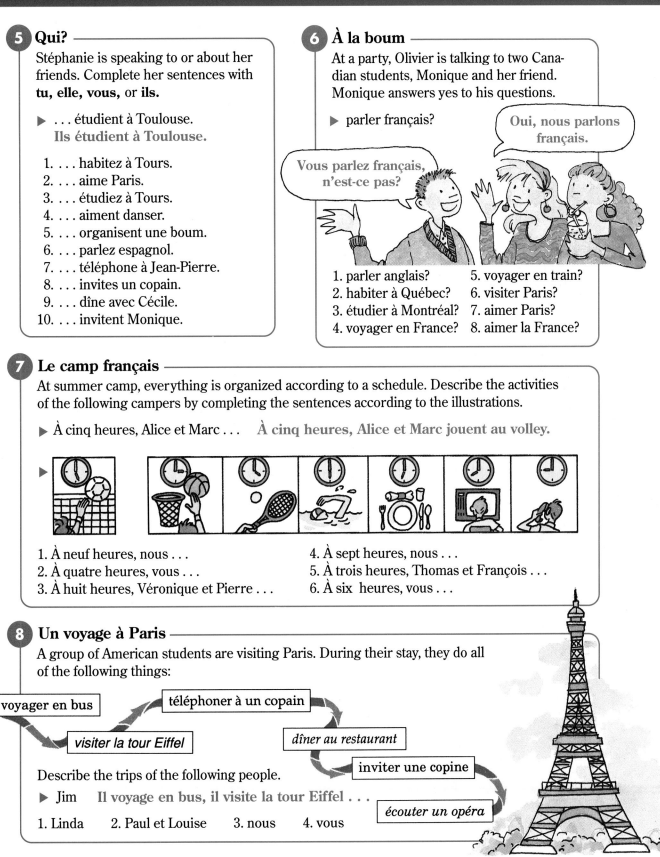

1. parler anglais?
2. habiter à Québec?
3. étudier à Montréal?
4. voyager en France?
5. voyager en train?
6. visiter Paris?
7. aimer Paris?
8. aimer la France?

7 Le camp français

At summer camp, everything is organized according to a schedule. Describe the activities of the following campers by completing the sentences according to the illustrations.

▶ À cinq heures, Alice et Marc ...   **À cinq heures, Alice et Marc jouent au volley.**

1. À neuf heures, nous ...
2. À quatre heures, vous ...
3. À huit heures, Véronique et Pierre ...
4. À sept heures, nous ...
5. À trois heures, Thomas et François ...
6. À six heures, vous ...

8 Un voyage à Paris

A group of American students are visiting Paris. During their stay, they do all of the following things:

voyager en bus

téléphoner à un copain

visiter la tour Eiffel

dîner au restaurant

inviter une copine

écouter un opéra

Describe the trips of the following people.

▶ Jim   **Il voyage en bus, il visite la tour Eiffel ...**

1. Linda   2. Paul et Louise   3. nous   4. vous

FORMS

Compare the affirmative and negative forms of **parler.**

AFFIRMATIVE	NEGATIVE
je **parle** tu **parles** il/elle **parle**	je **ne parle pas** tu **ne parles pas** il/elle **ne parle pas**
nous **parlons** vous **parlez** ils/elles **parlent**	nous **ne parlons pas** vous **ne parlez pas** ils/elles **ne parlent pas**

REMEMBER: The negative form of the verb follows the pattern:

SUBJECT + **ne** + VERB + **pas** ↓ **n'** (+ VOWEL SOUND)	Il **ne** travaille **pas** ici. Je **n'**invite **pas** Pierre.

Il <u>ne</u> travaille <u>pas</u>.

Ils <u>n'</u>écoutent <u>pas</u>.

Elle <u>ne</u> chante <u>pas</u> bien.

USES

In the present tense, French verbs have several English equivalents:

Je **joue** au tennis.
{ *I **play** tennis.*
*I **do play** tennis.*
*I **am playing** tennis.*

Je **ne joue pas** au tennis.
{ *I **do not play** tennis. (I **don't** play tennis.)*
*I **am not playing** tennis. (I'm **not playing** tennis.)*

> Studying French helps you better appreciate how the English language works.

9 Non!

One cannot do everything. From the following list of activities, select at least three that you do *not* do.

▶ **Je ne joue pas au bridge.**

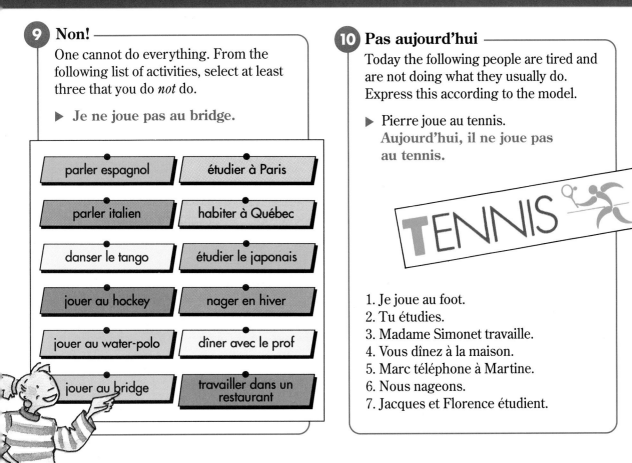

parler espagnol	étudier à Paris
parler italien	habiter à Québec
danser le tango	étudier le japonais
jouer au hockey	nager en hiver
jouer au water-polo	dîner avec le prof
jouer au bridge	travailler dans un restaurant

10 Pas aujourd'hui

Today the following people are tired and are not doing what they usually do. Express this according to the model.

▶ Pierre joue au tennis.
   Aujourd'hui, il ne joue pas au tennis.

TENNIS

1. Je joue au foot.
2. Tu étudies.
3. Madame Simonet travaille.
4. Vous dînez à la maison.
5. Marc téléphone à Martine.
6. Nous nageons.
7. Jacques et Florence étudient.

11 Un jeu: Weekend!

On weekends, people like to do different things. For each person, pick an activity and say what that person does. Select another activity and say what that person does not do.

▶ **Antoine et Isabelle dansent.**
   Ils ne regardent pas la télé.

je
tu
ma cousine
nous
Antoine et Isabelle
Monsieur Leblanc
Madame Jolivet
vous
le professeur

Vocabulaire: Mots utiles

bien	*well*	Je joue **bien** au tennis.
très bien	*very well*	Je ne chante pas **très bien.**
mal	*badly, poorly*	Tu joues **mal** au volley.
beaucoup	*a lot, much, very much*	Paul aime **beaucoup** voyager.
un peu	*a little, a little bit*	Nous parlons **un peu** français.
souvent	*often*	Charles invite **souvent** Nathalie.
toujours	*always*	Je travaille **toujours** en été.
aussi	*also, too*	Je téléphone à Marc. Je téléphone **aussi** à Véronique.
maintenant	*now*	J'étudie **maintenant.**
rarement	*rarely, seldom*	Vous voyagez **rarement.**

➡ In French, the above expressions *never* come *between* the subject and the verb. They usually come *after* the verb. Compare their positions in French and English.

Nous parlons **toujours** français.	We **always** speak French.
Tu joues **bien** au tennis.	You play tennis **well.**

12 Expression personnelle

Complete the following sentences with an expression from the list below.

bien	mal	très bien	toujours	souvent	rarement	un peu	beaucoup

1. Je chante . . .
2. Je nage . . .
3. Je regarde . . . la télé.
4. Je mange . . .

5. Je voyage . . . en bus.
6. Le prof parle . . . français.
7. Nous parlons . . . français en classe.

8. Les Rolling Stones chantent . . .
9. Michael Jordan joue . . . au basket.
10. Les Yankees jouent . . . au baseball.

Expressions pour la conversation

How to express approval or regret:

Super!	*Terrific!*	Tu parles français? **Super!**
Dommage!	*Too bad!*	Tu ne joues pas au tennis? **Dommage!**

Tu parles français?

Oui, je parle français.

Super!

13 Conversation

Ask your classmates if they do the following things. Then express approval or regret, according to their answers.

▶ parler français? —**Est-ce que tu parles français?**
—**Oui, je parle français. (Non, je ne parle pas français.)**
—**Super! (Dommage!)**

1. parler espagnol?
2. jouer au tennis?
3. danser bien?
4. voyager beaucoup?
5. dîner souvent au restaurant?
6. inviter souvent ton copain?

D. La construction: verbe + infinitif

Note the use of the infinitive in the following sentences.

J'aime **parler** français.	*I like **to speak** French. I like **speaking** French.*
Nous aimons **voyager.**	*We like **to travel**. We like **traveling.***
Tu n'aimes pas **étudier.**	*You don't like **to study**. You don't like **studying.***
Ils n'aiment pas **danser.**	*They don't like **to dance**. They don't like **dancing.***

To express what they like and don't like to do, the French use these constructions:

SUBJECT + PRESENT TENSE + INFINITIVE . . . of **aimer**		SUBJECT + **n'** + PRESENT TENSE + **pas** + INFINITIVE . . . of **aimer**	
Nous	**aimons** **voyager.**	Nous	**n'aimons pas** **voyager.**

➡ Note that in this construction, the verb **aimer** may be affirmative or negative:

> AFFIRMATIVE: Jacques **aime** voyager.   NEGATIVE: Philippe **n'aime pas** voyager.

➡ The above construction is used in questions: Est-ce que Paul **aime voyager?**

OBSERVATION: The infinitive is also used after the following expressions:

Je préfère . . .	*I prefer . . .*	**Je préfère travailler.**
Je voudrais . . .	*I would like . . .*	**Je voudrais voyager.**
Je (ne) veux (pas) . . .	*I (don't) want . . .*	**Je veux jouer** au foot.
Est-ce que tu veux . . .	*Do you want . . .*	**Est-ce que tu veux danser?**
Je (ne) peux (pas) . . .	*I can (I can't) . . .*	**Je ne peux pas dîner** avec toi.
Je dois . . .	*I have to . . .*	**Je dois étudier.**

14 Dialogue

Ask your classmates if they like to do the following things.

▶ chanter?
—**Est-ce que tu aimes chanter?**
—**Oui, j'aime chanter.**   (**Non, je n'aime pas chanter.**)

1. étudier?   4. danser?   7. nager en hiver?
2. voyager?   5. parler français en classe? 8. travailler le week-
3. téléphoner?   6. nager en été?   end *(on weekends)*?

15 Une excellente raison *(An excellent reason)*

The following people are doing certain things. Say that they like these activities.

▶ Thomas voyage.   **Il aime voyager.**

1. Monique chante.   7. Lise et Rose jouent au frisbee.
2. Charles étudie la musique.   8. Éric et Denis écoutent la radio.
3. Henri téléphone.   9. Nous travaillons.
4. Isabelle organise une boum.   10. Nous parlons espagnol.
5. Marc et Sophie nagent.   11. Vous regardez la télé.
6. Annie et Vincent dansent.   12. Vous mangez.

Prononciation

Les voyelles /i/ et /u/

/u/ **où?**   /i/ **ici!**

The vowel sounds /i/ and /u/ are easy to say. Remember to pronounce the French "**i**" as in **Mimi** and not as in the English *him*.

Répétez:
/i/ **ici** **Philippe** **il**
      Mimi **Sylvie** **visite**
Philippe visite Paris avec Sylvie.

/u/ **où** **nous** **vous**
      écoute **joue** **toujours**

Vous jouez au foot avec nous?

À votre tour!

1 Allô!

Sophie is phoning some friends. Match her questions on the left with her friends' answers on the right.

1. Est-ce que Marc est canadien?
2. Est-ce que tu joues au tennis?
3. Ton frère est à la maison?
4. Ta mère est en vacances?
5. Tu invites Christine et Juliette à la boum?

a. Non, elle travaille.
b. Oui, mais pas très bien.
c. Bien sûr! Elles aiment beaucoup danser.
d. Oui, il habite à Montréal.
e. Non, il dîne au restaurant avec un copain.

2 Créa-dialogue

Find out how frequently your classmates do the following activities. They will respond using one of the expressions on the scale.

NON	OUI		
	un peu →	souvent →	beaucoup

— **Robert**, est-ce que tu **joues au tennis?**
— Non, je **ne joue pas au tennis.**
— Est-ce que tu **écoutes la radio?**
— Oui, j'**écoute souvent la radio.**

3 Qu'est-ce qu'ils font?
(What do they do?)

Look at what the following students have put in their lockers and say what they like to do.

Éric aime jouer au tennis.
Il aime aussi . . .

4 Message illustré

Marc wrote about certain activities, using pictures. On a separate sheet, write out his description replacing these pictures with the missing words.

À la maison, ma soeur Catherine à une copine. Mon frère Éric . En général, nous à sept heures et demie. Après° le dîner, mes° parents . Moi, j' pour la classe de français. En vacances, nous . Je . Éric et Catherine . Parfois° mes parents au restaurant.

Après *After*   **mes** *my*   **Parfois** *Sometimes*

5 Point de vue personnel

Select one of the following situations. On a separate sheet of paper, or on a computer, write two things you do and one thing you do not do in that situation. Use complete sentences.

En classe, je...

À la maison,...

En vacances, . . .

Avec mes (my) copains,...

Avec mes Parents, . . .

LEÇON 16

Une interview

Nicolas is a reporter for *La Gazette des Étudiants,* the student newspaper. He has decided to write an article on the foreign students who attend his school. Today he is interviewing Fatou, a student from Senegal.

NICOLAS:	Bonjour, Fatou. Est-ce que je peux <u>te poser quelques questions</u>?	*ask you some questions*
FATOU:	Oui, bien sûr.	
NICOLAS:	Tu es <u>sénégalaise</u>, n'est-ce pas?	*Senegalese*
FATOU:	Oui, je suis sénégalaise.	
NICOLAS:	Où est-ce que tu habites?	
FATOU:	Je suis de Dakar, mais maintenant j'habite à Paris avec ma famille.	
NICOLAS:	<u>Pourquoi</u> est-ce que vous habitez à Paris?	*Why*
FATOU:	<u>Parce que</u> ma mère travaille pour l'Unesco.	*Because*
NICOLAS:	Est-ce que tu aimes Paris?	
FATOU:	J'adore Paris.	
NICOLAS:	<u>Qu'est-ce que tu fais le weekend</u>?	*What do you do on weekends?*
FATOU:	<u>Ça</u> dépend! Je regarde la télé ou je joue au tennis avec <u>mes</u> copains.	*That* *my*
NICOLAS:	Merci beaucoup, Fatou.	
FATOU:	C'est <u>tout</u>?	*all*
NICOLAS:	Oui, c'est tout!	

■ NOTES ■ CULTURELLES

1 Le Sénégal

Senegal is a country in western Africa, whose capital is Dakar. Its population includes twelve different tribes, all speaking their own dialects. Because of the historical and cultural ties between Senegal and France, French has been adopted as the official language.

Most of the people of Senegal are Muslims. Some common names are **Awa** and **Fatou** (for girls), **Babacar** and **Mamadou** (for boys).

FATOU:	Bon. <u>Alors</u>, maintenant c'est mon <u>tour</u>! Est-ce que je peux te poser une question?	*So / turn*
NICOLAS:	Bien sûr!	
FATOU:	Qu'est-ce que tu fais samedi?	
NICOLAS:	Euh . . . <u>je ne sais pas</u>.	*I don't know*
FATOU:	Alors, est-ce que tu veux <u>aller</u> à un concert de musique africaine?	*to go*
NICOLAS:	Avec qui?	
FATOU:	Avec moi, bien sûr!	
NICOLAS:	D'accord! Où? <u>Quand</u>? Et à quelle heure?	*When*

2 L'Unesco

UNESCO (United Nations Educational Scientific and Cultural Organization) was founded in 1946 to promote international cooperation in education, science, and the arts. The organization has its headquarters in Paris and is staffed by people from all member countries.

Compréhension: Vrai ou faux?

Read the following statements and say whether they are true (**C'est vrai!**) or false (**C'est faux!**).

1. Fatou est française.
2. Elle habite à Paris.
3. Le père de Fatou travaille pour l'Unesco.
4. Le weekend, Fatou aime jouer au tennis.
5. Nicolas invite Fatou à un concert.
6. Fatou accepte l'invitation.

A. Les questions d'information

The questions below ask for specific information and are called INFORMATION QUESTIONS. The INTERROGATIVE EXPRESSIONS in heavy print indicate what kind of information is requested.

—**Où** est-ce que tu habites?   ***Where** do you live?*
—J'habite **à Nice.**   *I live **in Nice.***

—**À quelle heure** est-ce que vous dînez?   ***At what time** do you eat dinner?*
—Nous dînons **à sept heures.**   *We eat **at seven.***

In French, information questions may be formed according to the pattern:

> INTERROGATIVE EXPRESSION **+ est-ce que** + SUBJECT + VERB . . . ?
>
> **À quelle heure**   **est-ce que**   vous   travaillez?

➡ **Est-ce que** becomes **est-ce qu'** before a vowel sound.
Quand **est-ce qu'**Alice et Roger dînent?

➡ In information questions, your voice rises on the interrogative expression and then falls until the last syllable.

Quand est-ce que tu travailles?   **À quelle heure** est-ce que vous dînez?

OBSERVATION: In casual conversation, French speakers frequently form information questions by placing the interrogative expression at the end of the sentence. The voice rises on the interrogative expression.

Vous habitez **où?**   Vous dînez **à quelle heure?**

Vocabulaire: Expressions interrogatives

où	*where?*	**Où** est-ce que vous travaillez?
quand?	*when?*	**Quand** est-ce que ton copain organise une boum?
à quelle heure?	*at what time?*	**À quelle heure** est-ce que tu regardes la télé?
comment?	*how?*	**Comment** est-ce que tu chantes? Bien ou mal?
pourquoi?	*why?*	—**Pourquoi** est-ce que tu étudies le français?
parce que	*because*	—**Parce que** je veux voyager en France.

➡ **Parce que** becomes **parce qu'** before a vowel sound.
Juliette invite Olivier **parce qu'**il danse bien.

1 Le Club International

The president of the International Club wants to know where some of the members are from. The secretary tells her where each one lives.

▶ Sylvie (à Québec)

LA PRÉSIDENTE: **Où est-ce que Sylvie habite?**

LE SECRÉTAIRE: **Elle habite à Québec.**

1. Jacques (à Montréal)
2. Awa (à Dakar)
3. Marc et Frédéric (à Toulouse)
4. Jean-Pierre (à Genève)
5. Sophie et Michèle (à Nice)
6. Isabelle (à Paris)

2 Curiosité

At a party in Paris, Nicolas meets Béatrice, a Canadian student. He wants to know more about her. Play both roles.

▶ où / habiter? (à Québec)

NICOLAS: **Où est-ce que tu habites?**

BÉATRICE: **J'habite à Québec.**

1. où/étudier? (à Montréal)
2. où/travailler? (dans [*in*] une pharmacie)
3. quand/parler français? (toujours)
4. quand/parler anglais? (souvent)
5. comment/jouer au tennis? (bien)
6. comment/danser? (très bien)
7. pourquoi/être en France? (parce que j'aime voyager)
8. pourquoi/être à Paris? (parce que j'ai [*I have*] un copain ici)

Expression pour la conversation

How to express surprise or mild doubt:

Ah bon? *Oh? Really?* —Stéphanie organise une soirée.
—**Ah bon?** Quand?

---

3 Au téléphone

When Philippe phones his cousin Michèle, he likes to tell her what his plans are. She asks him a few questions. Play both roles.

J'organise une soirée.

Ah bon? Quand est-ce que tu organises une soirée?

Samedi.

▶ organiser une soirée (quand? samedi)

1. organiser un pique-nique (quand? dimanche)
2. dîner avec Pauline (quand? lundi)
3. dîner avec Caroline (où? au restaurant Belcour)
4. regarder «Batman» (à quelle heure? à 9 heures)
5. jouer au tennis (quand ? demain)
6. inviter Brigitte (où? à un concert)
7. parler espagnol (comment? assez bien)
8. étudier l'italien (pourquoi? je veux voyager en Italie)

4 Questions personnelles

1. Où est-ce que tu habites? *(name of your city)*
2. Où est-ce que tu étudies? *(name of your school)*
3. À quelle heure est-ce que tu dînes?
4. À quelle heure est-ce que tu regardes la télé?
5. Quand est-ce que tu nages?
6. Quand est-ce que tu joues au tennis? (en mai? en juillet?)
7. Comment est-ce que tu chantes? (bien? très bien? mal?)
8. Comment est-ce que tu nages?

B. Les expressions interrogatives avec *qui*

To ask about PEOPLE, French speakers use the following interrogative expressions:

qui?	*who(m)?*	**Qui** est-ce que tu invites au concert?
à qui?	*to who(m)?*	**À qui** est-ce que tu téléphones?
de qui?	*about who(m)?*	**De qui** est-ce que vous parlez?
avec qui?	*with who(m)?*	**Avec qui** est-ce que Pierre étudie?
pour qui?	*for who(m)?*	**Pour qui** est-ce que Laure organise la boum?

To ask *who is doing something*, French speakers use the construction:

qui + VERB . . . ?	
Qui habite ici?	*Who lives here?*
Qui organise la boum?	*Who is organizing the party?*

5 Précisions *(Details)*

Anne is telling Hélène what certain people are doing. She asks for more details. Play both roles.

▶ Alice dîne. (avec qui? avec une copine)

1. Jean-Pierre téléphone. (à qui? à Sylvie)
2. Frédéric étudie. (avec qui? avec un copain)
3. Madame Masson parle. (à qui? à Madame Bonnot)
4. Monsieur Lambert travaille. (avec qui? avec Monsieur Dumont)
5. Juliette danse. (avec qui? avec Georges)
6. François parle à Michèle. (de qui? de toi)

> Alice dîne.

> Elle dîne avec une copine.

> Ah bon? Avec qui est-ce qu'elle dîne?

6 Un sondage *(A poll)*

Take a survey to find out how your classmates spend their free time. Ask who does the following things.

▶ écouter la radio
Qui écoute la radio?

1. voyager souvent
2. aimer chanter
3. nager
4. aimer danser
5. regarder la télé
6. jouer au tennis
7. jouer au foot
8. travailler
9. regarder les clips *(music videos)*
10. parler italien
11. étudier beaucoup
12. visiter souvent New York

7 Questions

Prepare short dialogues with your classmates, using the information in the illustrations.

▶ —Où est-ce que tu dînes?
—Je dîne à la maison.

où?
à la maison

1. à quelle heure?
à 8 heures

2. quand?
en septembre

3. comment?
BONJOUR!
très bien

4. avec qui?
avec Denise

5. à qui?
à mon cousin

6. de qui?
BLA BLA BLA...
de toi

7. pour qui?
pour M. Lambert

C. Qu'est-ce que?

Note the use of the interrogative expression **qu'est-ce que** *(what)* in the questions below.

Qu'est-ce que tu regardes?   Je regarde un match de tennis.
Qu'est-ce qu'Alice mange?   Elle mange une pizza.

To ask *what people are doing,* the French use the following construction:

qu'est-ce que + SUBJECT + VERB + . . . ?	**Qu'est-ce que** tu fais?
qu'est-ce qu' (+ VOWEL SOUND)	**Qu'est-ce qu'**elle fait?

8 La Boutique-Musique

People in Column A are at the Boutique-Musique, a local music shop. Use a verb from Column B to ask what they are listening to or looking at. A classmate will answer you, using an item from Column C.

A	**B**	**C**
tu	écouter?	une guitare
vous	regarder?	un poster
Alice		un compact (CD) de jazz
Éric		une cassette de rock
Antoine et Claire		un album de Paul Simon

Qu'est-ce qu'Éric écoute?

Il écoute un album de Paul Simon.

D. Le verbe *faire*

Faire *(to do, make)* is one of the most useful French verbs. It is an IRREGULAR verb since it does not follow a predictable pattern. Note the forms of **faire** in the present tense.

faire *(to do, make)*		
je **fais**	Je **fais** un sandwich.	
tu **fais**	Qu'est-ce que tu **fais** maintenant?	
il/elle **fait**	Qu'est-ce que ton copain **fait** samedi?	
nous **faisons**	Nous **faisons** une pizza.	
vous **faites**	Qu'est-ce que vous **faites** ici?	
ils/elles **font**	Qu'est-ce qu'elles **font** pour la boum?	

Vocabulaire: Expressions avec *faire*

faire un match	to play a game (match)	Mes cousins **font un match** de tennis.
faire une promenade	to go for a walk	Caroline **fait une promenade** avec Olivier.
faire un voyage	to take a trip	Ma copine **fait un voyage** en France.
faire attention	to pay attention	Est-ce que tu **fais attention** quand le professeur parle?

9 La boum de Juliette

Juliette's friends are helping her prepare food for a party. Use the verb **faire** to say what everyone is doing.

▶ Je . . . une crêpe.

Je fais une crêpe.

1. Nous . . . une salade.
2. Tu . . . une salade de fruits.
3. Vous . . . une tarte *(pie)*.
4. Cécile et Marina . . . un gâteau *(cake)*.
5. Christine . . . une pizza.
6. Marc . . . un sandwich.
7. Patrick et Thomas . . . une omelette.
8. Pierre et Karine . . . une quiche.

10 Qu'est-ce qu'ils font?

Read the descriptions below and say what the people are doing. Use the verb **faire** and an expression from the list below. Be logical.

un voyage   une promenade   une pizza   un match   attention

▶ Madame Dumont est en Chine.
Elle fait un voyage.

1. Nicolas travaille dans *(in)* un restaurant.
2. Nous sommes en ville.
3. Hélène et Jean-Paul jouent au tennis.
4. Je suis dans la cuisine *(kitchen)*.
5. Marc est dans le train Paris–Nice.
6. Vous jouez au volley.
7. Je suis dans le parc.
8. Monsieur Lambert visite Tokyo.
9. Nous écoutons le prof.

E. L'interrogation avec inversion

Learning about language

In conversational French, questions are usually formed with **est-ce que.** However, when the subject of the sentence is a pronoun, French speakers often use INVERSION, that is, they invert or reverse the order of the subject pronoun and the verb.

REGULAR ORDER: **Vous parlez** français.
           SUBJECT   VERB

INVERSION: **Parlez-vous** anglais?
           VERB   SUBJECT

Look at the two sets of questions below. They both ask the same thing. Compare the position of the subject pronouns in heavy print.

Est-ce que **tu** parles anglais?   Parles-**tu** anglais?   *Do you speak English?*
Est-ce que **vous** habitez ici?   Habitez-**vous** ici?   *Do you live here?*

Où est-ce que **nous** dînons?   Où dînons-**nous?**   *Where are we having dinner?*
Où est-ce qu'**il** est?   Où est-**il?**   *Where is he?*

Inverted questions are formed according to the patterns:

YES / NO	VERB / SUBJECT PRONOUN . . . ?	
QUESTION	**Voyagez-vous**	souvent?

INFORMATION	INTERROGATIVE EXPRESSION + VERB / SUBJECT PRONOUN . . . ?		
QUESTION	**Avec qui**	**travaillez-vous**	demain?

➡ In inversion, the verb and the subject pronoun are connected by a hyphen.

OBSERVATION: In inversion, liaison is required before **il/elle** and **ils/elles.** If a verb in the singular ends on a vowel, the letter "**t**" is inserted between the verb and the subject pronoun so that liaison can occur:

Où travaille-**t**-il?   Où travaille-**t**-elle?
Avec qui dîne-**t**-il?   Avec qui dîne-**t**-elle?

11 Conversation

Get better acquainted with your class-mates by asking them a few questions. Use inversion.

▶ où / habiter? —**Où habites-tu?**
                     —J'habite à (Boston).

1. à quelle heure / dîner?
2. à quelle heure / regarder la télé?
3. avec qui / parler français?
4. à qui / téléphoner souvent?
5. comment / nager?
6. avec qui / étudier?

Prononciation   /y/

La voyelle /y/

The vowel sound /y/ – represented by the letter "**u**" – does not exist in English. Here is a helpful trick for producing this new sound.

S<u>u</u>per!

First say the French word **si.** Then round your lips as if to whistle and say **si** with rounded lips: /sy/. Now say **si-per.** Then round your lips as you say the first syllable: **super!**

Répétez: /y/   **s<u>u</u>per   t<u>u</u>   ét<u>u</u>die   bien s<u>û</u>r**
                     L<u>u</u>cie   L<u>u</u>c
                     T<u>u</u> ét<u>u</u>dies avec L<u>u</u>cie.

▶ ▶

À votre tour!

1 Allô!

Awa is phoning some friends. Match her questions on the left with her friends' answers on the right.

1. Qu'est-ce que tu fais?
2. Qu'est-ce que vous faites samedi?
3. Où est ton père?
4. Quand est-ce que tu veux jouer au tennis avec moi?
5. Qui est-ce que tu invites au cinéma?
6. Pourquoi est-ce que tu étudies l'anglais?

a. Il fait une promenade.
b. Ma cousine Alice.
c. Dimanche. D'accord?
d. J'étudie.
e. Nous faisons un match de tennis.
f. Parce que je voudrais habiter à New York.

2 Les questions

The following people are answering questions. Read what they say and figure out what questions they were asked.

Je chante très mal.

▶ Comment est-ce que tu chantes?

1. J'habite à Québec.
2. Je dîne à sept heures.
3. Nous dînons à l'Hippopotame.
4. Je mange une pizza.
5. Je regarde un film.
6. J'invite Catherine.

3 Créa-dialogue

Ask your classmates what they do on different days of the week. Carry out conversations similar to the model. Note: "??" means you can invent your own answers.

▶ —Qu'est-ce que tu fais <u>lundi</u>?
—Je <u>joue au tennis</u>.
—Ah bon? À quelle heure est-ce que tu <u>joues</u>?
—<u>À deux heures</u>.
—Et avec qui?
—Avec <u>Anne-Marie</u>.

▶	lundi	mardi	mercredi	jeudi	vendredi	samedi	dimanche
ACTIVITÉ						??	??
À QUELLE HEURE?	2 heures	6 heures	??	??	??	??	??
AVEC QUI?	avec Anne-Marie	avec un copain	??	??	??	??	??

4 Faisons connaissance!
(Let's get acquainted!)

Get better acquainted with a classmate that you don't know very well. Ask questions in French. For instance:

- Where does he/she live?
- Does he/she study much at home?
- Does he/she speak French at home? (with whom?)
- Does he/she watch TV? (at what time?)
- Does he/she like to phone? (whom? [**à qui?**])

5 Interview

A famous rock star is visiting the United States. You are going to interview her for your school paper (perhaps even on the Internet!). Write out five questions you would want to ask the singer, addressing her as **vous.** For example, you may want to know . . .

- where she is singing
- why she is visiting your city
- how she is traveling
- how (well) she speaks English

6 Curiosité

Imagine that a French friend has just made the following statements. For each one, write down three or four related questions you could ask him or her.

Je joue au foot demain.

Je joue au tennis. **1**

2 Je dîne avec un copain.

▶ • Avec qui est-ce que tu joues?
• Où est-ce que vous jouez?
• À quelle heure est-ce que vous jouez?
• Pourquoi est-ce que vous jouez au foot?

3 Je fais une promenade.

4 J'organise une soirée.

Vive la différence!

Les activités quotidiennes

Nous sommes américains, français, anglais, canadiens . . . Nos° cultures ont° beaucoup de points communs, mais elles ne sont pas identiques.

Parlons° de la vie quotidienne.° Nous faisons les mêmes choses,° mais souvent nous faisons ces° choses un peu différemment.° Voici plusieurs° questions. Répondez° à ces questions. À votre avis,° quelles° sont les réponses des jeunes Français?°

1 Quel jour de la semaine est-ce que vous préférez?
- le lundi
- le vendredi
- le samedi
- le dimanche

Et les Français, quel jour est-ce qu'ils préfèrent?

2 Pendant° la semaine, qu'est-ce que vous préférez faire quand vous n'étudiez pas?
- Je préfère regarder la télé.
- Je préfère lire.°
- Je préfère jouer au basket.
- Je préfère téléphoner à mes° copains.

Et les jeunes Français, qu'est-ce qu'ils préfèrent faire?

3 Voici quatre sports. Quel sport est-ce que vous pratiquez le plus?°
- Je nage.
- Je joue au basket.
- Je fais du jogging.
- Je joue au football.

Et les jeunes Français, quel sport est-ce qu'ils pratiquent le plus?

4 À quelle heure est-ce que vous dînez en général?
- entre° cinq heures et demie et six heures
- entre six heures et sept heures
- entre sept heures et huit heures
- après huit heures

Et les Français, à quelle heure est-ce qu'ils dînent?

5 En moyenne,° combien d'heures° par jour° est-ce que vous regardez la télé?
- une heure
- deux heures
- trois heures
- quatre heures ou plus°

Et les jeunes Français? Combien d'heures par jour est-ce qu'ils regardent la télé?

6 Qu'est-ce que vous préférez regarder à la télé?
- les sports
- les films
- la publicité°
- les feuilletons°

Et les jeunes Français, qu'est-ce qu'ils préfèrent regarder?

Et les Français?

1. Ils préfèrent le samedi. 2. Ils préfèrent regarder la télé. 3. Ils jouent au football. 4. Ils dînent entre sept heures et huit heures. 5. Ils regardent la télé deux heures par jour. 6. Ils préfèrent regarder les films.

Nos *Our* **ont** *have* **Parlons** *Let's talk* **vie quotidienne** *daily life* **mêmes choses** *same things* **ces** *these* **différemment** *differently* **plusieurs** *several* **Répondez** *Answer* **À votre avis** *In your opinion* **quelles** *what* **jeunes Français** *young French people* **Pendant** *During* **lire** *to read* **mes** *my* **le plus** *the most* **entre** *between* **En moyenne** *On the average* **combien d'heures** *how many hours* **par jour** *per day* **plus** *more* **publicité** *commercials* **feuilletons** *series*

EN FRANCE

À la télé, ce weekend

In France, TV viewers have a choice of seven main channels: **TF1**, **France 2**, **France 3**, **Arte**, **La Cinq**, **M6**, and **Canal Plus**. (People who want to watch **Canal Plus** need to have a special decoding machine for which they pay a monthly fee.)

Note that in TV listings, times are expressed using a 24-hour clock. In this system, 8 P.M. is **20.00** (**vingt heures**); 10 P.M. is **22.00** (**vingt-deux heures**).

Imagine that you are spending a month in Paris with a French family. This Friday and Saturday you have decided to stay home and watch TV. Look at the program listings at the right.

- Which programs would you like to watch on Friday? When do they start?
- Which programs would you choose on Saturday evening? When do they start?
- Your French hosts are soccer fans. What program would they want to watch and when? Which teams are playing? (Locate these cities on the map of France.)
- What program is featured on **France 2** on Saturday evening? Who are the guests on this program? Do you know any of them?
- How many different movies are being shown over the weekend? How many of these movies are American? Which movie would you choose to see? At what time and on which channel?
- You are interested in watching a French TV series. Which program would you select? On which channel? According to its title, what kind of a series do you think it is?

SÉLECTION DE LA SEMAINE

	VEN	SAM
TF1	**20.30** VARIÉTÉS **SALUT L'ARTISTE** Émission présentée par Yves Noël et Ophélie Winter **22.05** DOCUMENT **HISTOIRES NATURELLES**	**20.35** SPECTACLE **HOLIDAY ON ICE** Mis en scène par Jérôme Savary **22.10** SÉRIE **DANS LA CHALEUR DE LA NUIT**
2 France	**20.35** SÉRIE **HÔTEL DE POLICE** LE GENTIL MONSIEUR de Claude Barrois avec Cécile Magnet **23.20** FILM **ALICE DANS LES VILLES** de Wim Wenders	**20.40** VARIÉTÉS **CHAMPS-ÉLYSÉES** Invités: Elton John, Isabelle Adjani, Tom Cruise **22.25** SÉRIE **MÉDECINS DE NUIT**
France 3	**21.30** SÉRIE **LE MASQUE** MADEMOISELLE EVELYNE de Jean-Louis Fournier **23.45** CONCERT **MUSIQUES, MUSIQUE**	**20.35** JEUNESSE **SAMDYNAMITE** DESSINS ANIMÉS Série: **BATMAN** **22.25** ENTRETIEN **LE DIVAN** Pierre Dumayet
arte	**20.15** DOCUMENTAIRE **Cent ans de cinéma japonais** **23.20** MAGAZINE **Une vidéo inédite de Bob Dylan**	**20.40** SÉRIE **Comédie visuelle** **21.45** DOCUMENTAIRE **Le monde des animaux**
M6	**20.30** FILM TV **COPACABANA** de Warris Hussein avec Barry Manilow, Annette O'Toole **22.05** THÉÂTRE **LE SEXE FAIBLE**	**20.35** FILM TV **L'ÉCLOSION DES MONSTRES** de J. Piquer Simon avec Yan Sera **22.20** SÉRIE **LE COMTE DE MONTE-CRISTO**
CANAL+	**20.30** FOOTBALL **CAEN - TOULOUSE** Championnat de France 28e journée **22.40** FILM **MALCOM X** de Spike Lee	**20.30** FILM **ALIENS, LE RETOUR** de James Cameron avec Sigourney Weaver **22.45** FILM **UNE NUIT À L'ASSEMBLÉE NATIONALE** de Jean-Pierre Mocky

Entre amis: Bonjour, Patrick!

Qu'est-ce que vous aimez faire? Dans° une lettre, Patrick répond° à cette question. Voici la lettre de Patrick.

Bonjour!

Je m'appelle Patrick Lacaze. J'ai 14 ans. J'habite à Tours avec ma famille. Je suis élève° de troisième.° J'étudie beaucoup, mais je n'étudie pas tout le temps.° Voici ce que° j'aime faire.

J'aime les boums parce que j'adore danser.

J'aime la musique. J'aime surtout° le rock. J'aimerais° jouer de la guitare, mais je ne sais pas.°

J'aime les sports. En hiver je skie et en été je nage et je joue au tennis. (Je ne suis pas un champion, mais je joue assez° bien.) J'aime jouer au basket, mais je préfère jouer au foot. (J'aime jouer au babyfoot, mais ce n'est pas un sport.) J'aime faire des promenades à vélo° le weekend avec mes copains.

J'aime mon école.° J'aime surtout l'anglais parce que le prof est sympa.° (Il s'appelle Mr. Ross, mais il est très gentil.°) Je n'aime pas trop° les maths.

À la maison, j'aime regarder la télé. J'adore les séries américaines! J'aime aussi écouter mes cassettes.

J'aime téléphoner à ma copine, mais je ne téléphone pas souvent. (Mon père n'aime pas ça.°)

J'aime jouer aux jeux° sur le Minitel!

Et vous, qu'est-ce que vous aimez faire? Répondez-moi° vite.°

Amicalement,°
Patrick Lacaze

Dans *In*   **répond** *answers*   **élève** *student*   **troisième** *ninth grade*   **tout le temps** *all the time*   **ce que** *what*
surtout *especially*   **aimerais** *would like*   **je ne sais pas** *I don't know how*   **assez** *rather*
promenades à vélo *bike rides*   **école** *school*   **sympa** *nice*   **gentil** *nice*   **trop** *too much*   **ça** *that*   **jeux** *games*
Répondez-moi *Answer me*   **vite** *quickly*   **Amicalement** *Cordially (In friendship)*

■ NOTES ■
CULTURELLES

1 Tours

Tours is an attractive city located about 150 miles southwest of Paris. It is the capital of Touraine, an area of France known for its beautiful castles.

Paris

Tours

2 Le babyfoot

Babyfoot is a tabletop soccer game in which two teams of two people each try to score goals by manipulating rows of toy players. **Babyfoot** is very popular among French teenagers, who play it in cafés or in youth clubs.

Comment lire *(Reading hints)*
GETTING THE MEANING

When you read French, try to understand the meaning. Don't look for a word-for-word English translation for each sentence.

- Sometimes the two languages use different constructions.

   Je m'appelle . . .   *(I call myself . . .)*   *My name is . . .*

- Sometimes French uses some words that English leaves out.

   J'aime <u>le</u> rock.   *I love rock.*
   J'aime jouer <u>de</u> la guitare.   *I like to play the guitar.*

- And sometimes French leaves out words that English uses.

   Je suis élève de troisième.   *I am <u>a</u> student in ninth <u>grade</u>.*

- Word order may also be different.

   des promenades à vélo   *bike rides*

Enrichissez votre vocabulaire
COGNATES

You have already discovered that there are many words in French that look like English words and have similar meanings. These are called COGNATES. Cognates let you increase your vocabulary effortlessly. But be sure to pronounce them the French way!

- Sometimes the spelling is the same, or almost the same.

   la radio   *radio*
   un champion   *champion*

- Sometimes the spelling is a little different.

   américain   *American*

Activité
Read the letter from Patrick again and find five more French-English cognates.

Activité: Une lettre à Patrick
You are writing a letter to Patrick in which you introduce yourself and explain what you like to do. You may tell him:

- if you like music (and what kind)
- what sports you like to do in fall or winter
- what sports you like to do in spring or summer
- what you like to do at home
- whether or not you like French and math
- what you like to do on weekends
- what programs you like to watch on TV

> You may start your letter with the words:
> **Mon cher Patrick,**
> *(My dear Patrick)*
> and end it with:
> **Amicalement,**

Mon cher Patrick,

Amicalement,

■ NOTE ■
CULTURELLE

Le Minitel/Internet

If you lived in Paris and wanted to find the phone number or address of a friend, you wouldn't call information. You would turn to your **Minitel.** The **Minitel** is a small computer terminal connected to the telephone. By entering certain codes, you can gain access to a large variety of services. The most popular is the **annuaire électronique** (*computerized phone directory*).

However, the **Minitel** has much more to offer. You can check plane and train schedules, reserve theater tickets, and send electronic messages. For recreation, there are all sorts of games sponsored by various companies. If you answer a certain number of questions correctly, for example, you can win prizes like a pair of movie tickets or even a trip abroad.

But there is a catch! Although the **Minitel** terminals are distributed free of charge, users are billed each month according to the services used and time spent on the line. Because the **Minitel** may become expensive, French parents insist on limiting its use.

Internet/CD-ROM

French teens are also interested in CD-ROM and the internet. **Le Net** is becoming an exciting place for **les internautes:** there are cafés in Paris where you can **naviguer** or **netsurfer/surfer sur le Net** while having lunch!

PASSEPORT TOURISME MINITEL

Le Louvre Fr CD *#06831*
F.ht **330** (391,38 F.ttc)
Découvrez avec ce CD intéractif le plus grand musée du monde. Naviguez à travers le temps et les collections, attardez vous sur les détails des oeuvres grâce à la loupe, consultez les animations et commentaires.

Napoléon, l'Europe et l'Empire Fr CD
F.ht **329** (390,19 F.ttc)
Vous serez surpris par la qualité et la richesse historique et artistique de ce CD-Rom. Découvrez aux travers de liens hypertexte et du multimédia toute la vie de Napoléon, ses batailles, les évenements marquants de son époque, ses rencontres mises en scène grâce à des récits animés, ainsi que des anecdotes et citations. Infograme ...#07391

L'album des arts et métiers Fr CD *#06829*
F.ht **290** (343,94 F.ttc)
Plus de 1000 fiches décrivant les objets et la collection du Musée, 2000 photos ou gravures, 150 citations sonores et 150 animations font de ce CD un superbe album intéractif.

Internet : bienvenue sur la planète virtuelle !

Variétés

Cinq portraits

Cinq jeunes parlent de ce qu'ils font,° mais ils ne révèlent pas leur° identité. Est-ce que vous pouvez° identifier chacun?° Lisez° les paragraphes suivants° et faites correspondre° chaque° paragraphe à une photo.

Moussa Dembila
Abidjan, Côte d'Ivoire

1 Je ne suis pas français, mais je parle français. Je parle anglais aussi, mais je préfère parler français. J'aime les sports. Je joue au volley et au basket, mais mon sport préféré° est le hockey. Je m'appelle . . .

2 Je suis française, mais je n'habite pas à Paris. J'habite dans une île tropicale. Au lycée, j'étudie beaucoup. Mon sujet préféré est la biologie. (Je voudrais être médecin.°) J'aime la musique. J'aime beaucoup le reggae et j'adore chanter. J'aime les sports. Je nage souvent. Là où j'habite je peux nager en toute saison.° Je m'appelle . . .

Catherine Miguel
Bordeaux, France

3 Je n'habite pas à Paris. J'habite dans° une grande° ville° à 600 kilomètres de Paris. Je suis élève° dans un lycée. J'étudie beaucoup. Mes sujets préférés sont l'espagnol, la gymnastique, le français et la musique. J'aime beaucoup le jazz et le rock. J'adore danser. Je m'appelle . . .

Laurent Arnold
Genève, Suisse

4 Je n'habite pas en France, mais un jour je voudrais étudier à Paris. J'habite en Afrique. Je suis élève au Collège Moderne du Plateau. J'étudie l'anglais, les maths et la physique. Mon ambition est d'être architecte. Je m'appelle . . .

Isabelle Lamy
Trois Îlets, Martinique

5 J'habite dans un petit° pays° européen. Dans mon pays les gens° parlent des langues différentes. Moi, je parle français. En classe j'étudie l'anglais et l'allemand.° J'aime voyager. Je voudrais visiter le Canada. Ma cousine Christine habite là-bas. Je m'appelle . . .

Denis Lévêque
Montréal, Québec

ce qu'ils font *what they do*   **leur** *their*   **pouvez** *can*   **chacun** *each one*   **Lisez** *Read*
suivants *following*   **faites correspondre** *match*   **chaque** *each*   **préféré** *favorite*
médecin *doctor*   **en toute saison** *all year round (in any season)*   **dans** *in*
grande *large*   **ville** *city*   **élève** *student*   **petit** *small*   **pays** *country*   **gens** *people*
allemand *German*

UNITE 5

Le monde personnel et familier

THÈME ET OBJECTIFS

People and possessions

When you meet French teenagers, you will want to share information about yourself, your friends, and your possessions.

In this unit, you will learn . . .
- to talk about yourself: your personality and what you look like
- to describe your friends and other people
- to describe your room
- to talk about everyday objects that you own or use
- to describe these objects: their size and color

You will also be able . . .
- to express your opinion about what you see or hear
- to identify colors

17

Les personnes et les objets

Accent sur . . . Les Français

France has a population of 57 million people. France is a European country, but its population includes people of many different ethnic backgrounds and cultural origins. There are many French citizens whose families have come from North Africa and French-speaking West Africa, as well as from Vietnam, Laos, and Cambodia.

- France is a country of Catholic tradition, but it also has:
  — the largest Jewish population of Western Europe (about 600,000 people).
  — the largest Muslim population of Western Europe (about five million people).

- France is a young country. Thirty percent of its population is under the age of 20.

- French young people tend to be idealists. They believe in freedom and democracy. They also believe in friendship and family. In fact, they rank these values far above money and material success.

- French young people in general have a positive attitude toward Americans. They like American music and would enjoy visiting the United States.

- Because language study is required in French secondary schools, many French teenagers can communicate in a second language, such as English or German.

Au Café Montparnasse
Stéphanie parle avec ses amis.

Chez le marchand de glaces
Philippe est chez le marchand
de glaces avec une copine.

À Paris
Des jeunes font une promenade
sur les Champs-Élysées.

Chez des amis
Stéphanie écoute des
disques avec un copain.

C'est un copain.

A. La description des personnes

▶ *How to describe someone:*

Qui est-ce?
C'est un copain.

Comment s'appelle-t-il?
Il s'appelle Marc.

Quel âge a-t-il?
Il a seize ans.

Comment est-il?
Il est petit.
Il est blond.

Qui est-ce?
C'est une copine.

Comment s'appelle-t-elle?
Elle s'appelle Sophie.

Quel âge a-t-elle?
Elle a quinze ans.

Comment est-elle?
Elle est grande.
Elle est brune.

Les personnes

une **personne**

		une **personne**
un **étudiant**	*(student)*	une **étudiante**
un **élève**	*(pupil)*	une **élève**
un **camarade**	*(classmate)*	une **camarade**
un **homme**	*(man)*	une **femme** *(woman)*
un **professeur,** un **prof**	*(teacher)*	un **professeur,** une **prof**
un **voisin**	*(neighbor)*	une **voisine**

➡ **Une personne** is always feminine whether it refers to a male or female person.

➡ **Un professeur** is always masculine whether it refers to a male or female teacher. However, in casual French, one distinguishes between **un prof** (male) and **une prof** (female).

La description physique

Il est . . .

grand · petit · brun · blond · **beau** *handsome, good-looking* · **jeune** *young*

Elle est . . .

grande · petite · brune · blonde · **belle** *beautiful* · **jolie** *pretty* · jeune

1 Oui ou non?

Describe the people below in affirmative or negative sentences.

▶ Michael Jordan / petit?
Michael Jordan n'est pas petit.

▶ Geena Davis / grande?
Geena Davis est grande.

1. Dennis Rodman / grand?
2. Tom Hanks / blond?
3. Dracula / beau?
4. mon copain / brun?
5. mon père / petit?
6. mon voisin / jeune?
7. la princesse Diana / belle?
8. Meryl Streep / jeune?
9. Oprah Winfrey / grande?
10. ma copine / petite?
11. ma mère / brune?
12. ma voisine / jolie?

2 Vacances à Québec

You spent last summer in Quebec and have just had your photographs developed. Describe each of the people, giving name, approximate age, and two or three characteristics.

blond(e)	petit(e)
brun(e)	beau (belle)
grand(e)	jeune

▶ Il s'appelle Alain.
Il est brun.
Il a seize ans.
Il n'est pas grand.
Il est petit.

▶ **Alain**

1. **Anne-Marie**
2. **Jean-Pierre**
3. **Claire**
4. **Mademoiselle Lévêque**
5. **Madame Paquette**
6. **Monsieur Beliveau**

B. Les objets

Qu'est-ce que c'est?

▶ *How to identify something:*

Qu'est-ce que c'est?	*What is it? What's that?*	—**Qu'est-ce que c'est?**
C'est . . .	*It's . . . , That's . . .*	—**C'est** une radio.

▶ *How to say that you know or do not know:*

Je sais.	*I know.*
Je ne sais pas.	*I don't know.*

▶ *How to point out something:*

—**Regarde ça.**	*Look at that.*
—**Quoi?**	*What?*
—**Ça,** là-bas.	*That, over there.*

Quelques objets *(A few objects)*

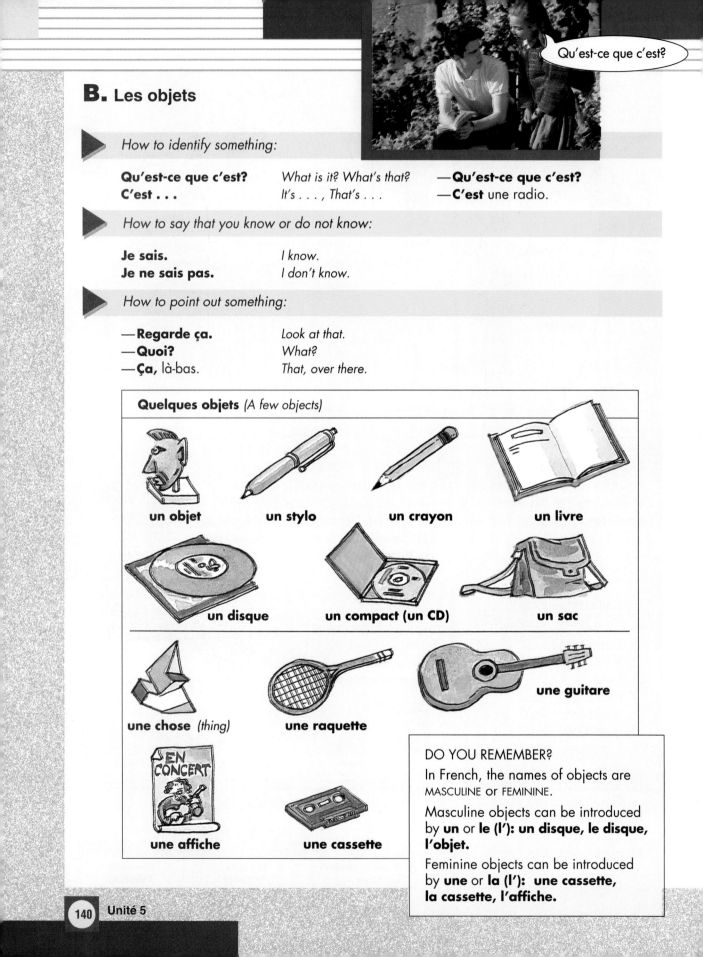

un objet   un stylo   un crayon   un livre

un disque   un compact (un CD)   un sac

une chose *(thing)*   une raquette   une guitare

une affiche   une cassette

DO YOU REMEMBER?

In French, the names of objects are
MASCULINE or FEMININE.

Masculine objects can be introduced
by **un** or **le (l')**: **un disque, le disque,
l'objet.**

Feminine objects can be introduced
by **une** or **la (l')**: **une cassette,
la cassette, l'affiche.**

— QU'EST-CE QUE
C'EST QUE ÇA?
— QUOI?
— ÇA, LÀ-BAS!
— C'EST UNE TÉLÉ.

— OH LÀ LÀ, NON!
REGARDE! C'EST
UN EXTRA-
TERRESTRE!

3 Qu'est-ce que c'est?

Ask a classmate to identify the following objects.

Qu'est-ce que c'est?

C'est un stylo.

4 S'il te plaît

Ask a classmate to give you the following objects.

▸ —S'il te plaît, donne-moi
   la cassette.
   —Voilà la cassette.
   —Merci.

C'EST VUARNET!

VUARNET
FRANCE

C. Les possessions personnelles

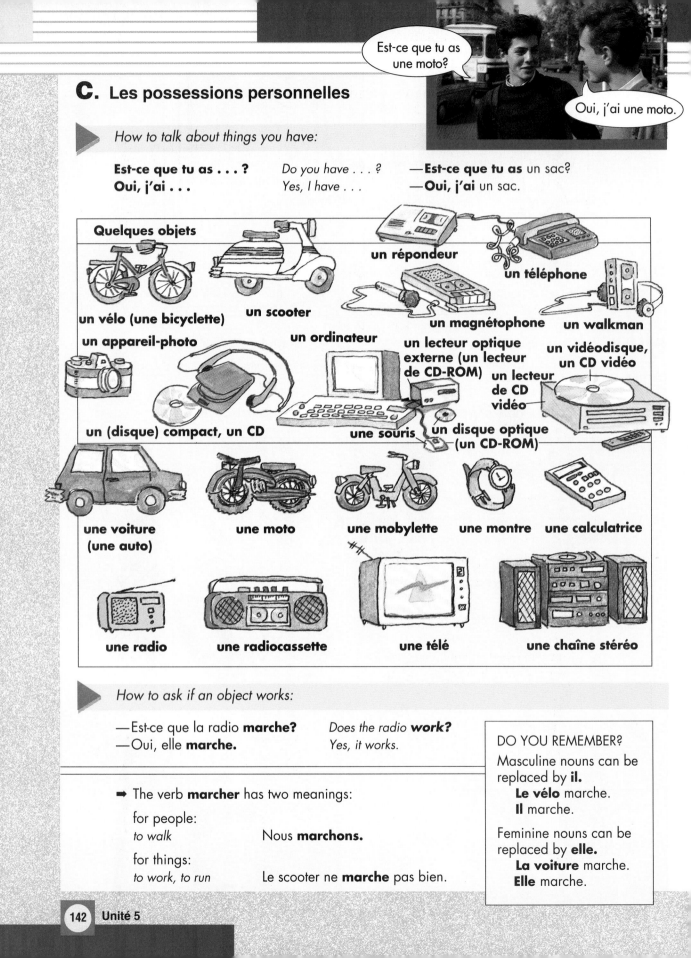

Est-ce que tu as une moto?

Oui, j'ai une moto.

How to talk about things you have:

Est-ce que tu as . . . ?	Do you have . . . ?	—**Est-ce que tu as** un sac?
Oui, j'ai . . .	Yes, I have . . .	—**Oui, j'ai** un sac.

Quelques objets

un vélo (une bicyclette) un scooter un répondeur un téléphone

un magnétophone un walkman

un appareil-photo un ordinateur un lecteur optique externe (un lecteur de CD-ROM) un vidéodisque, un CD vidéo

un lecteur de CD vidéo

un (disque) compact, un CD une souris un disque optique (un CD-ROM)

une voiture (une auto) une moto une mobylette une montre une calculatrice

une radio une radiocassette une télé une chaîne stéréo

How to ask if an object works:

—Est-ce que la radio **marche?**	Does the radio **work?**
—Oui, elle **marche.**	Yes, it works.

➡ The verb **marcher** has two meanings:

for people:
to walk

Nous **marchons.**

for things:
to work, to run

Le scooter ne **marche** pas bien.

DO YOU REMEMBER?

Masculine nouns can be replaced by **il.**
Le vélo marche.
Il marche.

Feminine nouns can be replaced by **elle.**
La voiture marche.
Elle marche.

5 **Et toi?**

1. J'ai . . .
   (Name 3 objects you own.)
2. Je voudrais . . .
   (Name 3 things you would like to have.)
3. Pour Noël / Hanoukka, je voudrais . . .
   (Name 2 gifts you would like to receive.)

6 **Joyeux anniversaire**
(Happy birthday)

For your birthday, a rich aunt is giving you the choice between different possible gifts. Indicate your preferences.

▶ vélo ou scooter?

1. mobylette ou moto?
2. montre ou radio?
3. appareil-photo ou walkman?
4. radiocassette ou chaîne stéréo?
5. télé ou ordinateur?
6. magnétophone ou calculatrice?

Je préfère le vélo.

Je préfère le scooter.

7 **Qu'est-ce que tu as?**

Philippe asks Christine if she has the following objects. She says that she does. Play both roles.

▶ PHILIPPE: **Est-ce que tu as une guitare?**
CHRISTINE: **Oui, j'ai une guitare.**

8 **Est-ce qu'il marche bien?**

Tell your classmates that you own the following objects. They will ask you if the objects are working. Answer according to the illustrations.

▶ —J'ai un vélo.
—Est-ce qu'il marche bien?
—Non, il ne marche pas bien.

▶ —J'ai une télé.
—Est-ce qu'elle marche bien?
—Oui, elle marche très bien.

D. Ma chambre *(My room)*

> Dans ma chambre il y a une télé.

▶ How to talk about what there is in a place:

il y a   there is   Dans *(In)* ma chambre, **il y a** une télé.
               there are   Dans le garage, **il y a** deux voitures.

est-ce qu'il y a . . . ?   is/are there . . . ?   **Est-ce qu'il y a** un ordinateur dans la classe?

qu'est-ce qu'il y a . . . ?   what is there . . . ?   **Qu'est-ce qu'il y a** dans le garage?

Dans ma chambre

une fenêtre

une porte

un lit

un bureau   une chaise   une table

▶ How to say where something or someone is:

Où est Félix?
Félix est . . .

dans le lit

sur le lit

sous le lit

devant le lit

derrière le lit

9 Qu'est-ce qu'il y a?

Describe the various objects that are in the pictures.

1. Sur la table, il y a . . .   2. Sous le lit, il y a . . .   3. Dans le garage, il y a . . .

10 Ma chambre

Describe the various objects (pieces of furniture and personal belongings) that are in your room.

▶ **Il y a une radio, . . .**
  Il y a aussi . . .

11 Où est le téléphone?

Michèle is looking for the telephone. Jean-Claude tells her where it is.

▶   MICHÈLE: **Où est le téléphone?**
   JEAN-CLAUDE: **Il est sur la table.**

12 C'est étrange! *(It's strange!)*

Funny things sometimes happen. Describe these curious happenings by selecting an item from Column A and putting it in one of the places listed in Column B.

▶ Il y a un éléphant sous le lit!

▶ Il y a . . .

A	B
un rhinocéros	dans la classe
un éléphant	sur le bureau
une girafe	sous la table
un crabe	sous le lit
une souris *(mouse)*	derrière la porte
un ami de King Kong	sur la tour Eiffel
	dans le jardin *(garden)*
un extra-terrestre	devant le restaurant

13 La chambre de Nicole

Florence wants to borrow a few things from Nicole's room. Nicole tells her where each object is.

▶ la raquette

1. la télé
2. la guitare
3. le livre
4. le vélo
5. l'ordinateur

6. le sac
7. la radio
8. le compact
9. la cassette

14 Pauvre Monsieur Vénard *(Poor Mr. Vénard)*

Today Monsieur Vénard left on vacation, but he soon ran out of luck. Describe the four cartoons by completing the sentences below.

Le voyage de Monsieur Vénard

1. M. Vénard est ___ la voiture.

2. M. Vénard est ___ la voiture.

3. M. Vénard est ___ la voiture.

4. La contractuelle° est ___ la voiture.

la contractuelle   *meter maid*

À votre tour!

1 Créa-dialogue

Daniel is showing Nathalie his recent photographs, and she is asking questions about the various people. Create similar dialogues and act them out in class.

un copain

Éric/14

▶ —Qui est-ce?
—C'est <u>un copain</u>.
—Comment s'appelle-t-<u>il</u>?
—<u>Il</u> s'appelle <u>Éric</u>.
—Quel âge a-t-<u>il</u>?
—<u>Il</u> a <u>quatorze</u> ans.

1. une cousine	2. un camarade	3. une camarade	4. un voisin	5. une voisine	6. un professeur
Valérie/20	Philippe Boucher/13	Nathalie Masson/15	Monsieur Dumas/70	Madame Smith/51	Monsieur Laval/35

2 Conversation dirigée

Olivier is visiting his new friend Valérie. Act out the dialogue according to the instructions.

Olivier

Valérie

Olivier		Valérie
asks Valérie if she has a boom box	⇄	answers affirmatively
asks her if it works well	⇄	says that it works very well and asks why
says he would like to listen to his new (**sa nouvelle**) cassette	→	says that the boom box is on the table in the living room (**le salon**)

3 Mes possessions

Imagine that your family is going to move to another city. Prepare for the move by making a list of the objects you own. Use a separate sheet of paper.

4 Composition: Un objet

Write a short paragraph describing a real or an imaginary object. You may want to include a picture. (Use only vocabulary that you know.) You may begin your sentences with the following phrases:

▶ Voici mon/ma...
Il/Elle est...
Il/Elle marche (ne marche pas)...

18

Vive la différence!

We are not necessarily like our friends. Caroline, a French girl from Montpellier, describes herself. She also talks about her friend Jean-Pierre.

Caroline

Jean-Pierre

Je m'appelle Caroline.
J'habite à Montpellier.
J'ai des frères.

J'ai un chien.

J'ai un scooter.

J'aime le cinéma.
J'aime les films de science-fiction.
J'aime les sports.
J'étudie l'anglais.

Il s'appelle Jean-Pierre.
Il habite à Strasbourg.
Il n'a pas de frère,
    mais il a des soeurs.

Il n'a pas de chien,
    mais il a deux horribles chats.

Il a une moto.

Il préfère le théâtre.
Il préfère les westerns.
Il préfère la musique.
Il étudie l'espagnol.

Jean-Pierre et moi, nous sommes très différents . . . mais nous sommes copains.

C'est l'essentiel, non?

Compréhension

Answer the questions below with the appropriate names: **Caroline, Jean-Pierre,** or **Caroline et Jean-Pierre.**

1. Qui habite en France?
2. Qui a des soeurs?
3. Qui n'a pas de frère?

4. Qui a un animal domestique?
5. Qui aime jouer au volley?
6. Qui préfère écouter un concert?

7. Qui étudie
    une langue *(language)*?

Et toi?

Describe yourself and your best friend by completing the sentences below with a phrase of your choice.

1. J'ai . . .
   Mon copain (ma copine) a . . .
   - un frère
   - une soeur
   - des frères
   - des soeurs

2. J'ai . . .
   Mon copain (ma copine) a . . .
   - un chien
   - un chat
   - un perroquet *(parrot)*
   - un poisson rouge *(goldfish)*

3. J'ai . . .
   Mon copain (ma copine) a . . .
   - un vélo
   - une moto
   - un scooter
   - une mobylette

4. J'aime . . .
   Mon copain (ma copine) aime . . .
   - le cinéma
   - le théâtre
   - la musique
   - les sports

5. Je préfère . . .
   Mon copain (ma copine) préfère . . .
   - les westerns
   - les comédies
   - les films d'aventures
   - les films de science-fiction

6. J'étudie . . .
   Mon copain (ma copine) étudie . . .
   - l'espagnol
   - le français
   - l'italien
   - l'allemand *(German)*

7. Mon ami(e) et moi,
   nous sommes . . .
   - assez *(rather)* différent(e)s
   - très différent(e)s
   - assez semblables *(similar)*
   - très semblables

NOTE CULTURELLE

Montpellier et Strasbourg

Montpellier and Strasbourg are two very different cities.

- Montpellier is a city of more than 200,000 inhabitants located in southern France near the Mediterranean. It is an important university center with a School of Medicine founded in 1221.

- Strasbourg, a city of 255,000 inhabitants, is the capital of the French province of Alsace. Because of its location near Germany and Switzerland, it has always been an international city. Strasbourg is now the seat of important European institutions.

Paris ★
Strasbourg
Montpellier

A. Le verbe *avoir*

The verb **avoir** *(to have, to own)* is irregular. Note the forms of this verb in the present tense.

avoir	to have	
j' **ai**	I have	J'**ai** une copine à Québec.
tu **as**	you have	Est-ce que tu **as** un frère?
il/elle **a**	he/she has	Philippe **a** une cousine à Paris.
nous **avons**	we have	Nous **avons** un ordinateur.
vous **avez**	you have	Est-ce que vous **avez** une moto?
ils/elles **ont**	they have	Ils n'**ont** pas ton appareil-photo.

➡ There is liaison in the forms: **nous avons, vous avez, ils ont, elles ont.**

Vocabulaire: Expressions avec *avoir*

avoir faim	*to be hungry*	J'**ai faim.** Et toi, est-ce que tu **as faim?**
avoir soif	*to be thirsty*	Paul **a soif.** Sylvie n'**a** pas **soif.**
avoir . . . ans	*to be . . . (years old)*	J'**ai** 14 **ans.** Le prof **a** 35 **ans.**

1 Les voitures

The people below own cars made in the countries where they live. Match each car with its owner.

▶ Monsieur Sato habite à Tokyo.

une Alfa Roméo
une Jaguar
une Renault
une Chevrolet
une Volvo
une Mercedes
une Toyota

Il a une Toyota.

1. Tu habites à Boston.
2. Vous habitez à Munich.
3. Madame Ericson habite à Stockholm.
4. J'habite à Paris.
5. Nous habitons à Oxford.
6. Mes cousines habitent à Rome.

2 Expression personnelle

How old are the following people? Complete the sentences below. If you don't know the exact age, make a guess.

1. J'ai . . .
2. *(The student on your right)* Tu as . . .
3. *(The teacher)* Vous . . .
4. Mon copain . . .
5. Ma copine . . .
6. La voisine . . .

3 Faim ou soif?

You are at a party with your classmates. Offer them the following foods and beverages. They will accept or refuse by saying whether they are hungry or thirsty.

1. une crêpe
2. un soda
3. un hamburger
4. un jus d'orange
5. un croissant
6. un jus de raisin
7. une pizza
8. un Perrier

▶ un sandwich
▶ une limonade

Tu veux un sandwich?

Oui, merci! J'ai faim.

(Non, merci! Je n'ai pas faim.)

Tu veux une limonade?

Oui, merci! J'ai soif.

(Non, merci! Je n'ai pas soif.)

B. Les noms et les articles: masculin et féminin

NOUNS

- Nouns designating PEOPLE

  Nouns that designate male persons
  are almost always *masculine:*

  un garçon   **un ami**

  Nouns that designate female persons
  are almost always *feminine:*

  une fille   **une amie**

> *Learning about language*
>
> NOUNS are words that designate people, animals, objects, and things.
>
> In French, all nouns have GENDER: they are either MASCULINE or FEMININE.

⇒ EXCEPTIONS:

une personne is always feminine (even when it refers to a male)

un professeur is always masculine (even when it refers to a woman)

- Nouns designating ANIMALS, OBJECTS, and THINGS

  There is no systematic way to determine whether these nouns are
  masculine or feminine. Therefore, it is very important to learn these
  nouns with their articles.

MASCULINE:	**un** disque	**un** vélo	**un** ordinateur
FEMININE:	**une** cassette	**une** moto	**une** affiche

ARTICLES

Note the forms of the articles in the chart below.

	MASCULINE		FEMININE			
INDEFINITE ARTICLE	**un**	*a, an*	**une**	*a, an*	**un** garçon	**une** fille
DEFINITE ARTICLE	**le**	*the*	**la**	*the*	**le** garçon	**la** fille

> *Learning about language*
>
> Nouns are often introduced by ARTICLES. In French, ARTICLES have the *same* gender as the nouns they introduce.

⇒ Both **le** and **la** become **l'** before a vowel sound:

le garçon   **l'ami**

la fille   **l'amie**

PRONOUNS

> *Learning about language*
>
> Nouns may be replaced by PRONOUNS. In French, PRONOUNS have the *same* gender as the nouns they replace.

Note the forms of the pronouns in the chart below.

MASCULINE	**il**	*he* / *it*	Où est **le** garçon?	**Il** est en classe.
			Où est **le** disque?	**Il** est sur la table.
FEMININE	**elle**	*she* / *it*	Où est **la** fille?	**Elle** est en ville.
			Où est **la** voiture?	**Elle** est là-bas.

4 Les célébrités

You and Jean-Pierre have been invited to a gala dinner attended by many American celebrities. Jean-Pierre asks you who each person is. Answer him using **un** or **une,** as appropriate.

▶ Connie Chung / journaliste

Tiens, voilà Connie Chung!

Qui est-ce?

Une journaliste.

1. Peter Jennings / journaliste
2. Jodie Foster / actrice
3. Johnny Depp / acteur
4. Whoopi Goldberg / comédienne
5. Whitney Houston / chanteuse *(singer)*
6. Michael Jordan / athlète
7. Denzel Washington / acteur
8. Stevie Wonder / chanteur

5 Sur la table ou sous la table?

Caroline is looking for the following objects. Cécile tells her where each one is: on or under the table.

▶ walkman
   CAROLINE: **Où est le walkman?**
   CÉCILE: **Le walkman? Il est sur la table.**

1. ordinateur   3. affiche   5. raquette   7. radiocassette
2. sac   4. calculatrice 6. disque   8. télé

C. Les noms et les articles: le pluriel

Compare the singular and plural forms of the articles and nouns in the sentences below.

SINGULAR	PLURAL
Tu as **le disque?**	Tu as **les disques?**
Qui est **la fille** là-bas?	Qui sont **les filles** là-bas?
Voici **un livre.**	Voici **des livres.**
J'invite **une copine.**	J'invite **des copines.**

PLURAL NOUNS

In written French, the plural of most nouns is formed as follows:

> SINGULAR NOUN + **s** = PLURAL NOUN

➡ If the noun ends in -s in the singular, the singular and plural forms are the same.
   Voici **un Français.**   Voici **des Français.**
➡ In spoken French, the final -s of the plural is always silent.
➡ NOTE: **des gens** *(people)* is always plural. Compare:

| **une personne** | *person* | Qui est **la personne** là-bas? |
| **des gens** | *people* | Qui sont **les gens** là-bas? |

Les sacs

SINGULAR AND PLURAL ARTICLES

The forms of the articles are summarized in the chart below.

	SINGULAR	PLURAL	
DEFINITE ARTICLE	le (l') *the* la (l')	les *the*	les garçons les ordinateurs les filles les affiches
INDEFINITE ARTICLE	un *a, an* une	des *some*	des garçons des ordinateurs des filles des affiches

➡ There is liaison after **les** and **des** when the next word begins with a vowel sound.

➡ **Des** corresponds to the English article *some*. While *some* is often omitted in English, **des** MUST be expressed in French. Contrast:

Il y a *There are*	des *some*	livres sur la table. *books on the table.*

Je dîne avec *I'm having dinner with*	des . . .	amis. *friends.*

---

6 **Pluriel, s'il vous plaît**

Give the plurals of the following nouns.

▶ une copine
   des copines

1. un copain
2. une amie
3. un homme
4. une femme
5. un vélo
6. une affiche

▶ l'ami
   les amis

7. le voisin
8. l'élève
9. la cousine
10. le livre
11. l'ordinateur
12. la voiture

---

8 **Qu'est-ce qu'il y a?**

Explain what there is in the following places. Complete the sentences with **il y a** and a noun from the box. Be sure to use the appropriate articles: **un, une, des.** Be logical. Often several choices are possible.

▶ Dans le garage, . . .

> **Dans le garage, il y a une moto (des voitures . . .).**

1. Sur le bureau, . . .
2. À la boum, . . .
3. Dans la classe, . . .
4. Au café, sur la table, . . .
5. Dans ma chambre, . . .
6. Dans la classe de maths, . . .

limonade   stylo   livres   affiches   moto professeur   lit   croissants   voitures   filles ordinateur   garçons   élèves   table

---

7 **Shopping**

You are in a department store in Montpellier looking for the following items. Ask the salesperson if he or she has these items. The salesperson will answer affirmatively.

▶ —**Pardon, monsieur (madame). Est-ce que vous avez des sacs?**
—**Bien sûr, nous avons des sacs.**

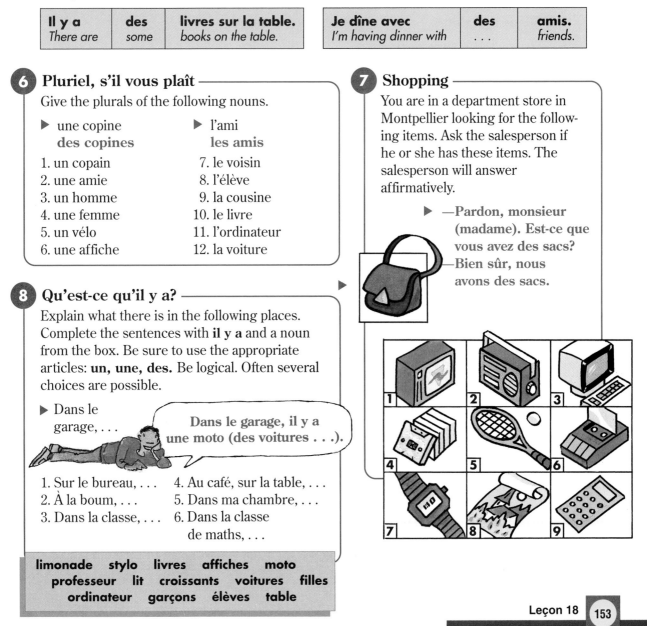

D. L'article indéfini dans les phrases négatives

Compare the forms of the indefinite article in affirmative and negative sentences.

AFFIRMATIVE	NEGATIVE	
Tu as **un** vélo?	Non, je n'ai **pas de** vélo.	*No, I don't have a bike.*
Est-ce que Paul a **une** radio?	Non, il n'a **pas de** radio.	*No, he doesn't have a radio.*
Vous invitez **des** copains demain?	Non, nous n'invitons **pas de** copains.	*No, we are not inviting any friends.*

After a NEGATIVE verb:

> **pas + un, une, des** becomes **pas de**

➡ Note that **pas de** becomes **pas d'** before a vowel sound.

Alice a un ordinateur. Paul n'a **pas d'**ordinateur.

J'ai des amis à Québec. Je n'ai **pas d'**amis à Montréal.

➡ The negative form of **il y a** is **il n'y a pas:**

Dans ma chambre,

il y a une radio. **Il n'y a pas de** télé. *There is no TV.*

il y a des affiches. **Il n'y a pas de** photos. *There are no photographs.*

➡ After **être,** the articles **un, une,** and **des** do NOT change.

Philippe est un voisin. Éric n'est **pas un** voisin.

Ce sont des vélos. Ce ne sont **pas des** mobylettes.

---

9 Possessions

Ask your classmates if they own the following.

▶ un ordinateur

Est-ce que tu as un ordinateur?

Oui, j'ai un ordinateur.

(Non, je n'ai pas d'ordinateur.)

1. un appareil-photo
2. une moto
3. une mobylette
4. une clarinette
5. des disques de jazz
6. des affiches
7. un boa
8. un alligator
9. des hamsters

10 Oui et non

One cannot have everything. Say that the following people do not have what is indicated in parentheses.

▶ Paul a un vélo. (un scooter)
Il n'a pas de scooter.

1. Julien a un scooter. (une voiture).
2. J'ai une radio. (une télé)
3. Vous avez des cassettes. (des compacts)
4. Vous avez des frères. (une soeur)
5. Nous avons un chien. (des chats)
6. Tu as des copains à Bordeaux. (des copains à Lyon)
7. Marc a un oncle à Québec. (un oncle à Montréal)
8. Nathalie a des cousins à San Francisco. (des cousins à Los Angeies)

11 Le grenier *(The attic)*

Your friend is cleaning the attic. Ask if the following items are up there. Your friend (a classmate) will answer according to the illustration.

▶ une raquette?
—**Est-ce qu'il y a une raquette?**
—**Non, il n'y a pas de raquette.**

1. des vélos?
2. une guitare?
3. des livres?
4. un magnétophone?
5. des disques?

6. des cassettes?
7. une télé?
8. une radiocassette?
9. un bureau?
10. une table?

Tu n'as pas de chaîne stéréo?

Si! J'ai une chaîne stéréo.

Expression pour la conversation

How to contradict a negative statement or question:

Si! *Yes!* —Tu n'as pas de chaîne stéréo?
—**Si!** J'ai une chaîne stéréo.

12 Contradictions!

Contradict all of the following negative statements.

▶ Tu ne parles pas anglais!   **Si, je parle anglais!**

1. Tu ne parles pas français!
2. Tu n'étudies pas!
3. Tu ne joues pas au basket!

4. Tu n'aimes pas les sports!
5. Tu n'aimes pas la musique!
6. Tu n'écoutes pas le professeur!

E. L'usage de l'article défini dans le sens général

In French, the definite article (le, la, les) is used more often than in English. Note its use in the following sentences.

J'aime **la musique**.   *(In general) I like **music**.*
Tu préfères **le tennis** ou **le golf?**   *(Generally) do you prefer **tennis** or **golf?***
Pauline aime **les westerns**.   *(In general) Pauline likes **westerns**.*
Nous aimons **la liberté**.   *(In general) we love **liberty**.*

The definite article (le, la, les) is used to introduce ABSTRACT nouns, or nouns used in a GENERAL or COLLECTIVE sense.

J' ❤ le français

13 Expression personnelle

Say how you feel about the following things, using one of the suggested expressions.

Je n'aime pas . . .
J'aime un peu . . .
J'aime beaucoup . . .

▶ **Je n'aime pas la violence.**

la musique	le français	la violence	le théâtre
la nature	les maths	l'injustice	le cinéma
les sports	les sciences	la liberté	la danse
le camping			la photo
			(photography)

Elle m'aime...

Il m'aime...

passionnément
à la folie
beaucoup
pas du tout
un peu

14 C'est évident! *(It's obvious!)*

Read about the following people and say what they like. Choose the appropriate item from the list. (Masculine nouns are in blue. Feminine nouns are in red.)

▶ Cécile écoute des cassettes.
Cécile aime la musique.

art   cinéma   danse   français   musique   nature   tennis

1. Jean-Claude a une raquette.
2. Vous faites une promenade dans la forêt.
3. Les touristes visitent un musée *(museum)*.
4. Tu regardes un film.
5. Nous étudions en classe de français.
6. Véronique et Roger sont dans une discothèque.

F. L'usage de l'article défini avec les jours de la semaine

Compare the following sentences.

REPEATED EVENTS	SINGLE EVENT
Le samedi, je dîne avec des copains.	**Samedi,** je dîne avec mon cousin.
(On) Saturdays (in general), I have	*(On) Saturday (that is, this Saturday),*
dinner with friends.	*I am having dinner with my cousin.*

To indicate a repeated or habitual event, French uses the construction:

> **le** + DAY OF THE WEEK

➡ When an event happens only once, no article is used.

15 Questions personnelles

1. Est-ce que tu étudies le samedi?
2. Est-ce que tu dînes au restaurant le dimanche? Si *(If)* oui, avec qui?
3. Est-ce que tu as une classe de français le lundi? le mercredi?
4. Est-ce que tu regardes les matchs de football américain le samedi? le dimanche?
5. Quel programme de télé est-ce que tu regardes le vendredi? le jeudi?
6. Est-ce que tu travailles? Où? *(Name of place or store)* Quand?

16 L'emploi du temps

	LUNDI	MARDI	MERCREDI	JEUDI	VENDREDI
9 h	français	physique	sciences	biologie	
10 h		histoire		maths	anglais
11 h	maths	sciences	anglais		français

The following students all have the same morning schedule. Complete the sentences accordingly.

▶ **Nous avons une classe de français le lundi** . . .

1. J'ai une classe de maths _____ .
2. Tu as une classe de sciences _____ .
3. Jacques a une classe de physique _____ .
4. Thérèse a une classe d'histoire _____ .
5. Vous avez une classe de biologie _____ .
6. Les élèves ont une classe d'anglais _____ .

Prononciation	**le** /lə/ **les** /le/

Les articles *le* et *les*

Be sure to distinguish between the pronunciation of **le** and **les**. In spoken French, that is often the only way to tell the difference between a singular and a plural noun.

le sac   **les sacs**

Répétez:	/lə/	le	le sac	le vélo	le disque	le copain	le voisin
	/le/	les	les sacs	les vélos	les disques	les copains	les voisins

À votre tour!

1 Allô!

Jean-Marc is phoning some friends. Match his questions on the left with his friends' answers on the right.

1. Quel âge a ton copain?
2. Est-ce qu'Éric a un scooter?
3. Où est l'appareil-photo?
4. Tu as des cassettes?
5. Est-ce que tu aimes étudier l'anglais?
6. Tu as soif?

a. Oui, mais je n'ai pas de magnétophone.
b. Il est sur la table.
c. Quatorze ans.
d. Oui, je voudrais une limonade.
e. Oui, mais je préfère l'espagnol.
f. Non, mais il a une moto.

2 Un sondage

A French consumer research group wants to know what things American teenagers own. Conduct a survey in your class asking who has the objects on the list. Count the number of students who raise their hands for each object, and report your findings on a separate piece of paper.

Qui a des cassettes?... Quinze élèves ont des cassettes.

UN SONDAGE

15

3 Créa-dialogue

Ask your classmates if they like the following things. Then ask if they own the corresponding object.

le tennis

1. la musique	2. le jogging	3. les maths	4. la photo	5. les matchs de baseball	6. l'exercice

▶ —Tu aimes le tennis? —Tu as une raquette?
—Oui, j'aime le tennis. —Oui, j'ai une raquette.
(Non, je n'aime pas le tennis.) (Non, je n'ai pas de raquette.)

4 Quelle est la différence?

Sophie went away with her family for the weekend and she took some of her belongings with her. Describe what is in her room on Friday and what is missing on Saturday.

VENDREDI SAMEDI

▶ Il y a . . . ▶ Il n'y a pas de . . .

5 Inventaire *(Inventory)*

Write a short paragraph naming two things that may be found in each of the following places. Also indicate one thing that is usually not found in that place.

▶ **Dans le salon, il y a une télé et des chaises. Il n'y a pas de lit.**

- dans ma chambre
- dans mon sac
- dans le garage
- dans la rue *(street)*
- sur la table

6 Composition: Ma semaine

In a short paragraph, describe what you do (or do not do) regularly on various days of the week. Select three days and two different activities for each day. Use only vocabulary that you know. Perhaps you might want to exchange paragraphs with a friend by FAX or modem.

Le lundi, j'ai une classe de français.
Je regarde «La roue de la for...
(Wheel of For...

Le lundi, j'ai une classe de français.
Je regarde « La roue de la fortune»
(Wheel of Fortune) à la télé.

Le samedi, je n'étudie pas. Je dîne
au restaurant avec mon copain.

Le copain de Mireille

Nicolas and Jean-Claude are having lunch at the school cafeteria. Nicolas is looking at the students seated at the other end of their table.

NICOLAS:	Regarde la fille là-bas!
JEAN-CLAUDE:	La fille blonde?
NICOLAS:	Oui! Qui est-ce?
JEAN-CLAUDE:	C'est Mireille Labé.
NICOLAS:	Elle est <u>mignonne</u>!
JEAN-CLAUDE:	Elle est aussi <u>amusante</u>, intelligente et <u>sympathique</u>.
NICOLAS:	Est-ce qu'elle a un copain?
JEAN-CLAUDE:	Oui, elle a un copain.
NICOLAS:	Il est sympathique?
JEAN-CLAUDE:	Oui . . . Très sympathique!
NICOLAS:	Et intelligent?
JEAN-CLAUDE:	Aussi!
NICOLAS:	Dommage! . . . Qui est-ce?
JEAN-CLAUDE:	C'est moi!
NICOLAS:	Euh . . . oh . . . Excuse-moi et <u>félicitations</u>!

cute

fun / nice

congratulations

● **Compréhension**

1. Qui est-ce que Nicolas regarde?
2. Comment s'appelle la fille?
3. Est-ce qu'elle est jolie?
4. Est-ce qu'elle a d'autres *(other)* qualités?
5. Est-ce qu'elle a un copain?
6. Qui est le copain de Mireille *(Mireille's boyfriend)*?

■ NOTE ■
CULTURELLE

L'amitié *(Friendship)*

For the French, friendship is very important. It is high on the scale of values such as family, freedom, justice, love, and money.

What qualities do French young people expect in their friends? As in the United States, friends must be fun to be with, since French teenagers like to do things as a group with their **bande de copains.** Friends should be helpful and understanding because when French teenagers have a problem, they tend to talk to their friends before talking to their parents. And, of course, friends must be loyal, because the French tend to remain close to their high school friends for the rest of their lives.

A. Les adjectifs: masculin et féminin

Compare the forms of the adjectives in heavy print as they describe masculine and feminine nouns.

MASCULINE	FEMININE
Le scooter est **petit.**	La voiture est **petite.**
Patrick est **intelligent.**	Caroline est **intelligente.**
L'ordinateur est **moderne.**	La télé est **moderne.**

In written French, feminine adjectives are usually formed as follows:

> MASCULINE ADJECTIVE + **-e** = FEMININE ADJECTIVE

➡ If the masculine adjective ends in **-e,** there is no change in the feminine form.

Jérôme est **timide.**   Juliette est **timide.**

➡ Adjectives that follow the above patterns are called REGULAR adjectives. Those that do not are called IRREGULAR adjectives. For example:

Marc est **beau.**   Sylvie est **belle.**
Paul est **canadien.**   Marie est **canadienne.**

NOTE: French dictionaries list adjectives by their masculine forms. For irregular adjectives, the feminine form is indicated in parentheses.

NOTES DE PRONONCIATION:

• If the masculine form of an adjective ends in a silent consonant, that consonant is pronounced in the feminine form.
• If the masculine form of an adjective ends in a vowel or a pronounced consonant, the masculine and feminine forms sound the same.

DIFFERENT PRONUNCIATION		SAME PRONUNCIATION	
petit	petite	timide	timide
blond	blonde	joli	jolie
français	française	espagnol	espagnole

1 Vive la différence!

People can be friends and yet be quite different. Describe the girls named in parentheses, indicating that they are not like their friends.

▶ Jean-Claude est brun. (Nathalie)
Nathalie n'est pas brune.

1. Jean-Louis est blond. (Carole)
2. Paul est petit. (Mireille)
3. Éric est beau. (Marthe)
4. Jérôme est grand. (Louise)
5. Michel est riche. (Émilie)
6. André est français. (Lisa)
7. Antonio est espagnol. (Céline)
8. Bill est américain. (Julie)

Vocabulaire: La description

Voici Jean-Claude. **Voici Mireille.**

ADJECTIFS

amusant	*amusing, fun*	Il est **amusant.**	Elle est **amusante.**
intelligent	*intelligent*	Il est **intelligent.**	Elle est **intelligente.**
intéressant	*interesting*	Il est **intéressant.**	Elle est **intéressante.**
méchant	*mean, nasty*	Il n'est pas **méchant.**	Elle n'est pas **méchante.**
bête	*silly, dumb*	Il n'est pas **bête.**	Elle n'est pas **bête.**
sympathique	*nice, pleasant*	Il est **sympathique.**	Elle est **sympathique.**
timide	*timid*	Il est **timide.**	Elle n'est pas **timide.**
gentil (gentille)	*nice, kind*	Il est **gentil.**	Elle est **gentille.**
mignon (mignonne)	*cute*	Il est **mignon.**	Elle est **mignonne.**
sportif (sportive)	*athletic*	Il est **sportif.**	Elle est **sportive.**

ADVERBES

assez	*rather*	Nous sommes **assez** intelligents.
très	*very*	Vous n'êtes pas **très** sportifs!

2 Oui ou non?

In your opinion, do the following people have the suggested traits? (Note: These traits are given in the masculine form only.)

> Il est intéressant.

> Il n'est pas intéressant.

▶ le prince Charles / intéressant? ▶

1. le Président / sympathique?
2. Steffi Graf / sportif?
3. ma copine / gentil?
4. Meg Ryan / mignon?
5. Oprah Winfrey / intelligent?
6. Einstein / bête?
7. Jay Leno / amusant?
8. le prof / méchant?

3 Descriptions

Select one of the following characters. Using words from the **Vocabulaire,** describe this character in two affirmative or negative sentences.

▶ Frankenstein
Il est très méchant.
Il n'est pas très mignon.

1. Tarzan
2. King Kong
3. Big Bird
4. Batman
5. Miss Piggy
6. Wonder Woman
7. Charlie Brown
8. Blanche-Neige *(Snow White)*
9. Garfield
10. Snoopy

4 L'idéal

Now you have the chance to describe your ideal people. Use two adjectives for each one.

1. Le copain idéal est . . . et . . .
2. La copine idéale est . . . et . . .
3. Le professeur idéal est . . . et . . .
4. L'étudiant idéal est . . . et . . .
5. L'étudiante idéale est . . . et . . .

B. Les adjectifs: le pluriel

Compare the forms of the adjectives in heavy print as they describe singular and plural nouns.

SINGULAR	PLURAL
Paul est **intelligent** et **timide**.	Paul et Éric sont **intelligents** et **timides**.
Alice est **intelligente** et **timide**.	Alice et Claire sont **intelligentes** et **timides**.

In written French, plural adjectives are usually formed as follows:

> SINGULAR ADJECTIVE + **-s** = PLURAL ADJECTIVE

➡ If the masculine singular adjective already ends in **-s,** there is no change in the plural form.

Patrick est **français.**   Patrick et Daniel sont **français.**

BUT: Anne est **française.**   Anne et Alice sont **françaises.**

NOTE DE PRONONCIATION: Because the final **-s** of plural adjectives is silent, singular and plural adjectives sound the same.

SUMMARY: Forms of regular adjectives

	MASCULINE	FEMININE	*also:*
SINGULAR	**–** **grand**	**-e** **grande**	timide timide
PLURAL	**-s** **grands**	**-es** **grandes**	français françaises

---

5 **Une question de personnalité**

Indicate whether or not the following people exhibit the personality traits in parentheses. (These traits are given in the masculine singular form only. Make the necessary agreements.)

Elles ne sont pas timides.

▸ Alice et Thérèse aiment parler en public. (timide?)

1. Claire et Valérie sont très populaires. (amusant?)
2. Robert et Jean-Luc n'aiment pas danser. (timide?)
3. Catherine et Martine aiment jouer au foot. (sportif?)
4. Laure et Gisèle ont un «A» en français. (intelligent?)
5. Thomas et Vincent n'aiment pas le jogging. (sportif?)
6. Les voisins n'aiment pas parler avec nous. (sympathique?)

Vocabulaire: Les adjectifs de nationalité

américain	American	**italien (italienne)**	Italian
mexicain	Mexican	**canadien (canadienne)**	Canadian
français	French	**japonais**	Japanese
anglais	English	**chinois**	Chinese
espagnol	Spanish		
suisse	Swiss		

➡ Words that describe nationality are adjectives and take adjective endings.

Monsieur Katagiri est **japonais.**

Kumi et Michiko sont **japonaises.**

Expression pour la conversation

How to introduce a conclusion:

alors *so, then* —J'habite à Québec.

—**Alors,** tu es canadien!

> J'habite à Québec.

> Alors, tu es canadien.

6 Quelle nationalité?

Your classmate wants to know more about the following people: where they live and what their nationality is. Act out the dialogues.

▶ —Où habitent Janet et Barbara?
—Elles habitent à San Francisco.
—Alors, elles sont américaines?
—Mais oui, elles sont américaines.

Janet et Barbara	**1. Jim et Bob**	**2. Laure et Céline**
San Francisco	Liverpool	Toulouse
américain	anglais	français
3. Luisa et Teresa	**4. Éric et Vincent**	**5. ??**
Madrid	Montréal	??
espagnol	??	??

7 Les nationalités

Read the descriptions of the following people and give their nationalities.

▶ Silvia et Maria sont étudiantes à Rome.
Elles sont italiennes.

1. Lise et Nathalie étudient à Québec.
2. Michael et Dennis sont de Liverpool.
3. Luis et Paco étudient à Madrid.
4. Isabel et Carmen travaillent à Acapulco.
5. Yoko et Liliko sont étudiantes à l'université de Tokyo.
6. Monsieur et Madame Chen habitent à Beijing.
7. Jean-Pierre et Claude sont de Genève.
8. Françoise et Sylvie travaillent à Paris.

C. La place des adjectifs

Note the position of the adjectives in the sentences on the right.

Philippe a une voiture.   Il a une voiture **anglaise.**
Denise invite des copains.   Elle invite des copains **américains.**
Voici un livre.   Voici un livre **intéressant.**
J'ai des amies.   J'ai des amies **sympathiques.**

In French, adjectives usually come AFTER the noun they modify, according to the pattern:

ARTICLE	+	NOUN	+	ADJECTIVE
une		voiture		**française**
des		copains		**intéressants**

R.S.V.P.
Le Club de Correspondance

Étudiant français, 16 ans, brun, grand, sportif, assez intelligent, un peu timide, voudrait correspondre avec étudiante américaine sportive et sympathique.

Envoyez votre message à :
Correspondants
13 rue de la Cerisaie
75004 Paris

8 Préférences personnelles

For each person or object below, choose among the characteristics in parentheses. Indicate your preference.

▶ avoir un copain (sympathique, intelligent, sportif)
Je préfère avoir un copain intelligent.

1. avoir une copine (amusante, mignonne, intelligente)
2. avoir un professeur (gentil, intelligent, amusant)
3. avoir des voisins (sympathiques, intéressants, riches)
4. avoir une voiture (moderne, confortable, rapide)
5. avoir une calculatrice (japonaise, américaine, française)
6. avoir une montre (suisse, japonaise, française)
7. dîner dans un restaurant (italien, chinois, français)
8. regarder un film (intéressant, amusant, intelligent)
9. travailler avec des personnes (gentilles, amusantes, sérieuses)
10. faire un voyage avec des gens (amusants, riches, sympathiques)

9 Qui se ressemble . . .
(Birds of a feather . . .)
Say that the following people have friends, relatives, or acquaintances with the same personality or nationality.

▶ Claire est anglaise. (un copain)
Elle a un copain anglais.

1. Jean-Pierre est sympathique. (des cousines)
2. La prof est intelligente. (des étudiants)
3. Madame Simon est intéressante. (des voisines)
4. Alice est américaine. (des copines)
5. Véronique est amusante. (un frère)
6. Michel est sportif. (une soeur)
7. Pedro est espagnol. (des camarades)
8. Antonio est mexicain. (une copine)
9. Bernard est sportif. (un voisin)

Birds of a feather flock together.

10 **Préférences internationales** ————————

Choose an item from Column A and indicate
your preference as to country of origin by
choosing an adjective from Column B. Be sure to
make the necessary agreement.

Je préfère
les voitures italiennes.

A	B
la musique	anglais
la cuisine	américain
les voitures	français
Je préfère . . . les ordinateurs	mexicain
les appareils-photo	chinois
les compacts	japonais
les restaurants	italien

Prononciation

Les consonnes finales

/-/   /d/

As you know, when the last letter of a word
is a consonant, that consonant is often silent.
But when a word ends in "**e**," the consonant
before it is pronounced. As you practice the
following adjectives, be sure to distinguish
between the masculine and the feminine forms.

blond   **blonde**

	MASCULINE ADJECTIVE *(no final consonant sound)*		FEMININE ADJECTIVE *(final consonant sound)*
Répétez:	**blond**	/d/	**blonde**
	grand		**grande**
	petit	/t/	**petite**
	amusant		**amusante**
	français	/z/	**française**
	anglais		**anglaise**
	américain	/n/	**américaine**
	canadien		**canadienne**

Joli,
petit
et bon!

Bureau
195F

Table
325F

Jolie,
petite
et bonne!

IKEA *Miracle économique!*

À votre tour!

1 Allô!

Valérie is phoning some friends. Match her questions on the left with her friends' answers on the right.

1 Ton frère aime jouer au foot?

2 Cécile et Sophie sont mignonnes, n'est-ce pas?

3 Pourquoi est-ce que tu invites Olivier?

4 Tu aimes la classe?

5 Tu as des cousins?

a Oui, et intelligentes aussi!

b Parce qu'il est amusant et sympathique.

c Oui, j'ai un professeur très intéressant.

d Oui, il est très sportif.

e Oui, mais ils ne sont pas très sympathiques.

2 Créa-dialogue

With your classmates, talk about the people of different nationalities you may know or objects you may own.

des cousins

mignon?

—J'ai des <u>cousins mexicains</u>.
—<u>Ils sont mignons?</u>
—<u>Oui, ils sont très mignons.</u>

1. une voisine	2. un prof	3. des copines	4. un livre	5. une voiture
blond?	sympathique?	sportif?	intéressant?	grand?

ASTÉRIX

3 Une invitation

> Comment s'appelle ta cousine?
> Quel âge a-t-elle?

A French friend has invited you to go to a party with his/her cousin. You want to know as much as you can about this cousin. You may first ask your friend the cousin's name and age.

Then ask as many questions as you can about the cousin's physical appearance and personality traits. Act out your conversation with a classmate.

4 Avis de recherche

(Missing person's bulletin)

The two people in the pictures below have been reported missing. Describe each one as well as you can, using your imagination. Mention:

- the (approximate) age of the person
- the way he/she looks
- personality traits
- other features or characteristics

5 Composition: Descriptions

Describe one of the following well-known French people in a short paragraph, giving the person's name, profession, and approximate age. Also briefly describe the person's physical appearance.

Isabelle Adjani (actrice)

Surya Bonaly (athlète)

Jean-Jacques Goldman (chanteur)

Jacques Chirac (président)

6 Composition: Rencontres

Select two people whom you would like to meet (a man and a woman). These people may be famous singers, actors or actresses, sports figures, politicians, professional people, community leaders, etc. (You might even be able to contact them directly by e-mail!) Describe each person (physical traits and personality), using either affirmative or negative sentences.

```
Je voudrais
rencontrer X.
Il (Elle) est...
```

La voiture de Roger

Dans la <u>rue</u>, il y a une voiture <u>rouge</u>. *street / red*
C'est une petite voiture. C'est une voiture de sport.
Dans la rue, il y a aussi un café. Au café, il y a un jeune homme.
Il s'appelle Roger.
C'est le <u>propriétaire</u> de la voiture rouge. *owner*

Une jeune fille <u>entre dans</u> le café. *enters*
Elle s'appelle Véronique.
C'est <u>l'amie de Roger</u>. *Roger's friend*
Véronique parle à Roger.

VÉRONIQUE: Tu as une <u>nouvelle</u> voiture, n'est-ce pas? *new*

ROGER: Oui, j'ai une nouvelle voiture.

VÉRONIQUE: Est-ce qu'elle est grande ou petite?

ROGER: C'est une petite voiture.

VÉRONIQUE: De quelle couleur est-elle?

ROGER: C'est une voiture rouge.

VÉRONIQUE: Est-ce que c'est une voiture italienne?

ROGER: Oui, c'est une voiture italienne. Mais <u>dis donc</u>, Véronique, tu es <u>vraiment</u> très curieuse! *hey there / really*

VÉRONIQUE: Et toi, tu n'es pas <u>assez</u> <u>curieux</u>! *curious / enough*

ROGER: Ah bon? Pourquoi?

VÉRONIQUE: Pourquoi?! . . . Regarde la <u>contractuelle</u> là-bas! *meter maid*

ROGER: Ah, zut alors!

Compréhension

1. Qu'est-ce qu'il y a dans la rue?
2. Est-ce que la voiture est grande?
3. Comment s'appelle le jeune homme?
4. Où est-il?
5. Comment s'appelle la jeune fille?
6. De quelle couleur est la voiture?

■ N O T E ■
CULTURELLE

Les Français et l'auto

France is one of the leading producers of automobiles in the world. The two major automakers are **Renault** and **Peugeot.** They manufacture a variety of models ranging from sports cars to mini-vans and buses.

To obtain a driver's license in France, you must be eighteen years old and pass a very difficult driving test. French teenagers can, however, begin to drive at the age of sixteen, as long as they take lessons at an accredited driving school (**auto-école**) and are accompanied by an adult.

On the whole, because cars (even used cars) are expensive to buy and maintain, few French teenagers have cars. Instead, many get around on two-wheelers: motorcycles, scooters, and mopeds.

A. Les couleurs

Note the form and position of the color words in the following sentences:

Alice a un vélo **bleu**.　　　　　　*Alice has a **blue** bicycle.*
Nous avons des chemises **bleues**.　　*We have **blue** shirts.*

> Names of colors are ADJECTIVES and take adjective ENDINGS. Like most descriptive adjectives, they come *after* the noun.

Vocabulaire: Les couleurs

De quelle couleur . . . ?　　*What color . . . ?*　　—**De quelle couleur** est la moto?
　　　　　　　　　　　　　　　　　　　　　　　—Elle est rouge.

| blanc (blanche) | noir (noire) | bleu (bleue) | rouge (rouge) | jaune (jaune) | vert (verte) | gris (grise) | marron (marron) | orange (orange) | rose (rose) |

➡ The colors **orange** and **marron** are INVARIABLE. They do not take any endings.
　　un sac **orange**　　des sacs **orange**
　　un tee-shirt **marron**　　une chemise **marron**

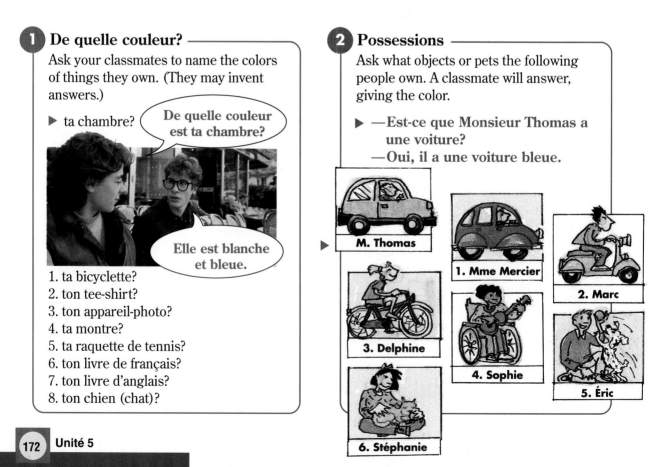

1 De quelle couleur?

Ask your classmates to name the colors of things they own. (They may invent answers.)

▶ ta chambre?

De quelle couleur est ta chambre?

Elle est blanche et bleue.

1. ta bicyclette?
2. ton tee-shirt?
3. ton appareil-photo?
4. ta montre?
5. ta raquette de tennis?
6. ton livre de français?
7. ton livre d'anglais?
8. ton chien (chat)?

2 Possessions

Ask what objects or pets the following people own. A classmate will answer, giving the color.

▶ —Est-ce que Monsieur Thomas a une voiture?
　—Oui, il a une voiture bleue.

M. Thomas

1. Mme Mercier
2. Marc
3. Delphine
4. Sophie
5. Éric
6. Stéphanie

3 **L'arche de Noé**

Noah's ark has just landed. Give the colors
of the animals as they get off the ship.

▶ le chien   **Le chien est blanc.**

1. le chat
2. l'éléphant *(m.)*
3. la panthère
4. le zèbre
5. le flamant
6. le cardinal
7. le lion
8. le perroquet

B. La place des adjectifs avant le nom

Compare the position of the adjectives in the following sentences.

Voici une voiture **française.**   Voici une **petite** voiture.
Paul est un garçon **intelligent.**   Pierre est un **beau** garçon.

▌ A few adjectives like **petit** and **beau** come BEFORE the noun they modify.

⇒ The article **des** often becomes **de** before an adjective. Compare:
   des voitures   →   **de** petites voitures

Vocabulaire: Les adjectifs qui précèdent le nom

beau (belle)	*beautiful, handsome*	Regarde la **belle** voiture!
joli	*pretty*	Qui est la **jolie** fille avec André?
grand	*big, large, tall*	Nous habitons dans un **grand** appartement.
petit	*little, small, short*	Ma soeur a un **petit** ordinateur.
bon (bonne)	*good*	Tu es un **bon** copain.
mauvais	*bad*	Patrick est un **mauvais** élève.

⇒ There is a LIAISON after the above adjectives when the noun which follows begins with a vowel sound. Note that in liaison:

• the "**d**" of **grand** is pronounced /t/: **un grand appartement**
• **bon** is pronounced like **bonne: un bon élève**

---

4 **Opinions personnelles**

Give your opinion about the following people and things, using the adjectives **bon** or **mauvais**.

▶ Meryl Streep est (une) actrice *(actress)*.
Meryl Streep est une bonne actrice (une mauvaise actrice).

1. *Rambo* est un film.
2. «Star Trek» est un programme de télé.
3. Whitney Houston est (une) chanteuse *(singer)*.
4. Denzel Washington est (un) acteur.
5. Cybil Shepherd est (une) actrice.

6. Dracula est une personne.
7. McDonald's est un restaurant.
8. Les Yankees sont une équipe *(team)* de baseball.
9. Les Lakers sont une équipe de basket.
10. Je suis [un(e)] élève.

Expressions pour la conversation

How to get someone's attention:

Dis!	*Say! Hey!*	**Dis,** Éric, est-ce que tu as une voiture?
Dis donc!	*Hey there!*	**Dis donc,** est-ce que tu veux faire une promenade avec moi?

---

5 **Dialogue**

Christine asks her cousin Thomas if he has certain things. He responds affirmatively, describing each one. Play both roles.

▶ un ordinateur (petit)　　　　　▶ une voiture (anglaise)

1. une télé (petite)
2. une guitare (espagnole)
3. un vélo (rouge)
4. une calculatrice (petite)

5. un sac (grand)
6. des livres (intéressants)
7. une copine (amusante)
8. une mobylette (bleue)

9. une montre (belle)
10. un copain (bon)
11. une cousine (jolie)
12. une radio (japonaise)

C. Il est ou c'est?

When describing a person or thing, French speakers use two different constructions,
il est (elle est) and **c'est.**

		Il est + ADJECTIVE **Elle est** + ADJECTIVE	**C'est** + ARTICLE + NOUN (+ ADJECTIVE)
Roger	*He is . . .*	**Il est** amusant.	**C'est** un copain. **C'est** un copain amusant.
Véronique	*She is . . .*	**Elle est** sportive.	**C'est** une amie. **C'est** une bonne amie.
un scooter	*It is . . .*	**Il est** joli.	**C'est** un scooter français. **C'est** un bon scooter.
une voiture	*It is . . .*	**Elle est** petite.	**C'est** une voiture anglaise. **C'est** une petite voiture.

➡ Note the corresponding plural forms:

    (Pierre et Marc)   *They are . . .*   **Ils sont** amusants.   **Ce sont** des copains.
    (Claire et Anne)   *They are . . .*   **Elles sont** timides.   **Ce sont** des copines.

➡ In negative sentences, **c'est** becomes **ce n'est pas.**

    Ce n'est pas un mauvais élève.   ***He's not a bad student.***
    Ce n'est pas une Peugeot.   ***It's not a Peugeot.***

➡ **C'est** is also used with names of people

    C'est Véronique.   **C'est** Madame Lamblet.

SCOOTERS PEUGEOT

6 Descriptions

Complete the following descriptions with **Il est, Elle est,** or **C'est,** as appropriate.

A. Roger
1. _____ grand.
2. _____ brun.
3. _____ un garçon sympathique.
4. _____ un mauvais élève.

B. Véronique
5. _____ une fille brune.
6. _____ une amie sympathique.
7. _____ très amusante.
8. _____ assez grande.

C. La voiture de Roger
9. _____ une voiture moderne.
10. _____ une petite voiture.
11. _____ rouge.
12. _____ très rapide.

D. Le scooter de Véronique
13. _____ bleu et blanc.
14. _____ très économique.
15. _____ un joli scooter.
16. _____ assez confortable.

D. Les expressions impersonnelles avec *c'est* —————————————

Note the use of **c'est** in the following sentences.

J'aime parler français.   **C'est** intéressant.   *It's interesting.*

Je n'aime pas travailler le weekend.   **Ce n'est pas** amusant.   *It's no(t) fun.*

To express an opinion on a general topic, the French use the construction:

> **C'est**
> **Ce n'est pas** } + MASCULINE ADJECTIVE

Vocabulaire: Opinions

| **C'est . . .** | *It's . . . , That's . . .* |
| **Ce n'est pas . . .** | *It's not . . . , That's not . . .* |

vrai	*true*	**chouette**	*neat*
faux	*false*	**super**	*great*
		extra	*terrific*
facile	*easy*	**pénible**	*a pain, annoying*
difficile	*hard, difficult*	**drôle**	*funny*

➡ To express an opinion, the French also use adverbs like **bien** and **mal.**

| **C'est bien.** | *That's good.* | Tu étudies? **C'est bien.** |
| **C'est mal.** | *That's bad.* | Alain n'étudie pas. **C'est mal.** |

---

 7 **Vrai ou faux?** ————————————————————————

Imagine that your little sister is talking about where certain cities are located. Tell her whether her statements are right or wrong.

1. Paris est en Italie.
2. Los Angeles est en Californie.
3. Genève est en Italie.
4. Dakar est en Afrique.
5. Fort-de-France est au Canada.
6. Québec est en France.

8 Opinion personnelle

Ask your classmates if they like to do the following things. They will answer, using an expression from the **Vocabulaire**.

▶ parler français

Tu aimes parler français?

Oui, c'est extra!

(Non, c'est difficile!)

1. téléphoner
2. parler en public
3. nager
4. danser
5. voyager
6. dîner en ville
7. regarder «Star Trek»
8. étudier le weekend
9. écouter la musique classique

Prononciation   ch /ʃ/

Les lettres «ch»

The letters "**ch**" are usually pronounced like the English "*sh.*"

Répétez: **chien   chat   chose   marche
chouette   chocolat   affiche
Michèle a un chat et deux chiens.**

chien

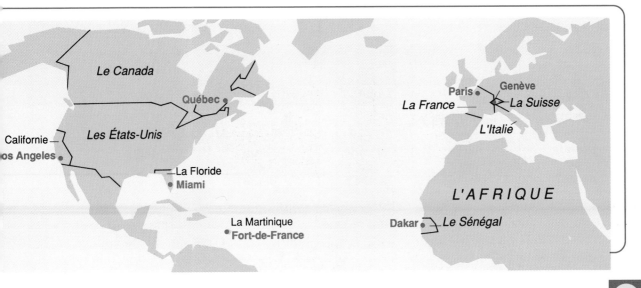

Le Canada

Québec

Les États-Unis

Californie

Los Angeles

La Floride
Miami

La Martinique
Fort-de-France

Paris — Genève
La France — La Suisse
L'Italie

L'AFRIQUE

Dakar — Le Sénégal

À votre tour!

1 Allô!

Christophe is phoning some friends. Match his questions on the left with his friends' answers on the right.

1. De quelle couleur est ton vélo?
2. Ta raquette est bleue?
3. Tu aimes regarder la télé?
4. C'est un magazine français?
5. Philippe n'aime pas parler en public?

a. Non, il est canadien.
b. C'est vrai! Il est très timide.
c. Non, elle est blanche.
d. Oui, c'est amusant.
e. Il est vert.

2 Créa-dialogue

There has been a burglary in the rue Saint-Pierre. By walkie-talkie, two detectives are describing what they see. Play both roles.

(le)	1. (la)	2. (la)	3. (le)	4. (le)	5. (la)
CAFÉ	PHARMACIE+	LIBRAIRIE	Restaurant	CINÉMA	fontaine
grande ou petite?	rouge ou bleue?	grande ou petite?	brun ou blond?	anglais ou français?	noir ou jaune?

▶ DÉTECTIVE 1: **Qu'est-ce qu'il y a devant <u>le café</u>?**   DÉTECTIVE 1: **<u>Elle</u> est <u>grande</u> ou <u>petite</u>?**
  DÉTECTIVE 2: **Il y a <u>une voiture</u>.**   DÉTECTIVE 2: **C'est <u>une petite voiture</u>.**

3 **Faisons connaissance!**

Try to find out which students have the same
interests you do. Select two activities you enjoy
from Column A and ask a classmate if he/she
likes to do them. Your classmate will answer
yes or no, using an appropriate expression from
Column B.

Tu aimes voyager?

Oui, c'est amusant.

A	**B**
chanter	chouette
danser	super
nager	extra
téléphoner	amusant
voyager	intéressant
jouer au foot	pénible
jouer au volley	drôle
organiser des boums	difficile
parler avec les voisins	facile
parler français en classe	
dîner au restaurant	

Tu aimes parler français en classe?

Non, c'est difficile.

4 **Composition: La chambre de Véronique**

Look at the picture of Véronique's
room. Write a short paragraph in which
you describe five of the following items.
You may want to mention color or size
(grand? petit?), and perhaps give your
opinion **(joli? beau? drôle? bon?,** etc.)

  la chambre
  la porte
  le lit
  la table
  la chaise
  la radiocassette
  la guitare
  l'affiche

▶ La chambre de Véronique est
  bleue et blanche. Elle a un grand
  lit. . . .

5 **Composition: Ma chambre**

Write a short description of your own room: real or imaginary. Use only vocabulary that you
know. You may use the suggestions about Véronique's room as a guide.

Vive la différence!
Le monde personnel

Parlons° de votre monde° personnel. Répondez aux questions suivantes.° D'après° vous, quelles sont les réponses des jeunes Français en général à ces° questions?

1 Combien de télés est-ce qu'il y a chez vous?°

- zéro
- une
- deux
- trois ou plus°

Et dans une maison française typique, combien est-ce qu'il y a de télés?

2 Combien de livres est-ce qu'il y a chez vous?

- dix
- cinquante
- cent
- plus de° cent cinquante

Et dans une maison française typique, combien de livres est-ce qu'il y a?

3 Dans la classe de français, quel est le pourcentage d'élèves qui ont un walkman?

- moins de° 25% (vingt-cinq pour cent)
- entre° 26% et 50%
- entre 51% et 75%
- entre 76% et 100% (cent pour cent)

Selon° vous, quel est le pourcentage de jeunes Français qui ont un walkman?

4 En général, comment sont vos relations avec vos parents?

- très bonnes
- bonnes
- assez bonnes
- mauvaises

Et en France, comment sont les relations entre parents et enfants?°

5 Quand vous avez une chose importante à discuter° (par exemple, un problème personnel), à qui est-ce que vous préférez parler?

- à votre frère ou à votre soeur
- à votre père ou à votre mère
- à un copain ou à une copine
- à un professeur

Et les jeunes Français, à qui est-ce qu'ils préfèrent parler de leurs° problèmes?

6 En général, qu'est-ce que vous pensez° de vos professeurs?

- Ils sont «cool».
- Ils sont compréhensifs.°
- Ils sont sévères.°
- Ils sont sympathiques.

Et les élèves français, qu'est-ce qu'ils pensent de leurs professeurs?

7 Quelle est la chose la plus° importante dans votre vie?°

- l'argent°
- l'amitié°
- l'indépendance
- les études°

Et pour les jeunes Français, quelle est la chose la plus importante?

Et les Français?

1. La majorité des familles françaises ont seulement *(only)* une télé.   2. Les Français aiment lire *(to read)*. Ils ont en moyenne *(on the average)* plus de cent livres par famille.
3. 41% (quarante et un pour cent)   4. La majorité des jeunes Français ont de très bonnes relations avec leurs parents.   5. En général, ils préfèrent parler à un copain ou à une copine.   6. En général, ils pensent que leurs professeurs sont sympathiques.
7. C'est l'amitié.

Parlons *Let's talk*   **monde** *world*   **suivantes** *following*   **D'après** *According to*
ces *these*   **chez vous** *in your home*   **plus** *more*   **plus de** *more than*
moins de *less than*   **entre** *between*   **Selon** *According to*   **enfants** *children*
discuter *to discuss*   **leurs** *their*   **pensez** *think*   **compréhensifs** *understanding*
sévères *strict*   **la plus** *the most*   **vie** *life*   **argent** *money*   **amitié** *friendship*
études *studies*

EN FRANCE

La mobylette

Because mopeds or cyclomoteurs are easy and fun to drive, they are very popular with French teenagers. During the week, many students go to school on their mopeds. On weekends, they take their mopeds to go downtown or to go for a ride in the country with their friends.

Although the term mobylette is a trade name, students tend to use the term (or its shortened form mob) to refer to any type of moped. In France, you can drive a mobylette at age 14, and the only restrictions are that you must wear a helmet and cannot exceed 45 kilometers per hour.

Look at the ads on the right. Which moped would you like to have? Describe it using words that you know. (What color is it? What country is it from? Is it big or small?)

Entre amis: Bonjour, Brigitte!

Chers° copains américains,

Je m'appelle Brigitte Lavie. J'ai quatorze ans. Voici ma photo. Je ne suis pas très grande, mais je ne suis pas petite. Je suis de taille° moyenne.° Je suis brune mais j'ai les yeux° verts. Je suis sportive. J'aime le ski, le jogging et la danse moderne.

J'habite à Toulouse avec ma famille. Mon père travaille dans l'industrie aéronautique. Il est ingénieur.° Ma mère travaille dans une banque. Elle est directrice° du personnel.

J'ai une soeur et un frère. Ma petite soeur s'appelle Ariane. Elle a cinq ans. Elle est très mignonne. Mon frère s'appelle Jérôme. Il a treize ans. Il est pénible. J'ai un chien. Il s'appelle Attila mais il est très gentil. (Il est plus gentil que° mon frère!) J'ai aussi deux poissons rouges.° Ils n'ont pas de nom.°

J'ai une chaîne stéréo et des quantités de compacts. J'ai aussi une mobylette. Le weekend, j'adore faire des promenades° à mobylette avec mes copains. J'ai beaucoup de copains, mais je n'ai pas de « petit copain ».° Ça n'a pas d'importance!° Je suis heureuse° comme ça !°

Amitiés,
Brigitte

Chers *Dear* **taille** *size* **moyenne** *average* **yeux** *eyes* **ingénieur** *engineer* **directrice** *director*
plus gentil que *nicer than* **poissons rouges** *goldfish* **nom** *name* **faire des promenades** *go for rides*
petit copain *boyfriend* **Ça n'a pas d'importance!** *It doesn't matter!* **heureuse** *happy* **comme ça** *like that*

■ NOTE ■
CULTURELLE

★ Paris

● Toulouse

Toulouse

Toulouse, with a population of over half a million people, is the center of the French aeronautic and space industry. It is in Toulouse that the Airbus planes and the Ariane rockets are being built in cooperation with other European countries.

Comment lire
GUESSING FROM CONTEXT

- As you read French, try to guess the meanings of unfamiliar words before you look at the English equivalents. Often the context provides good hints. For example, Brigitte writes:

  Je ne suis pas très grande, mais je ne suis pas petite.
  Je suis <u>de taille moyenne</u>.

  She is neither tall nor short. She must be about average:

  de taille moyenne = *of medium height or size*

- Sometimes you know what individual words in an expression mean, but the phrase does not seem to make sense. Then you have to guess at the real meaning. For example, Brigitte writes that she has:

  deux poissons rouges *??red fish??*

  If you guessed that these are most likely *goldfish,* you are right!

Enrichissez votre vocabulaire
MORE ON COGNATES

- Some words are PARTIAL COGNATES. The English word may help you remember the regular meaning. For example:

gentil	looks like	*gentle*	but means	*nice*
grand	looks like	*grand*	but means	*tall, big*
j'adore	looks like	*I adore*	but means	*I love*

- Some cognates are spelled differently in the two languages. Knowing cognate patterns makes it easier to identify new words. For example:

FRENCH	ENGLISH	FRENCH	ENGLISH
-ique	*-ic*	**aéronautique**	*aeronautic, aeronautical*
-ique	*-ical*	**typique**	*typical*
-té	*-ty*	**quantité**	*quantity*

Activité

Can you identify the English equivalents of the following French words?

la musique classique, une personne dynamique, un film comique, une guitare électrique, une société, une activité, une possibilité, la curiosité, la beauté

Activité: Une lettre à Brigitte

Write a letter to Brigitte in which you describe yourself and your family. You may tell her:

- your name and how old you are
- if you are tall or short
- if you like sports
- if you have brothers and sisters (If so, give their names and ages.)

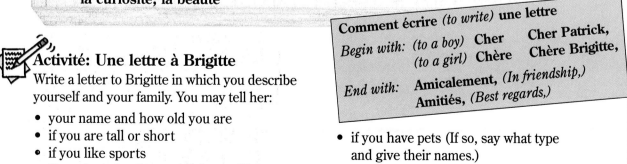

Comment écrire *(to write)* **une lettre**

Begin with: *(to a boy)* **Cher**   **Cher Patrick,**
(to a girl) **Chère**   **Chère Brigitte,**

End with: **Amicalement,** *(In friendship,)*
Amitiés, *(Best regards,)*

- if you have pets (If so, say what type and give their names.)
- a few things you own
- a few things you like to do with your friends

Variétés

Petit catalogue des compliments et des insultes

1

Elle est sympa!

C'est une chic fille!

2

Il est formidable!

Il est génial!

Il est sensationnel!

Il est super!

C'est un champion.

3 CONCERT

Elle est cool.

Elle est formidable!

Elle est super.

Elle est sensationnelle!

Elle est géniale!

4

Crétin!

Idiot!

Imbécile!

LES ANIMAUX
ET
LE LANGAGE

Selon° toi, est-ce que les animaux ont une personnalité? Pour les Français, les animaux ont des qualités et des défauts,° comme° nous. Devine° comment on° complète les phrases suivantes° en français.

1 Philippe n'aime pas étudier. Il préfère dormir.° Il est paresseux° comme° . . .

2 Charlotte adore parler. Elle est bavarde° comme . . .

3 Isabelle est une excellente élève. Elle a une mémoire extraordinaire. Elle a une mémoire d' (de) . . .

4 Le petit frère de Christine est jeune, mais il est très intelligent. Il est malin° comme . . .

5 Où est Jacques? Il n'est pas prêt!° Oh là là! Il est lent° comme . . .

6 Nicole a très, très faim. Elle a une faim de (d') . . .

un tigre un chat un lézard

une poule une pie un lion

éléphant hippopotame kangourou

un cheval un singe une girafe

une tortue un poisson un rhinocéros

lion ours loup

Voici les réponses:

1. un lézard 2. une pie 3. un éléphant 4. un singe 5. une tortue 6. loup

---

Selon *According to* **défauts** *shortcomings* **comme** *like* **Devine** *Guess* **on** *one* **phrases suivantes** *following sentences* **dormir** *to sleep* **paresseux** *lazy* **comme** *as* **bavarde** *talkative* **malin** *clever* **prêt** *ready* **lent** *slow*

REFERENCE SECTION

CONTENTS

APPENDIX 1

Maps

The French-Speaking World

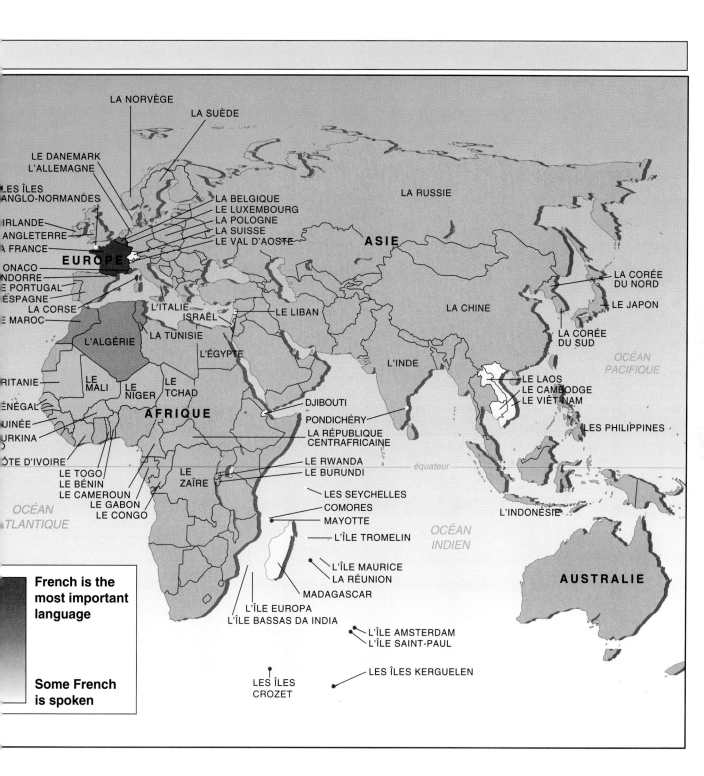

LA NORVÈGE
LA SUÈDE
LE DANEMARK
L'ALLEMAGNE
LES ÎLES
ANGLO-NORMANDES
IRLANDE
ANGLETERRE
A FRANCE
EUROPE
ONACO
NDORRE
E PORTUGAL
ESPAGNE
LA CORSE
E MAROC
L'ALGÉRIE
RITANIE
LE MALI
LE NIGER
LE TCHAD
ÉNÉGAL
UINÉE
URKINA
ÔTE D'IVOIRE
AFRIQUE
LE TOGO
LE BÉNIN
LE CAMEROUN
LE GABON
LE CONGO
OCÉAN
TLANTIQUE
LE ZAÏRE

LA BELGIQUE
LE LUXEMBOURG
LA POLOGNE
LA SUISSE
LE VAL D'AOSTE
L'ITALIE
ISRAËL
LA TUNISIE
L'ÉGYPTE
LE LIBAN

ASIE

LA RUSSIE

LA CHINE

LA CORÉE
DU NORD
LE JAPON

LA CORÉE
DU SUD

OCÉAN
PACIFIQUE

L'INDE

DJIBOUTI
PONDICHÉRY
LA RÉPUBLIQUE
CENTRAFRICAINE
LE RWANDA
LE BURUNDI

LE LAOS
LE CAMBODGE
LE VIÊT-NAM

LES PHILIPPINES

équateur

L'INDONÉSIE

LES SEYCHELLES
COMORES
MAYOTTE
L'ÎLE TROMELIN

L'ÎLE MAURICE
LA RÉUNION
MADAGASCAR
L'ÎLE EUROPA
L'ÎLE BASSAS DA INDIA

OCÉAN
INDIEN

AUSTRALIE

L'ÎLE AMSTERDAM
L'ÎLE SAINT-PAUL

LES ÎLES KERGUELEN

LES ÎLES
CROZET

**French is the
most important
language**

**Some French
is spoken**

France

L'ANGLETERRE

LA BELGIQUE

L'ALLEMAGNE

LA MANCHE

NORD[2]

Lille•

LE LUXEMBOURG

LES VOSGES

Le Havre•

HAUTE-
NORMANDIE

•Rouen

PICARDIE

LORRAINE

Meuse

Caen•

Nancy•

ALSACE

Strasbourg•

BASSE-
NORMANDIE

Versailles•⊛Paris

RÉGION
PARISIENNE[1]

CHAMPAGNE-
ARDENNE

Colmar•

Rhin

BRETAGNE

Seine

Rennes•

PAYS DE
LA LOIRE

CENTRE

Loire

Dijon•

FRANCHE-
COMTÉ

LA SUISSE

•Nantes

•Tours

BOURGOGNE

Saône

OCÉAN
ATLANTIQUE

POITOU-
CHARENTES

AUVERGNE

Vichy•

Annecy•

LIMOUSIN

Clermont-
Ferrand•

•Lyon

RHÔNE-ALPES

LES ALPES

L'ITALIE

Grenoble•

Bordeaux•

LE MASSIF

Garonne

CENTRAL

Rhône

AQUITAINE

Albi•

Nîmes•

Avignon•

MONACO

PROVENCE-
CÔTE D'AZUR[3]

Nice•

MIDI-PYRÉNÉES

Montpellier•

Cannes

Toulouse•

LANGUEDOC-
ROUSSILLON

Marseille•

Saint-
Tropez•

Toulon•

LES PYRÉNÉES

LA CORSE

L'ESPAGNE

MER MÉDITERRANÉE

[1]Also known as Île-de-France
[2]Also known as Nord-Pas-de-Calais
[3]Also known as Provence-Alpes-Côte d'Azur *(Bottin 1989)*

Vowels

Sound	Spelling	Examples
/a/	a, à, â	Madame, là-bas, théâtre
/i/	i, î	visite, Nice, dîne
	y (initial, final, or between consonants)	Yves, Guy, style
/u/	ou, où, oû	Toulouse, où, août
/y/	u, û	tu, Luc, sûr
/o/	o (final or before silent consonant)	piano, idiot, Margot
	au, eau	jaune, Claude, beau
	ô	hôtel, drôle, Côte-d'Ivoire
/ɔ/	o	Monique, Noël, jolie
	au	Paul, restaurant, Laure
/e/	é	Dédé, Québec, télé
	e (before silent final z, t, r)	chez, et, Roger
	ai (final or before final silent consonant)	j'ai, mai, japonais
/ɛ/	è	Michèle, Ève, père
	ei	seize, neige, tour Eiffel
	ê	tête, être, Viêt-nam
	e (before two consonants)	elle, Pierre, Annette
	e (before pronounced final consonant)	Michel, avec, cher
	ai (before pronounced final consonant)	française, aime, Maine
/ə/	e (final or before single consonant)	je, Denise, venir
/ø/	eu, oeu	deux, Mathieu, oeufs
	eu (before final se)	nerveuse, généreuse, sérieuse
/œ/	eu (before final pronounced consonant except /z/)	heure, neuf, Lesieur
	oeu	soeur, coeur, oeuf
	oe	oeil

Nasal vowels

Sound	Spelling	Examples
/ɑ̃/	an, am	France, quand, lampe
	en, em	Henri, pendant, décembre
/ɔ̃/	on, om	non, Simon, bombe
/ɛ̃/	in, im	Martin, invite, impossible
	yn, ym	syndicat, sympathique, Olympique
	ain, aim	Alain, américain, faim
	(o) + in	loin, moins, point
	(i) + en	bien, Julien, viens
/œ̃/	un, um	un, Lebrun, parfum

Semi-vowels

Sound	Spelling	Examples
/j/	**i, y** (before vowel sound)	bien, piano, Lyon
	-il, -ill (after vowel sound), **-ll**	oeil, travaille, Marseille, fille
/ɥ/	**u** (before vowel sound)	lui, Suisse, juillet
/w/	**ou** (before vowel sound)	oui, Louis, jouer
/wa/	**oi, oî**	voici, Benoît
	oy (before vowel)	voyage

Consonants

Sound	Spelling	Examples
/b/	**b**	Barbara, banane, Belgique
/k/	**c** (before **a, o, u,** or consonant)	Coca-Cola, cuisine, classe
	ch(r)	Christine, Christian, Christophe
	qu, q (final)	Québec, qu'est-ce que, cinq
	k	kilo, Kiki, ketchup
/ʃ/	**ch**	Charles, blanche, chez
/d/	**d**	Didier, dans, médecin
/f/	**f**	Félix, franc, neuf
	ph	Philippe, téléphone, photo
/g/	**g** (before **a, o, u,** or consonant)	Gabriel, gorge, légumes, gris
	gu (before **e, i, y**)	vague, Guillaume, Guy
/ɲ/	**gn**	mignon, champagne, Allemagne
/ʒ/	**j**	je, Jérôme, jaune
	g (before **e, i, y**)	rouge, Gigi, gymnastique
	ge (before **a, o, u**)	orangeade, Georges, nageur
/l/	**l**	Lise, elle, cheval
/m/	**m**	Maman, moi, tomate
/n/	**n**	banane, Nancy, nous
/p/	**p**	peu, Papa, Pierre
/r/	**r**	arrive, rentre, Paris
/s/	**c** (before **e, i, y**)	ce, Cécile, Nancy
	ç (before **a, o, u**)	ça, garçon, déçu
	s (initial or before consonant)	sac, Sophie, reste
	ss (between vowels)	boisson, dessert, Suisse
	t (before **i** + vowel)	attention, Nations Unies, natation
	x	dix, six, soixante
/t/	**t**	trop, télé, Tours
	th	Thérèse, thé, Marthe
/v/	**v**	Viviane, vous, nouveau
/gz/	**x**	examen, exemple, exact
/ks/	**x**	Max, Mexique, excellent
/z/	**s** (between vowels)	désert, Louise, télévision
	z	Suzanne, zut, zéro

A. Cardinal numbers

0	zéro	18	dix-huit	82	quatre-vingt-deux
1	un (une)	19	dix-neuf	90	quatre-vingt-dix
2	deux	20	vingt	91	quatre-vingt-onze
3	trois	21	vingt et un (une)	100	cent
4	quatre	22	vingt-deux	101	cent un (une)
5	cinq	23	vingt-trois	102	cent deux
6	six	30	trente	200	deux cents
7	sept	31	trente et un (une)	201	deux cent un
8	huit	32	trente-deux	300	trois cents
9	neuf	40	quarante	400	quatre cents
10	dix	41	quarante et un (une)	500	cinq cents
11	onze	50	cinquante	600	six cents
12	douze	60	soixante	700	sept cents
13	treize	70	soixante-dix	800	huit cents
14	quatorze	71	soixante et onze	900	neuf cents
15	quinze	72	soixante-douze	1.000	mille
16	seize	80	quatre-vingts	2.000	deux mille
17	dix-sept	81	quatre-vingt-un (une)	1.000.000	un million

Notes:
1. The word **et** occurs only in the numbers 21, 31, 41, 51, 61, and 71:   **vingt et un** / **soixante et onze**
2. **Un** becomes **une** before a feminine noun: **trente et une filles**
3. **Quatre-vingts** becomes **quatre-vingt** before another number: **quatre-vingt-cinq**
4. **Cents** becomes **cent** before another number: **trois cent vingt**
5. **Mille** never adds an **-s:**   **quatre mille**

B. Ordinal numbers

1er (ère)	**premier (première)**	5e	**cinquième**	9e	**neuvième**
2e	**deuxième**	6e	**sixième**	10e	**dixième**
3e	**troisième**	7e	**septième**	11e	**onzième**
4e	**quatrième**	8e	**huitième**	12e	**douzième**

Note: **Premier** becomes **première** before a feminine noun: **la première histoire**

C. Metric equivalents

1 gramme	= 0.035 ounces		1 ounce	=	**28,349 grammes**
1 kilogramme	= 2.205 pounds		1 pound	=	**0,453 kilogrammes**
1 litre	= 1.057 quarts		1 quart	=	**0,946 litres**
1 mètre	= 39.37 inches		1 foot	=	**30,480 centimètres**
1 kilomètre	= 0.62 miles		1 mile	=	**1,609 kilomètres**

APPENDIX 4
Verbs

A. Regular verbs

Infinitive	Present		Passé composé	
parler *(to talk, speak)*	je **parle** tu **parles** il **parle**	nous **parlons** vous **parlez** ils **parlent**	j'ai **parlé** tu as **parlé** il a **parlé**	nous **avons parlé** vous **avez parlé** ils **ont parlé**
	IMPERATIVE: **parle, parlons, parlez**			
finir *(to finish)*	je **finis** tu **finis** il **finit**	nous **finissons** vous **finissez** ils **finissent**	j'ai **fini** tu as **fini** il a **fini**	nous **avons fini** vous **avez fini** ils **ont fini**
	IMPERATIVE: **finis, finissons, finissez**			
vendre *(to sell)*	je **vends** tu **vends** il **vend**	nous **vendons** vous **vendez** ils **vendent**	j'ai **vendu** tu as **vendu** il a **vendu**	nous **avons vendu** vous **avez vendu** ils **ont vendu**
	IMPERATIVE: **vends, vendons, vendez**			

B. -er verbs with spelling changes

Infinitive	Present		Passé composé
acheter *(to buy)*	j'**achète** tu **achètes** il **achète**	nous **achetons** vous **achetez** ils **achètent**	j'ai **acheté**
	Verb like **acheter**: amener *(to bring, take along)*		
espérer *(to hope)*	j'**espère** tu **espères** il **espère**	nous **espérons** vous **espérez** ils **espèrent**	j'ai **espéré**
	Verbs like **espérer**: célébrer *(to celebrate)*, préférer *(to prefer)*		
commencer *(to begin, start)*	je **commence** tu **commences** il **commence**	nous **commençons** vous **commencez** ils **commencent**	j'ai **commencé**
manger *(to eat)*	je **mange** tu **manges** il **mange**	nous **mangeons** vous **mangez** ils **mangent**	j'ai **mangé**
	Verbs like **manger**: nager *(to swim)*, voyager *(to travel)*		
payer *(to pay, pay for)*	je **paie** tu **paies** il **paie**	nous **payons** vous **payez** ils **paient**	j'ai **payé**
	Verbs like **payer**: nettoyer *(to clean)*		

Infinitive	Present		Passé composé
avoir *(to have, own)*	j'**ai** tu **as** il **a**	nous **avons** vous **avez** ils **ont**	j'ai **eu**
	IMPERATIVE: **aie, ayons, ayez**		
être *(to be)*	je **suis** tu **es** il **est**	nous **sommes** vous **êtes** ils **sont**	j'ai **été**
	IMPERATIVE: **sois, soyons, soyez**		
aller *(to go)*	je **vais** tu **vas** il **va**	nous **allons** vous **allez** ils **vont**	je **suis allé(e)**
	IMPERATIVE: **va, allons, allez**		
boire *(to drink)*	je **bois** tu **bois** il **boit**	nous **buvons** vous **buvez** ils **boivent**	j'ai **bu**
connaître *(to know)*	je **connais** tu **connais** il **connaît**	nous **connaissons** vous **connaissez** ils **connaissent**	j'ai **connu**
devoir *(to have to, should, must)*	je **dois** tu **dois** il **doit**	nous **devons** vous **devez** ils **doivent**	j'ai **dû**
dire *(to say, tell)*	je **dis** tu **dis** il **dit**	nous **disons** vous **dites** ils **disent**	j'ai **dit**
dormir *(to sleep)*	je **dors** tu **dors** il **dort**	nous **dormons** vous **dormez** ils **dorment**	j' ai **dormi**
écrire *(to write)*	j' **écris** tu **écris** il **écrit**	nous **écrivons** vous **écrivez** ils **écrivent**	j'ai **écrit**
	Verb like **écrire**: décrire *(to describe)*		
faire *(to make, do)*	je **fais** tu **fais** il **fait**	nous **faisons** vous **faites** ils **font**	j'ai **fait**
lire *(to read)*	je **lis** tu **lis** il **lit**	nous **lisons** vous **lisez** ils **lisent**	j'ai **lu**
mettre *(to put, place)*	je **mets** tu **mets** il **met**	nous **mettons** vous **mettez** ils **mettent**	j'ai **mis**
	Verb like **mettre**: promettre *(to promise)*		

Infinitive	Present		Passé composé
ouvrir *(to open)*	j'**ouvre** tu **ouvres** il **ouvre**	nous **ouvrons** vous **ouvrez** ils **ouvrent**	j'ai **ouvert**

Verbs like **ouvrir**: découvrir *(to discover)*, offrir *(to offer)*

partir *(to leave)*	je **pars** tu **pars** il **part**	nous **partons** vous **partez** ils **partent**	je **suis parti(e)**
pouvoir *(to be able, can)*	je **peux** tu **peux** il **peut**	nous **pouvons** vous **pouvez** ils **peuvent**	j'ai **pu**
prendre *(to take)*	je **prends** tu **prends** il **prend**	nous **prenons** vous **prenez** ils **prennent**	j'ai **pris**

Verbs like **prendre**: apprendre *(to learn)*, comprendre *(to understand)*

savoir *(to know)*	je **sais** tu **sais** il **sait**	nous **savons** vous **savez** ils **savent**	j'ai **su**
sortir *(to go out, get out)*	je **sors** tu **sors** il **sort**	nous **sortons** vous **sortez** ils **sortent**	je **suis sorti(e)**
venir *(to come)*	je **viens** tu **viens** il **vient**	nous **venons** vous **venez** ils **viennent**	je **suis venu(e)**

Verb like **venir**: revenir *(to come back)*

voir *(to see)*	je **vois** tu **vois** il **voit**	nous **voyons** vous **voyez** ils **voient**	j'ai **vu**
vouloir *(to want)*	je **veux** tu **veux** il **veut**	nous **voulons** vous **voulez** ils **veulent**	j'ai **voulu**

aller *(to go)*	je **suis allé(e)**	**passer** *(to go by, through)*	je **suis passé(e)**
arriver *(to arrive, come)*	je **suis arrivé(e)**	**rentrer** *(to go home)*	je **suis rentré(e)**
descendre *(to go down)*	je **suis descendu(e)**	**rester** *(to stay)*	je **suis resté(e)**
entrer *(to enter, go in)*	je **suis entré(e)**	**revenir** *(to come back)*	je **suis revenu(e)**
monter *(to go up)*	je **suis monté(e)**	**sortir** *(to go out, get out)*	je **suis sorti(e)**
mourir *(to die)*	Il/elle **est mort(e)**	**tomber** *(to fall)*	je **suis tombé(e)**
naître *(to be born)*	je **suis né(e)**	**venir** *(to come)*	je **suis venu(e)**
partir *(to leave)*	je **suis parti(e)**		

VOCABULARY

French-English

The French-English vocabulary contains active and passive words from the text, as well as the important words of the illustrations used within the units. Obvious passive cognates have not been listed.

The numbers following an entry indicate the lesson in which the word or phrase is activated. (**B** stands for the photo essay that precedes **Niveau B;** and **E** stands for **Entracte.**)

Nouns: If the article of a noun does not indicate gender, the noun is followed by *m.* (*masculine*) or *f.* (*feminine*). If the plural (*pl.*) is irregular, it is given in parentheses.

Adjectives: Adjectives are listed in the masculine form. If the feminine form is irregular, it is given in parentheses. Irregular plural forms (*pl.*) are also given in parentheses.

Verbs: Verbs are listed in the infinitive form. An asterisk (*) in front of an active verb means that it is irregular. (For forms, see the verb charts in Appendix 4C.) Irregular present tense forms are listed when they are used before the verb has been activated. Irregular past participle (*p.p.*) forms are listed separately.

Words beginning with an **h** are preceded by a bullet (•) if the **h** is aspirate; that is, if the word is treated as if it begins with a consonant sound.

A

a: il y a there is, there are **17**
à at, in, to **14**
  à côté next door, next to
  à demain! see you tomorrow! **8**
  à partir de as of, beginning
  à samedi! see you Saturday! **8**
abolir to abolish
abondant plentiful, copious, large
un **abricot** apricot
absolument absolutely
un **accent** accent mark, stress
accepter to accept
un **accord** agreement
  d'accord okay, all right **13**
  être d'accord to agree **14**
un **achat** purchase
un **acteur, une actrice** actor, actress
une **activité** activity
l' **addition** *f.* check
adorer to love
une **adresse** address

l' **adresse électronique** e-mail address
adroit skilled, skillful
un(e) **adulte** adult
aéronautique aeronautic, aeronautical
un **aéroport** airport
affectueusement affectionately (*at the end of a letter*)
une **affiche** poster **17**
affirmativement affirmatively
l' **Afrique** *f.* Africa
l' **âge** *m.* age
  quel âge a-t-il/elle? how old is he/she? **17**
  quel âge as-tu? how old are you? **7**
  quel âge a ton père/ta mère? how old is your father/your mother? **7**
âgé old
une **agence** agency
  une agence de tourisme tourist office
  une agence de voyages travel agency
agiter to shake
agité agitated
ah! ah!, oh!

ah bon? oh? really? **16**
ah non! ah, no!
ai (*see* **avoir**)**: j'ai** I have **17**
  j'ai... ans I'm ... (years old) **7**
une **aile** wing
aimer to like **15**
  est-ce que tu aimes...? do you like ... ? **13**
  j'aime... I like ... **13**
  je n'aime pas... I don't like ... **13**
  j'aimerais I would like
ainsi thus
aîné older
  un frère aîné older brother
  une soeur aînée older sister
ajouter to add
l' **Algérie** *f.* Algeria (*country in North Africa*)
algérien (algérienne) Algerian
l' **Allemagne** *f.* Germany
allemand German
* **aller** to go
  allez (*see* **aller**)**: allez-vous-en!** go away!
  allez-y come on!, go ahead!, do it!

comment allez-vous? how are you? 3

allô! hello! *(on the telephone)*

alors so, then 19

une **alouette** lark

les **Alpes** *f.* (the) Alps

l' **alphabet** *m.* alphabet

l' **Alsace** *f.* Alsace *(province in eastern France)*

américain American 2, 19

à l'américaine American-style

un **Américain, une Américaine** American person

l' **Amérique** *f.* America

un **ami, une amie** *(close)* friend 5

amicalement love, cordially *(at the end of a letter)*

l' **amitié** *f.* friendship

amitiés best regards *(at the end of a letter)*

amusant funny, amusing 19

amuser to amuse

s'amuser to have fun

on s'est bien amusé! we had a good time!

un **an** year

avoir... ans to be . . . (years old) 18

il/elle a... ans he/she is . . . (years old) 7

j'ai... ans I'm . . . *(years old)* 7

l'an dernier last year

par an per year

un **ananas** pineapple

ancien (ancienne) former, old, ancient

un **âne** donkey

un **ange** angel

anglais English 2, 19

un **Anglais, une Anglaise** English person

un **animal** *(pl. animaux)* animal

une **animation** live entertainment

animé animated, lively

une **année** year 8

toute l'année all year long

un **anniversaire** birthday 8

c'est quand, ton anniversaire? when is your birthday? 8

joyeux anniversaire! happy birthday!

mon anniversaire est le (2 mars) my birthday is (March 2nd) 8

un **annuaire** telephone directory

un **anorak** ski jacket

les **antiquités** *f.* antiquities, antiques

août *m.* August 8

un **appareil-photo** *(pl. appareils-photo)* *(still)* camera 17

s' **appeller** to be named, called

comment s'appelle...? what's . . .'s name? 6

comment s'appelle-t-il/elle? what's his/her name? 17

comment t'appelles-tu? what's your name? 1

il/elle s'appelle... his/her name is . . . 6

je m'appelle... my name is . . . 1

apporter: apporte-moi (apportez-moi) bring me B

apprécier to appreciate

approprié appropriate

après after, afterwards

d'après according to

de l'après-midi in the afternoon, p.m. 4

l' **arabe** *m.* Arabic *(language)*

un **arbre** tree

un arbre généalogique family tree

l' **arche** *f.* **de Noé** Noah's Ark

l' **argent** *m.* money

l'argent de poche allowance, pocket money

arrêter to arrest; to stop

arriver to come, to arrive

j'arrive! I'm coming!

une **arrivée** arrival

un **arrondissement** district

un **artifice: le feu d'artifice** fireworks

un **artiste, une artiste** artist

as *(see avoir):* **est-ce que tu as...?** do you have . . . ? 17

un **ascenseur** elevator

un **aspirateur** vacuum cleaner

s' **asseoir: asseyez-vous!** sit down! B

assez rather, enough 19

associer to associate

l' **Atlantique** *m.* Atlantic Ocean

attention *f.:* **faire attention** to be careful, pay attention 16

attentivement carefully

au (à + le) to (the), at (the), in (the) 14

au revoir! good-bye! 3

une **auberge** inn

aucun: ne... aucun none, not any

aujourd'hui today 8

aujourd'hui, c'est... today is . . . 8

aussi also, too 2, 15

une **auto (automobile)** car, automobile 17

une auto-école driving school

l' **autobus** *m.* bus

l' **automne** *m.* autumn, fall

en automne in (the) autumn, fall 12

l' **autoroute** *f.* **de l'information** the information highway

autre other

d'autres others

un(e) autre another

avant before

avant-hier the day before yesterday

en avant let's begin

avantageux (avantageuse) reasonable, advantageous

avec with 14

avec moi, avec toi with me, with you 13

avec qui? with who(m)? 16

un **avis** opinion

un avis de recherche missing person's bulletin

à votre avis in your opinion

* **avoir** to have 18

avoir... ans to be . . . (years old) 18

avoir faim to be hungry 18

avoir lieu to take place

avoir soif to be thirsty 18

avril *m.* April 8

B

le **babyfoot** tabletop soccer game

le **babysitting: faire du babysitting** to baby-sit

les **bagages** *m.* bags, baggage

la **bande de copains** group of friends

une **bande dessinée** comic strip
des **bandes dessinées** comics

la **Bannière étoilée** Star-Spangled Banner

une **banque** bank

une **barbe: quelle barbe!** what a pain! *(colloq.)*

le **bas** the bottom
au bas at the bottom
basé based

le **basket (basketball)** basketball
jouer au basket to play basketball **13**

un **bateau-mouche** sightseeing boat

battre to beat

bavard talkative

beau (bel, belle; *m.pl.* beaux) handsome, good-looking, beautiful **17, 20**
il est beau he is good-looking, handsome **17**
il fait beau it's beautiful (nice) out **12**

un **beau-frère** stepbrother, brother-in-law

un **beau-père** stepfather, father-in-law

beaucoup (de) much, very much, many, a lot **15**

la **beauté** beauty

un **bec** beak

la **Belgique** Belgium
belle (*see* **beau**) beautiful **17, 20**
elle est belle she is beautiful **17**

une **belle-mère** stepmother, mother-in-law

une **belle-soeur** stepsister, sister-in-law

les **Bermudes** *f.* Bermuda

le **besoin** need

des **besoins d'argent** money needs

bête dumb, silly **19**

une **bicyclette** bicycle **17**

bien well, very well, carefully **15**
bien sûr of course **13**
ça va bien everything's fine (going well) **3**
ça va très bien I'm (everything's) very well **3**
c'est bien that's good (fine) **20**
je veux bien (...) I'd love to (...), I do, I want to **13**
oui, bien sûr... yes, of course ... **14**
très bien very well **15**

bientôt: à bientôt! see you soon!

bienvenue welcome

le **bifteck** steak
un bifteck de tortue turtle steak

bilingue bilingual

la **biologie** biology

une **bise** a kiss **1**

une **biscotte** dry toast

blaff de poisson *m.* fish stew

blanc (blanche) white **20**

Blanche-Neige Snow White

blanchir to blanch, turn white

bleu blue **20**

blond blond **17**
il/elle est blond(e) he/she is blond **17**

une **boisson** drink, beverage **10**

une **boîte** box

un **bol** deep bowl

bon (bonne) good **20**
ah bon? oh, really? **16**
de bonne humeur in a good mood
il fait bon the weather's good (pleasant) **12**

le **bonheur** happiness

bonjour hello **1, 3**

une **bouche** mouth **E3**

une **boucherie** butcher shop

le **boudin** sausage

une **boulangerie** bakery **3**

une **boum** a party **13, 15**

boxe: un match de boxe boxing match

un **bras** arm **E3**

brésilien (brésilienne) Brazilian

la **Bretagne** Brittany *(province in northwestern France)*

bricoler to do things around the house

broche: à la broche on the spit

bronzé tan

un **bruit** noise

brun brown, dark-haired **17**
il/elle est brun(e) he/she has dark hair **17**

brunir to turn brown

Bruxelles Brussels

le **bulletin de notes** report card

un **bureau** desk **B, 17**; office

un **bus** bus

un **but** goal; end

C

ça that, it
ça fait combien? ça fait... how much is that (it)? that (it) is ... **11**
ça, là-bas that (one), over there **17**
ça va? how's everything? how are you? **3**
ça va everything's fine, I'm OK **3**
ça va (très) bien, ça va bien everything's going very well, everything's fine (going well) **3**
ça va comme ci, comme ça everything's (going) so-so **3**
ça va (très) mal things are going (very) badly **3**
regarde ça look at that **17**

une **cabine d'essayage** fitting room

les **cabinets** *m.* toilet

un **cadeau** (*pl.* **cadeaux**) gift, present

cadet (cadette) younger
un frère cadet (a) younger brother
une soeur cadette (a) younger sister

le **café** coffee **10**

un **café au lait** coffee with hot milk

un **café** café (*French coffee shop*) **14**

    au café to (at) the café **14**

un **cahier** notebook **B, E3**

une **calculatrice** calculator **17**

un **calendrier** calendar

un **camarade, une camarade** classmate **17**

le **Cambodge** Cambodia (*country in Asia*)

un **cambriolage** burglary

un **cambrioleur** burglar

une **caméra** movie camera

la **campagne** the country(side)

    une auberge de campagne country inn

le **Canada** Canada

canadien (canadienne) Canadian **2, 19**

un **Canadien, une Canadienne** Canadian person

un **canard** duck

un **car** touring bus

    un car scolaire school bus

une **carotte** carrot

    des carottes râpées grated carrots

un **carré** square

    le Vieux Carré the French Quarter in New Orleans

une **carte** map **B**; card

une **carte postale** postcard

un **cas** case

    en cas de in case of

un **casque** headphones

une **cassette** cassette tape **B, 17**

le **catch** wrestling

une **cathédrale** cathedral

une **cave** cellar

un **CD (un compact)** CD, compact disc **B**

    un CD vidéo laserdisc, videodisc

    un lecteur de CD (vidéo) CD player (laserdisc player)

ce (c') this, that, it

    ce n'est pas that's/it's not **20**

    ce que that which, what

    ce sont these are, those are, they are **20**

une **cédille** cedilla

cela that

célèbre famous

cent one hundred **6**

une **centaine** about a hundred

un **centime** centime (*1/100 of a franc*)

un **centre** center

certain certain

    certains some of them

c'est (*see ce*)

    ce n'est pas it's (that's) not **20**

    c'est it's, that's **5, 17, 20**

    c'est + *day of the week* it's ... **8**

    c'est + *name or noun* it's ... **5**

    c'est bien/mal that's good/bad **20**

    c'est combien? how much is that/it? **11**

    c'est le (12 octobre) it's (October 12) **8**

    qu'est-ce 17

    qu'est-ce que c'est? what is it? what's that? **17**

    qui est-ce? who's that/this? **17**

chacun each one, each person

une **chaîne** (TV) channel

une **mini-chaîne** compact stereo

une **chaîne stéréo** stereo set **17**

une **chaise** chair **B, 17**

la **chaleur** heat, warmth

un **champion, une championne** champion

la **chance** luck

une **chanson** song

    chanter to sing **13, 15**

un **chanteur, une chanteuse** singer

une **chambre** bedroom

chaque each, every

charmant charming

un **chat** cat **7**

un **château** (*pl.* **châteaux**) castle

chaud warm, hot

    il fait chaud it's warm (hot) (weather) **12**

chauffer to warm, heat up

un **chauffeur** driver

un **chef** boss; chef

un **cheval** (*pl.* **chevaux**) horse **E5**

chic (*inv.*) nice; elegant, in style

    une chic fille a great girl

un **chien** dog **7**

la **chimie** chemistry

chinois Chinese **19**

le **chinois** Chinese (*language*)

le **chocolat** hot chocolate, cocoa **10**

    une glace au chocolat chocolate ice cream

un **choix** choice

    au choix choose one, your choice

une **chorale** choir

une **chose** thing **17**

    les mêmes choses the same things

chouette great, terrific **20**

le **cidre** cider

un **cinéaste, une cinéaste** film maker

le **cinéma** the movies

    au cinéma to (at) the movies, movie theater **14**

cinq five **1**

cinquante fifty **3**

une **circonstance** circumstance

cité: la Cité Interdite Forbidden City

une **classe** class

    en classe in class **14**

classique classical

le **clavier** keyboard

un **client, une cliente** customer

un **clip** music video

un **cochon** pig

un **coiffeur, une coiffeuse** hairdresser

un **coin** spot

une **coïncidence** coincidence

le **Colisée** the Coliseum (*a large stadium built by the Romans*)

un **collège** junior high school, middle school

une **colonie** colony

une **colonne** column

combien how much

    ça fait combien? how much is this (it)? **11**

c'est combien? how much is this (it)? **11**

combien coûte...? how much does . . . cost? **11**

combien de temps? how long?

combien d'heures? how many hours?

commander to order

comme like, as, for

comme ci, comme ça so-so

ça va comme ci, comme ça everything's so-so **3**

commencer to begin, start

comment? how? **16**; what?

comment allez-vous? how are you? **3**

comment est-il/elle? what's he/she like? what does he/she look like? **17**

comment lire reading hints

comment s'appelle...? what's . . .'s name? **6**

comment s'appelle-t-il/elle? what's his/her name? **17**

comment t'appelles-tu? what's your name? **1**

comment vas-tu? how are you? **3**

un **commentaire** comment, commentary

le **commérage** gossip

communiquer to communicate

un **compact disque (un CD)** compact disc **17**

compléter to complete

compréhensif understanding

* **comprendre** to understand

je (ne) comprends (pas) I (don't) understand **B**

compter to count (on); to expect, intend

concerne: en ce qui concerne as for

une **connaissance** acquaintance

faire connaissance (avec) to become acquainted (with)

* **connaître** to know, be acquainted

tu connais...? do you know . . .? are you acquainted with . . .? **6**

un **conseil** piece of advice, counsel

des conseils *m.* advice

un **conservatoire** conservatory

une **consonne** consonant

se **contenter** to limit oneself

le **contenu** contents

une **contradiction** disagreement

une **contravention** (traffic) ticket

cool cool, neat

un **copain, une copine** friend, pal **5**

un petit copain, une petite copine boyfriend, girlfriend

copier to copy

coréen (coréenne) Korean

un **corps** body

correspondant corresponding

correspondre to correspond, agree

la **Corse** Corsica *(French island off the Italian coast)*

un **costume** man's suit

la **Côte d'Azur** Riviera *(southern coast of France on the Mediterranean)*

la **Côte d'Ivoire** Ivory Coast *(French-speaking country in West Africa)*

côté: à côté (de) next door; next to

une **côtelette de porc** pork chop

le **cou** neck **E3**

une **couleur** color **20**

de quelle couleur...? what color . . .? **20**

un **couloir** hall, corridor

coup: dans le coup *(colloq.)* "with it"

courageux (courageuse) courageous

le **courrier électronique** e-mail, electronic mail

une **course** race

un **cousin, une cousine** cousin **7**

le **coût: le coût de la vie** the cost of living

coûter to cost

combien coûte...? how much does . . . cost? **11**

il (elle) coûte... it costs . . . **11**

un **couturier, une couturière** fashion designer

un **crabe** crab

des matoutou crabes stewed crabs with rice

la **craie** chalk

un morceau de craie piece of chalk **B**

un **crayon** pencil **17**

créer to create

une **crêpe** crepe *(pancake)* **9**

une **crêperie** crepe restaurant

un **crétin** idiot

une **crevaison** flat tire

une **croisade** crusade

un **croissant** crescent (roll) **9**

une **cuillère** spoon

une cuillère à soupe soup spoon

cuit cooked

culturel (culturelle) cultural

curieux (curieuse) curious, strange

la **curiosité** curiosity

le **Cyberespace** information highway, cyberspace

les **cybernautes** people who like to use the Internet

un **cyclomoteur** moped

D ▬▬▬▬▬▬▬▬

d'accord okay, all right

être d'accord to agree **14**

oui, d'accord yes, okay **13**

une **dame** lady, woman *(polite term)* **5**

dangereux (dangereuse) dangerous

dans in **17**

danser to dance **13, 15**

la **date** date **8**

quelle est la date? what's the date? **8**

de (d') of, from, about **14**

de l'après-midi in the afternoon **4**

de quelle couleur...? what color . . .? **20**

de qui? of whom? **16**

de quoi? about what?

de temps en temps from time to time

d'habitude usually

pas de not any, no **18**

débarquer to land

décembre *m.* December **8**

décider (de) to decide (to)

une **déclaration** statement

décoré decorated

* **découvrir** to discover

un **défaut** shortcoming

un **défilé** parade

dehors outside

en dehors de outside of

déjà already; ever

demain tomorrow **8**

à demain! see you tomorrow! **8**

demain, c'est... (jeudi) tomorrow is . . . (Thursday) **8**

demi half

...heure(s) et demie half past . . . **4**

midi et demi half past twelve (noon) **4**

minuit et demi half past midnight **4**

un **demi-frère** half-brother

une **demi-soeur** half-sister

un **démon** devil

une **dent** tooth

un **départ** departure

se **dépêcher: dépêchez-vous!** hurry up!

dépend: ça dépend (des) it depends (on)

une **dépense** expense

derrière behind, in back of **17**

des some, any **18**; of (the), from (the)

le **désert** desert

désirer to wish, want

vous désirez? what would you like? may I help you? **10**

désolé sorry

le **dessin** art, drawing

détester to hate, detest

un **dessin animé** cartoon

deux two **1**

le **deuxième étage** third floor

devant in front of **17**

développer to develop

deviner to guess

les **devoirs** *m.* homework

différemment differently

différent different

difficile hard, difficult **20**

la **dignité** dignity

dimanche *m.* Sunday **8**

dîner to have dinner **15**

dîner au restaurant to have dinner at a restaurant **13**

* **dire** to say, tell

comment dit-on... en français? How do you say . . . in French? **B**

directement straight

un **directeur, une directrice** director, principal

dirigé directed, guided

dis! (*see* dire) say!, hey! **20**

dis donc! say there!, hey there! **20**

discuter to discuss

une **dispute** quarrel, dispute

un **disque** record **17**

un (disque) compact compact disc **17**

le disque dur hard drive (computer)

un disque optique CD-ROM **B**

une **disquette** floppy disc **B**

dit (*p.p. of* dire) said

dix ten **1, 2**

dix-huit eighteen **2**

dix-neuf nineteen **2**

dix-sept seventeen **2**

un **docteur** doctor

dois (*see* devoir): **je dois** I have to (must) **13**

domestique domestic

les animaux *m.* **domestiques** pets **7**

dommage! too bad! **15**

donner to give

donne-moi... give me . . . **9**

donnez-moi... give me **10**

s'il te plaît, donne-moi... please, give me . . . **10**

doré golden brown

* **dormir** to sleep

douze twelve **2**

drôle funny **20**

du (*partitive*) of the

du matin in the morning, a.m. **4**

du soir in the evening, p.m. **4**

dur hard

des oeufs (*m.*) **durs** hard-boiled eggs

durer to last

dynamique dynamic

E

e-mail e-mail, electronic mail

un **échange** exchange

les **échecs** *m.* chess

une **éclosion** hatching

économiser to save money

écouter to listen to **B, 15**

écouter la radio to listen to the radio **13**

un **écran** screen (of a computer, TV)

l' **éducation** *f.* education

l'éducation civique civics

l'éducation physique physical education

égyptien (égyptienne) Egyptian

électronique electronic

une guitare électrique electric guitar

un **éléphant** elephant **E5**

élevé high

un(e) **élève** student (middle school, high school) **17**

elle she, it **11, 14, 18**

elle coûte... it costs . . . **11**

elle est (canadienne) she's (Canadian) **6**

elle s'appelle... her name is . . . **6**

embrasser: je t'embrasse love and kisses (*at the end of a letter*)

un **emploi du temps** time-table (*of work*)

emprunter à to borrow from

en in, on, to, by

en ce qui concerne as for

en face opposite, across (*the street*)

en fait in fact

en famille at home
en moyenne on the average
en plus in addition
en scène on stage
en solde on sale
un(e) **enfant** child
entier (entière) entire
l' **entracte** *m.* interlude
entre between
une **entrée** entry *(of a house)*
les **études** *f.* studies
un **entretien** discussion
envers toward
l' **envie** *f.* envy
envoyer to send
  envoyer quelque chose par e-mail to send something via e-mail
  envoyer quelque chose par la messagerie vocale to leave a voice mail message
épicé hot (spicy)
une **épicerie** grocery store
les **épinards** *m.* spinach
une **équipe** team
une **erreur** error, mistake
es *(see* **être**)
  tu es + *nationality* you are . . . 2
  tu es de...? are you from . . .? 2
un **escalier** staircase
un **escargot** snail
l' **Espagne** *f.* Spain
espagnol Spanish 19
  parler espagnol to speak Spanish 13
un **esprit** spirit
essayer to try on, to try
l' **essentiel** *m.* the important thing
est *(see* **être**)
  c'est... it's . . ., that's . . . 5, 7, 20
  c'est le + *date* it's . . . 8
  est-ce que (qu')...? phrase used to introduce a question 14
  il/elle est + *nationality* he/she is . . . 6
  n'est-ce pas...? isn't it? 14
  où est...? where is . . .? 14

quel jour est-ce? what day is it? 8
qui est-ce? who's that (this)? 5, 17
l' **est** *m.* east
et and 2, 14
  et demi(e), et quart half past, quarter past 4
  et toi? and you? 1
établir to establish
un **étage** floor of a building, story
les **États-Unis** *m.* United States
l' **été** *m.* summer
  en été in (the) summer 12
  l'heure d'été daylight savings time
étendre to spread
une **étoile** star
étrange strange
étranger (étrangère) foreign
* **être** to be 14
  être à to belong to
  être d'accord to agree 14
une **étude** study
un **étudiant, une étudiant(e)** (college) student 17
étudier to study 13, 15
eu *(p.p.* **avoir)**
  il y a eu there was
euh... er . . ., uh . . .
  euh non... well, no
européen (européenne) European
eux: eux-mêmes themselves
un **événement** event
un **examen** exam, test
  réussir à un examen to pass an exam, a test
un **exemple** example
  par exemple for instance
un **exercice** exercise
  faire des exercices to exercise
exiger to insist
exprimer to express
extérieur: à l'extérieur outside
extra terrific 20
extraordinaire extraordinary
  il a fait un temps extraordinaire! the weather was great!

F ▬▬▬▬▬▬▬▬▬

face: en face (de) opposite, across (the street) from
facile easy 20
faible weak
la **faim** hunger
  j'ai faim I'm hungry 9
  tu as faim? are you hungry? 9
* **faire** to do, make 16
  faire attention to pay attention, be careful 16
  faire correspondre to match
  faire partie de to be a member of
  faire sauter to flip
  faire un match to play a game (match) 16
  faire un voyage to take a trip 16
  faire une promenade to take a walk 16
fait *(see* **faire**): **ça fait combien?** how much is that (it)? 11
  ça fait... francs that's (it's) . . . francs 11
  en fait in fact
  il fait (beau, etc.) it's (beautiful, etc.) (weather) 12
  quel temps fait-il? what (how) is the weather? 12
familial with the family
une **famille** family 7
  en famille at home
un **fana, une fana** fan
un **fantôme** ghost
la **farine** flour
fatigué tired
faux (fausse) false 20
favori (favorite) favorite
un **fax-modem** fax machine
faxer to fax
les **félicitations** *f.* congratulations
une **femme** woman 17
une **fenêtre** window 17
fermer to close B
une **fête** party; holiday
le **feu** fire
  le feu d'artifice fireworks
une **feuille** sheet, leaf B
  une feuille de papier sheet of paper B

un **feuilleton** series, serial story (in newspaper, TV)

février *m.* February **8**

la **fièvre** fever

une **fille** girl **5**

un **film policier** detective movie

la **fin** end

flamand Flemish

un **flamant** flamingo

une **fleur** flower

un **fleuve** river

un **flic** cop (*colloq.*)

une **fois** time

à la **fois** at the same time

la **folie: à la folie** madly

folklorique: une chanson folklorique folksong

fonctionner to work, function

fondé founded

le **foot(ball)** soccer

jouer au foot to play soccer **13**

le **football américain** football

une **forêt** forest

formidable great!

fort strong

un **fouet** whisk

la **fourrure** fur

un **manteau de fourrure** fur coat

frais: il fait frais it's cool (weather) **12**

un **franc** franc (*monetary unit of France, Belgium, and Switzerland*) **11**

ça fait... francs that's (it's) ... francs **11**

le **français** French (language) **2, 9**

un **Français,** une **Française** French person

la **France** France **14**

en France in France **14**

francophone French-speaking

parler français to speak French **13**

un **frère** brother **7**

froid cold

il fait froid it's cold out (weather) **12**

le **fromage** cheese

un **sandwich au fromage** cheese sandwich

furieux (furieuse) furious

une **fusée** rocket

G

un **garçon** boy **5**; waiter

une **gare** train station

une **garniture** side dish

gauche left

une **gelée** jelly

généralement generally

généreux (généreuse) generous

la **générosité** generosity

génial brilliant

des **gens** *m.* people **18**

gentil (gentille) nice, kind **19**; sweet

la **géographie** geography

une **glace** ice cream **9**; mirror, ice

glacé iced

un **goûter** afternoon snack

une **goyave** guava

grand tall **17**; big, large **20**; big

une **grande surface** big store, self-service store

une **grand-mère** grandmother **7**

un **grand-père** grandfather **7**

grandir to get tall; to grow up

grec (grecque) Greek

un **grenier** attic

une **grillade** grilled meat

une **grille** grid

grillé: le pain grillé toast

une **tartine de pain grillé** buttered toast

la **grippe** flu

gris gray **20**

gros (grosse) fat, big

la **Guadeloupe** Guadeloupe (*French island in the West Indies*)

une **guerre** war

une **guitare** guitar **17**

un **gymnase** gym

H

habillé dressed

habiter to live **15**

Haïti Haiti (*French island in the West Indies*)

un **hamburger** hamburger **9**

la•**hâte** haste

en hâte quickly

•**haut** high

plus haut above

•**hélas!** too bad

hésiter to hesitate

l' **heure** *f.* time, hour; o'clock **4**

...heure(s) (dix) (ten) past ... **4**

...heure(s) et demie half past ... **4**

...heure(s) et quart quarter past ... **4**

...heure(s) moins (dix) (ten) of ... **4**

...heure(s) moins le quart quarter to ... **4**

à... heures at ... o'clock **14**

à quelle heure (est)...? at what time (is) ...? **4, 16**

combien d'heures? how many hours?

il est... heure(s) it's ... o'clock **4**

par heure per hour, an hour

quelle heure est-il? what time is it? **4**

heureux (heureuse) happy

hier yesterday

avant hier the day before yesterday

une **histoire** story, history

l' **hiver** *m.* winter **12**

en hiver in (the) winter **12**

•**hollandais** Dutch

un **homme** man **17**

honnête honest

une **horreur** horror

quelle horreur! what a scandal! how awful!

un•**hot dog** hot dog **9**

l' **huile** *f.* oil

•**huit** eight **1**

l' **humeur** *f.* mood

de bonne humeur in a good mood

un **hypermarché** shopping center

I

ici here 14
ignorer to be unaware of
il he, it 11, 14, 18
  est-ce qu'il y a...? is there, are there . . . ? 17
  il est it (he) is 20
  il/elle est + *nationality* he/she is . . . 6
  il y a there is, there are 17
  il n'y a pas de... there is/are no . . . 18
  il y a eu there was
  qu'est-ce qu'il y a...? what is there . . . ? 17
une **île** island
illustré illustrated
l' **impératif** *m.* imperative (command) mood
impoli impolite
l' **importance** *f.* importance
  ça n'a pas d'importance it doesn't matter
importé imported
impressionnant impressive
une **imprimante** printer
inactif (inactive) inactive
inclure to include
l' **indicatif** *m.* area code
les **informations** *f.* news
l' **informatique** *f.* computer science
s' **informer (de)** to find out about
l' **Inforoute** *f.* the information highway
un **ingénieur** engineer
un **inspecteur, une inspectrice** police detective
intelligent intelligent 19
interactif (interactive) interactive
intéressant interesting 19
l' **intérieur** *m.* interior, inside
les **internautes** people who like to use the Internet
Internet the Internet
interroger to question
interviewer to interview
inutilement uselessly
un **inventaire** inventory
un **invité, une invitée** guest
inviter to invite 15

israélien (israélienne) Israeli
italien (italienne) Italian 19
un **Italien, une Italienne** Italian person

J

j' (*see* je)
jamais ever; never
  jamais le dimanche! never on Sunday!
la **Jamaïque** Jamaica
janvier *m.* January 8
japonais Japanese 19
jaune yellow 20
jaunir to turn yellow
je I 14
je ne sais pas I don't know B, 17
j'ai un rendez-vous I have an appointment 4
un **jeu** (*pl.* jeux) game
  les jeux électroniques computer games
  les jeux télévisés TV game shows
jeudi *m.* Thursday 8
jeune young 17
les **jeunes** *m.* young people
un **job** (part-time) job
joli pretty (*for girls, women*) 17
  plus joli(e) que prettier than
jouer to play 15
  jouer au tennis (volley, basket, foot) to play tennis (volleyball, basketball, soccer) 13
un **jour** day 8
  le jour de l'an New Year's Day
  par jour per day, a day
  quel jour est-ce? what day is it? 8
un **journal** (*pl.* journaux) newspaper
une **journée** day, whole day
  bonne journée! have a nice day!
joyeux (joyeuse) happy
  joyeux anniversaire! happy birthday! 17
juillet *m.* July 8

le quatorze juillet Bastille Day (French national holiday)
juin *m.* June 8
un **jumeau** (*pl.* jumeaux), une **jumelle** twin
le **jus** juice
  le jus d'orange orange juice 10
  le jus de pomme apple juice 10
  le jus de raisin grape juice 10
  le jus de tomate tomato juice 10
jusqu'à until
juste right, fair
  le mot juste the right word

K

un **kangourou** kangaroo E5
un **kilo** kilogram

L

l' (see le, la)
la the 6, 18; her, it
là here, there 14
  là-bas over there 14
  ça, là-bas that (one), over there 17
  oh là là! uh, oh!; oh, dear!; wow!; oh, yes!
laid ugly
une **langue** language
large wide
se **laver** to wash (oneself), wash up
le the 6, 18
  le + *number* + *month* the . . . 8
  le (lundi) on (Mondays) 18
une **leçon** lesson
un **lecteur** reader, player
  un lecteur de CD vidéo, de (disque) compact laserdisc player, compact disc player
  un lecteur optique interne/ de CD-ROM internal CD-ROM drive B
lent slow

les *(pl.)* the **18**
une **lettre** letter
se **lever** to get up, stand
   lève-toi! (levez-vous!) stand up! **B**
un **lézard** lizard **E5**
le **Liban** Lebanon *(country in the Middle East)*
   libanais Lebanese
   libéré liberated
une **librairie** bookstore
   libre free
un **lieu** place, area
   avoir lieu to take place
une **ligne** line
   limité limited
la **limonade** lemon soda **10**
* **lire** to read
   comment lire reading hints
une **liste** list
   une liste des courses shopping list
un **lit** bed **17**
un **living** living room *(informal)*
un **livre** book **17**
   local *(m.pl.* **locaux**) local
une **location** rental
un **logiciel** software
   logique logical
   logiquement logically
   loin: loin d'ici far (from here)
le **loisir** leisure, free time
un **loisir** leisure-time activity
   Londres London
   longtemps (for) a long time
   moins longtemps que for a shorter time
le **loto** lotto, lottery, bingo
   lui-même: en lui-même to himself
   lundi *m.* Monday **8**
le **Luxembourg** Luxembourg
un **lycée** high school

M ▬▬▬▬▬▬▬▬▬▬▬

m' *(see* **me**)
M. (monsieur) Mr. (Mister) **3**
ma my **7**
   et voici ma mère and this is my mother **7**

ma chambre my bedroom **17**
une **machine** machine
   une machine à coudre sewing machine
   Madagascar Madagascar *(French-speaking island off of East Africa)*
   Madame (Mme) Mrs., ma'am **3**
   Mademoiselle (Mlle) Miss **3**
un **magasin** (department) store
   faire les magasins to go shopping *(browsing from store to store)*
   magnétique magnetic
un **magnétophone** tape recorder **17**
un **magnétoscope** VCR **B**
   magnifique magnificent
   mai *m.* May **8**
   maigre thin, skinny
une **main** hand **E3**
   maintenant now **15**
   mais but **14**
   j'aime…, mais je préfère… I like . . ., but I prefer . . . **13**
   je regrette, mais je ne peux pas… I'm sorry, but I can't . . . **13**
   mais oui! sure! **14**
   mais non! of course not! **14**
une **maison** house
   à la maison at home **14**
   mal badly, poorly **3, 15**
   ça va mal things are going badly **3**
   ça va très mal things are going very badly **3**
   c'est mal that's bad **20**
   malade sick
   malheureusement unfortunately
   malin clever
   manger to eat **13**
   j'aime manger I like to eat **13**
un **manteau** long coat
   un manteau de fourrure fur coat
un **marchand, une marchande** merchant, shopkeeper, dealer

un **marché** open-air market
   un marché aux puces flea market
   marcher to work, to run *(for objects)* **17**; to walk *(for people)* **17**
   il/elle (ne) marche (pas) bien it (doesn't) work(s) well **17**
   est-ce que la radio marche? does the radio work? **17**
   mardi *m.* Tuesday **8**
   le Mardi gras Shrove Tuesday
le **mariage** wedding, marriage
   marié married
une **marmite** covered stew pot
le **Maroc** Morocco *(country in North Africa)*
une **marque** brand (name)
une **marraine** godmother
   marrant fun
   marron *(inv.)* brown **20**
   mars *m.* March **8**
   martiniquais (person) from Martinique
la **Martinique** Martinique *(French island in the West Indies)*
un **match** game, (sports) match
   faire un match to play a game, (sports) match **16**
les **maths** *f.* math
le **matin** in the morning
   du matin in the morning, a.m. **4**
des **matoutou crabes** *m.* stewed crabs with rice
   mauvais bad **20**
   c'est une mauvaise idée that's a bad idea
   il fait mauvais it's bad (weather) **12**
   méchant mean, nasty **19**
un **médecin** doctor
   un médecin de nuit doctor on night duty
la **Méditerranée** Mediterranean Sea
   mélanger to mix, stir
   même same; even
   eux-mêmes themselves
   les mêmes choses the same things

une **mémoire** memory
mentionner to mention
merci thank you **3**
    oui, merci yes, thank you
    13
mercredi *m.* Wednesday **8**
une **mère** mother **7**
mériter to deserve
la **messagerie vocale** voice
    mail
le **métro** subway
mexicain Mexican **19**
midi *m.* noon **4**
mieux better
mignon (mignonne) cute **19**
militaire military
une **mini-chaîne** compact stereo
minuit *m.* midnight **4**
mixte mixed
Mlle Miss **3**
Mme Mrs. **3**
une **mob (mobylette)** motorbike,
    moped **17**
la **mode** fashion
moi me **1**
    avec moi with me **13**
    donne-moi give me **9**
    donnez-moi give me **10**
    moi, je m'appelle (Marc)
    myself, my name is
    (Marc) **1**
    prête-moi... lend me ... **11**
    s'il te plaît, donne-moi...
    please give me ... **10**
un **moine** monk
moins less
    ...heure(s) moins (dix)
    (ten) of ... **4**
    ...heure(s) moins le
    quart quarter of ... **4**
    moins de less than
un **mois** month **8**
    par mois per month, a month
mon (ma; mes) my **7**
    mon anniversaire est
    le... my birthday is the ...
    8
    voici mon père this is my
    father **7**
le **monde** world
    du monde in the world
    tout le monde everyone
la **monnaie** money; change
Monsieur (M.) Mr., sir **3**

un **monsieur** (*pl.* **messieurs**)
    gentleman, man (polite
    term) **5**
une **montre** watch **17**
un **morceau** piece
un **mot** word
une **moto** motorcycle **17**
la **moutarde** mustard
un **mouton** sheep
moyen (moyenne) average,
    medium
    en moyenne on the
    average
un **moyen** means
muet (muette) silent
le **multimédia** multimedia

N ▬▬▬▬▬▬▬▬▬▬

n' (*see* **ne**)
nager to swim **15**
    j'aime nager I like to
    swim **13**
une **nationalité** nationality **2**
naviguer to navigate
ne (n')
    ne... aucun none, not any
    ne... pas not **14**
    ne... plus no longer
    n'est-ce pas? right?, no?,
    isn't it (so)?, don't you?,
    aren't you? **14**
né(e) born
nécessaire necessary
négatif (négative) negative
négativement negatively
la **neige** snow
neiger to snow
    il neige it's snowing **12**
le **Net** the Internet
netsurfer/surfer sur le Net
    to "surf the Net"
neuf nine **1**
un **neveu** (*pl.* **neveux**) nephew
une **nièce** niece
un **niveau** (*pl.* **niveaux**) level
Noël *m.* Christmas
noir black **20**
un **nom** name; noun
un **nombre** number
nombreux (nombreuses)
    numerous
nommé named
non no **2, 14**

non plus neither
    mais non! of course not!
    14
le **nord** north
    le nord-est northeast
normalement normally
une **note** grade
nous we **14**
la **Nouvelle-Angleterre** New
    England
la **Nouvelle-Calédonie** New
    Caledonia (*French island
    in the South Pacific*)
novembre *m.* November **8**
    le onze novembre
    Armistice Day
la **nuit** night
un **numéro** number

O ▬▬▬▬▬▬▬▬▬▬

objectif (objective) objective
un **objet** object **17**
une **occasion** occasion;
    opportunity
occupé occupied
un **océan** ocean
octobre *m.* October **8**
une **odeur** odor
un **office: office de tourisme**
    tourist office
officiel (officielle) official
offert (*p.p. of* **offrir**) offered
* **offrir** to offer, to give
oh là là! uh,oh!, oh, dear!,
    wow!, oh, yes!
un **oiseau** (*pl.* **oiseaux**) bird
une **omelette** omelet **9**
on one, they, you
    comment dit-on... en
    français? how do you
    say ... in French?
    on est... today is ...
    on va dans un café? shall
    we go to a café?
    on y va let's go
un **oncle** uncle **7**
onze eleven **2**
opérer to operate
l' **or** *m.* gold
orange (*inv.*) orange (color)
    20
une **orange** orange (fruit)
    le jus d'orange orange
    juice **10**

un **poisson**
    un poisson rouge
    goldfish
    blaff de poisson fish stew
poli polite
un **politicien, une politicienne**
    politician
une **pomme** apple
    le jus de pomme apple
    juice **10**
    une purée de pommes
    de terre mashed
    potatoes
le **porc: une côtelette de porc**
    pork chop
une **porte** door **17**
un **porte-monnaie** change
    purse, wallet
portugais Portuguese
poser: poser une question
    to ask a question
une **possibilité** possibility
la **poste** post office
pouah! yuck! yech!
une **poule** hen **E5**
pour for **14**; in order to
    pour que so that
    pour qui? for whom? **16**
le **pourcentage** percentage
pourquoi why **16**
pratique practical
pratiquer to participate in
des **précisions** *f.* details
préférer
    je préfère I prefer **13**
    préféré favorite
    tu préférerais? would you
    prefer?
premier (première)
    c'est le premier juin it's
    June first **8**
    le premier de l'an New
    Year's Day
    le premier étage second
    floor *(in US)*
    le premier mai Labor
    Day *(in France)*
un **prénom** first name
près near
    près d'ici nearby, near
    here
    tout près very close
une **présentation** appearance

la **présentation**
    extérieure outward
    appearance
des **présentations** *f.*
    introductions
pressé in a hurry
prêt ready
un **prêt** loan
    prêter à to lend to, to loan
    prête-moi... lend me . . .
    11
principalement mainly
le **printemps** spring **12**
    au printemps in the
    spring **12**
un **prix** price
un **problème** problem
un **produit** product
un **prof, une prof** teacher
    (informal) **5**, **17**
un **professeur** teacher **17**
professionnel
    (professionnelle)
    professional
un **programme** program
un **projet** plan
une **promenade** walk
    faire une promenade à
    pied to go for a walk
    16
* **promettre** to promise
une **promo** special sale
proposer to suggest
propre (one's) own
un **propriétaire, une**
    propriétaire
    landlord/landlady, owner
la **Provence** Provence *(province*
    in southern France)
pu *(p.p.* **pouvoir)** **n'a pas pu**
    was not able to
public: un parc public city
    park
    un jardin public public
    garden
la **publicité** commercials,
    advertising, publicity
une **puce** flea
    un marché aux puces
    flea market
puis then, also
puisque since

les **Pyrénées** (the) Pyrenees
    (mountains between
    France and Spain)

Q

qu' *(see* **que)**
une **qualité** quality
quand when **16**
    c'est quand, ton
    anniversaire? when is
    your birthday? **8**
quarante forty **3**
un **quart** one quarter
    ...heure(s) et quart
    quarter past . . . **4**
    ...heure(s) moins le
    quart quarter of . . . **4**
quatorze fourteen **2**
quatre four **1**
quatre-vingt-dix ninety **6**
quatre-vingts eighty **6**
que that, which
    ce que that which, what
    qu'est-ce que (qu') what
    (phrase used to introduce
    a question) **16**
    qu'est-ce qu'il y a? what
    is there? **17**; what's the
    matter?
    qu'est-ce que c'est? what
    is it? what's that? **17**
    qu'est-ce que tu veux?
    what do you want? **9**
    qu'est-ce qui ne va pas?
    what's wrong?
un **Québécois, une Québécoise**
    person from Quebec
québécois from Quebec
quel (quelle)...! what a . . .!
    quel âge a ta mère/ton
    père? how old is your
    mother/your father? **7**
    quel âge a-t-il/elle? how
    old is he/she? **17**
    quel âge as-tu? how old
    are you? **7**
    quel jour est-ce? what
    day is it? **8**
    quel temps fait-il? what's
    (how's) the weather? **12**
    quelle est la date? what's
    the date? **8**

quelle heure est-il? what time is it? **4**

à quelle heure (est)...? at what time (is) ...? **4**

de quelle couleur...? what color is ...? **20**

quelques some, a few **17**

une **question** question

une **queue** tail

qui who, whom **16**

à qui? to whom? **16**

avec qui? with who(m)? **16**

c'est qui? who's that? (casual speech)

de qui? about who(m)? **16**

pour qui? for who(m)? **16**

qui est-ce? who's that (this)? **5, 17**

qui se ressemble... birds of a feather ...

quinze fifteen **2**

quoi? what? **17**

quotidien (quotidienne) daily

la vie quotidienne daily life

R

raconter to tell about

une **radio** radio **17**

écouter la radio to listen to the radio **13**

une **radiocassette** boom box **17**

un **raisin** grape

le jus de raisin grape juice **10**

une **raison** reason

rapidement rapidly

un **rapport** relationship

une **raquette** racket **17**

rarement rarely, seldom **15**

un **rayon** department *(in a store)*

réalisé made

récemment recently

une **recette** recipe

recherche: un avis de recherche missing person's bulletin

un **récital** *(pl. récitals)* *(musical)* recital

reconstituer to reconstruct

un **réfrigérateur** refrigerator

refuser to refuse

regarder to look at, watch **15**

regarde ça look at that **17**

regarder la télé to watch TV **13**

un **régime** diet

être au régime to be on a diet

régional *(m.pl. régionaux)* regional

regretter to be sorry

je regrette, mais... I'm sorry, but ... **13**

régulier (régulière) regular

une **reine** queen

une **rencontre** meeting, encounter

rencontrer to meet

un **rendez-vous**

j'ai un rendez-vous à... I have a date, appointment at ... **4**

rendre visite à to visit, come to visit (a person)

la **rentrée** first day back at school in fall

rentrer to go back, come back; to return

réparer to fix, repair

un **repas** meal

* **repeindre** to repaint

le **répondeur** answering machine

répondre (à) to answer, respond (to) **B**

répondez-lui (moi) answer him (me)

répondre que oui to answer yes

une **réponse** answer

un **reportage** documentary

représenter to represent

un **réseau** network

réservé reserved

une **résolution** resolution

un **restaurant** restaurant

au restaurant to (at) the restaurant **14**

dîner au restaurant to have dinner at a restaurant **13**

un restaurant trois étoiles three star restaurant

rose pink

rester to stay

retard: un jour de retard one day behind

en retard late

retourner to return; to turn over

réussir to succeed

réussir à un examen to pass an exam

* **revenir** to come back

revoir: au revoir! good-bye! **3**

le **rez-de-chaussée** ground floor

un **rhinocéros** rhinoceros

riche rich

rien (de) nothing

rien n'est parfait nothing is perfect

ne... rien nothing

une **rive** (river) bank

une **rivière** river, stream

le **riz** rice

une **robe** dress

le **roller** rollerblading

romain Roman

le **rosbif** roast beef

rose pink

rosse nasty *(colloq.)*

une **rôtie** toast (Canadian)

rôtir to roast

une **roue** wheel

rouge red **20**

rougir to turn red

rouler to roll

roux (rousse) red-head

une **rue** street

dans la rue (Victor Hugo) on (Victor Hugo) street

russe Russian

S

sa his, her

un **sac** bag, handbag **17**

sais *(see savoir)*

je sais I know **B, 17**

je ne sais pas I don't know **B, 17**

tu sais you know

une **saison** season **12**

en toute saison all year round (in every season)

une **salade** salad **9**; lettuce

un **salaire** salary

une **salle** hall, large room

  une salle à manger
  dining room

  une salle de bains
  bathroom

  une salle de séjour
  informal living room

un **salon** formal living room

salut hi!, good-bye! 3

une **salutation** greeting

samedi *m.* Saturday 8

  à samedi! see you
  Saturday! 8

  le samedi on Saturdays
  18

  samedi soir Saturday night

une **sandale** sandal

un **sandwich** sandwich 9

sans without

des **saucisses** *f.* sausages

le **saucisson** salami

 * **savoir** to know (information)

  je sais I know 17

  je ne sais pas I don't
  know 17

  tu sais you know

un **saxo (saxophone)**
  saxophone

une **scène** scene, stage

les **sciences** *f.* **économiques**
  economics

les **sciences** *f.* **naturelles**
  natural science

un **scooter** motorscooter 17

second second

seize sixteen 2

un **séjour** stay; informal living
  room

le **sel** salt

selon according to

  selon toi in your opinion

une **semaine** week 8

  cette semaine this week

  la semaine dernière last
  week

  la semaine prochaine
  next week

  par semaine per week, a
  week

semblable similar

le **Sénégal** Senegal *(French-
  speaking country in
  Africa)*

**sensationnel
  (sensationnelle)**
  sensational

séparer to separate

sept seven 1

septembre *m.* September
  8

septième seventh

une **série** series

sérieux (sérieuse) serious

un **serveur, une serveuse**
  waiter, waitress

servi served

une **serviette** napkin

ses his, her 24

seul alone, only; by oneself

seulement only, just

sévère strict, severe

un **short** shorts

si if, whether C

si! so, yes! *(to a negative
  question)* 18

un **signal** *(pl.* **signaux)** signal

un **signe** sign

  un signe orthographique
  spelling mark

un **singe** monkey

situé situated

six six 1

sixième sixth

un **skate** skateboard

le **ski** skiing

  le ski nautique
  waterskiing

  faire du ski to ski

  faire du ski nautique to
  go water-skiing

skier to ski

snob snobbish

la **Société Nationale des
  Chemins de Fer
  (SNCF)** French railroad
  system

une **société** society

un **soda** soda 10

une **soeur** sister 7

la **soie** silk

la **soif** thirst

  avoir soif to be thirsty

  j'ai soif I'm thirsty 10

  tu as soif? are you thirsty?
  10

un **soir** evening, night(time)

  ce soir this evening,
  tonight

  demain soir tomorrow
  night (evening)

  du soir in the evening,
  p.m. 4

  hier soir last night

  le soir in the evening

une **soirée** (whole) evening;
  (evening) party

soixante sixty 3, 5

soixante-dix seventy 5

un **soldat** soldier

un **solde** (clearance) sale

  en solde on sale

la **sole** sole (fish)

le **soleil** sun

  les lunettes *f.* **de soleil**
  sunglasses

sommes *(see* **être)**

  nous sommes... it is,
  today is . . . *(date)*

son (sa; ses) his, her

un **sondage** poll

une **sorte** sort, type, kind

 * **sortir** to leave, come out

un **souhait** wish

la **soupe** soup

une **souris** mouse (computer)

  un tapis de souris
  mousepad

sous under 17

le **sous-sol** basement

souvent often 15

soyez *(see* **être): soyez
  logique** be logical

les **spaghetti** *m.* spaghetti

spécialement especially

spécialisé specialized

une **spécialité** specialty

le **sport** sports

  faire du sport to play
  sports

  des vêtements *m.* **de
  sport** sports clothing

  une voiture de sport
  sports car

sportif (sportive) athletic 19

un **stade** stadium

un **stage** sports training camp;
  internship

une **station-service** gas station

un **steak** steak 9

un **steak-frites** steak and French
  fries 9

un **stylo** pen B, 17

le **sucre** sugar

le **sud** south
suggérer to suggest
suis (*see* **être**) (I) am . . . **2**
je suis + *nationality* I'm (*nationality*)
je suis de... I'm from . . . **2**
suisse Swiss **19**
la **Suisse** Switzerland
suivant following
suivi followed
un **sujet** subject, topic
super terrific **15**; great **20**
un **supermarché** supermarket
supersonique supersonic
supérieur superior
supplémentaire supplementary, extra
sur on **17**; about
sûr sure, certain
bien sûr! of course! **14**
oui, bien sûr... yes, of course . . .! **13**
tu es sûr(e)? are you sure?
sûrement surely
la **surface: une grande surface** big store, self-service store
surtout especially, above all
un **survêtement** jogging or track suit
un **sweat** sweatshirt
une **sweaterie** shop specializing in sweatshirts and sportswear
sympa nice, pleasant (*colloq.*)
sympathique nice, pleasant **19**
une **synagogue** Jewish temple or synagogue
un **synthétiseur** electronic keyboard, synthesizer

T ━━━━━━━━━━━━

t' (*see* **te**)
ta your **7**
une **table** table **B, 17**
mettre la table to set the table
un **tableau** (*pl.* **tableaux**) chalkboard **B**

Tahiti Tahiti (*French island in the South Pacific*)
la **taille** size
de taille moyenne of medium height or size
un **tailleur** woman's suit
se **taire: tais-toi!** be quiet!
une **tante** aunt **7**
un **tapis de souris** mousepad (for computer)
la **tarte** pie
une **tasse** cup
un **taxi** taxi
en taxi by taxi
te (to) you
un **tee-shirt** T-shirt
un **temple** Protestant church
le **temps** time; weather
combien de temps? how long?
de temps en temps from time to time
quel temps fait-il? what's (how's) the weather? **12**
tout le temps all the time
le **tennis** tennis
jouer au tennis to play tennis **13**
des **tennis** *m.* tennis shoes, sneakers **25**
la **télé** TV **B, 17**
à la télé on TV
regarder la télé to watch TV **13**
un **téléphone** telephone **17**
téléphoner (à) to call, phone **13, 15**
télévisé: des jeux *m.* **télévisés** TV game shows
un **terrain de sport** (playing) field
une **terrasse** outdoor section of a café, terrace
la **terre** earth
une pomme de terre potato
terrifiant terrifying
tes your
la **tête** head
le **thé** tea **10**
un thé glacé iced tea
un **théâtre** theater
le **thon** tuna
tiens! look!, hey! **5, 18**

un **tigre** tiger
timide timid, shy **19**
le **tissu** fabric
un **titre** title
toi you (*fam.*)
avec toi with you **13**
et toi? and you? **1**
les **toilettes** bathroom, toilet **21**
un **toit** roof
une **tomate** tomato
le jus de tomate tomato juice **10**
un **tombeau** tomb
ton (**ta; tes**) your **7**
c'est quand, ton anniversaire? when's your birthday? **8**
tort: avoir tort to be wrong
une **tortue** turtle
un bifteck de tortue turtle steak
toujours always **15**
je n'aime pas toujours... I don't always like . . . **13**
un **tour** turn
à votre tour it's your turn
la **Touraine** Touraine (*province in central France*)
le **tourisme: office de tourisme** tourist office
tourner to turn
la **Toussaint** All Saint's Day (*November 1*)
tout (**toute; tous, toutes**) all, every, the whole; completely, very
pas du tout not at all
tous les jours every day
tout ça all that
tout de suite right away
tout droit straight
tout le monde everyone
tout le temps all the time
tout près very close
toutes sortes all sorts, kinds
un **train** train
tranquille quiet
laisse-moi tranquille! leave me alone!
un **transistor** transistor radio
un **travail** (*pl.* **travaux**) job

travailler to work **13, 15**
une **traversée** crossing
treize thirteen **2**
trente thirty **3**
un **tréma** diaeresis
très very **19**
  ça va très bien things are going very well **3**
  ça va très mal things are going very badly **3**
  très bien very well **15**
trois three **1**
troisième third
  en troisième ninth grade *(in France)*
trop too, too much
trouver to find, to think of
  comment trouves-tu...? what do you think of . . .? how do you find . . .?
  s'y trouve is there
tu you **14**
la **Tunisie** Tunisia *(country in North Africa)*

U

un, une one **1**; a, an **5, 18**
unique only
uniquement only
une **université** university, college
l' **usage** *m.* use
un **ustensile** utensil
utile useful
utiliser to use **C**
  en utilisant (by) using
  utilisez... use . . . **C**

V

va *(see* **aller**)
  ça va? how are you? how's everything? **3**
  ça va! everything's fine (going well); fine, I'm OK **3**
  comment vas-tu? how are you? **3**
  on va dans un café? shall we go to a café?
  on y va! let's go!
  va-t'en! go away!

les **vacances** *f.* vacation
  bonnes vacances! have a nice vacation!
  en vacances on vacation **14**
  les grandes vacances summer vacation
une **vache** cow
vais *(see* **aller**)**: je vais** I'm going
la **vaisselle** dishes
  faire la vaisselle to do the dishes
valable valid
une **valise** suitcase
vanille: une glace à la vanille vanilla ice cream
varié varied
les **variétés** *f.* variety show
vas *(see* **aller**)
  comment vas-tu? how are you? **3**
  vas-y! come on!, go ahead!, do it!
le **veau** veal
une **vedette** star
un **vélo** bicycle **17**
  à vélo by bicycle
  faire une promenade à vélo to go for a bicycle ride
un **vendeur, une vendeuse** salesperson
vendre to sell
vendredi *m.* Friday **8**
vendu *(p.p. of* **vendre***)* sold
* **venir** to come
le **vent** wind
une **vente** sale
le **ventre** stomach
venu *(p.p. of* **venir***)* came, come
vérifier to check
la **vérité** truth
un **verre** glass
verser to pour
vert green **20**
  les • haricots *m.* **verts** green beans
une **veste** jacket
des **vêtements** *m.* clothing
  des vêtements de sport sports clothing
veut *(see* **vouloir***)***: que veut dire...?** What does . . . mean? **B**

veux *(see* **vouloir**)
  est-ce que tu veux...? do you want . . .? **13**
  je ne veux pas... I don't want . . . **13**
  je veux... I want . . . **13**
  je veux bien... I'd love to, I do, I want to . . . **13**
  qu'est-ce que tu veux? what do you want? **9**
  tu veux...? do you want . . .? **9**
la **viande** meat
une **vidéocassette** videocassette **B**
la **vie** life
  la vie quotidienne daily life
viens *(see* **venir**)
  viens... come . . . **B**
  oui, je viens yes, I'm coming along with you
vieux (vieil, vieille; *m.pl.* **vieux)** old
  le Vieux Carré the French Quarter in New Orleans
le **Viêt-nam** Vietnam *(country in Southeast Asia)*
vietnamien (vietnamienne) Vietnamese
une **vigne** vineyard
un **village** town, village
  un petit village small town
une **ville** city, town **6**
  en ville downtown, in town, in the city **14**
  une grande ville big city, town
le **vin** wine
vingt twenty **2, 3**
un **violon** violin
une **visite** visit
  rendre visite à to visit (a person)
visiter to visit (places) **15**
vite quickly
vite! fast!, quick!
vive: vive les vacances! three cheers for vacation!
* **vivre** to live
le **vocabulaire** vocabulary
voici... here is, this is . . ., here come(s) . . . **5**

voici + du, de la (*partitive*) here's some

voici mon père/ma mère here's my father/my mother **7**

voilà... there is . . ., there come(s) . . . **5**

voilà + du, de la (*partitive*) there's some

la **voile** sailing

faire de la voile to sail

la planche à voile windsurfing

* **voir** to see

voir un film to see a movie

un **voisin, une voisine** neighbor **17**

une **voiture** car **17**

une voiture de sport sports car

en voiture by car

faire une promenade en voiture to go for a drive by car

une **voix** voice

le **volley (volleyball)** volleyball

jouer au volley to play volleyball **13**

un **volontaire, une volontaire** volunteer

comme volontaire as a volunteer

vos your

votre (*pl.* **vos**) your

voudrais (*see* **vouloir**): **je voudrais** I'd like **9, 10, 13**

* **vouloir** to want

vouloir + du, de la (*partitive*) to want some (*some of something*)

vouloir dire to mean

voulu (*p.p. of* **vouloir**) wanted

vous you **14**; (to) you

vous désirez? what would you like? may I help you? **10**

s'il vous plaît please **10**

un **voyage** trip

bon voyage! have a nice trip!

faire un voyage to take a trip **16**

voyager to travel **13, 15**

vrai true, right, real **20**

c'est vrai! that's true! **16**

vraiment really

vu (*p.p. of* **voir**) saw, seen

une **vue** view

un point de vue point of view

W ▬▬▬▬▬▬▬▬▬▬

un **walkman** walkman **17**

les **WC** *m.* toilet

le **Web ("la toile d'araignée")** the World Wide Web

un **weekend** weekend

bon weekend! have a nice weekend!

ce weekend this weekend

le weekend on weekends

le weekend dernier last weekend

le weekend prochain next weekend

Y ▬▬▬▬▬▬▬▬▬▬

y there

allons-y! let's go!

est-ce qu'il y a...? is there . . .?, are there . . .? **17**

il y a there is, there are **17**

qu'est-ce qu'il y a? what is there? **17**

vas-y! come on!, go ahead!, do it!

le **yaourt** yogurt

les **yeux** *m.* (*sg.* **oeil**) eyes

Z ▬▬▬▬▬▬▬▬▬▬

le **Zaïre** Zaire (*French-speaking country in Central Africa*)

un **zèbre** zebra

zéro zero **1**

zut! darn! **3**

VOCABULARY
English-French

The English-French vocabulary contains active and passive words from the text, as well as the important words of the illustrations used within the units. Obvious passive cognates have not been listed.

The numbers following an entry indicate the lesson in which the word or phrase is activated. (**B** stands for the photo essay that precedes **Niveau B;** and **E** stands for **Entracte.**)

Nouns: If the article of a noun does not indicate gender, the noun is followed by *m. (masculine)* or

f. (feminine). If the plural (*pl.*) is irregular, it is given in parentheses.

Verbs: Verbs are listed in the infinitive form. An asterisk (*) in front of an active verb means that it is irregular. (For forms, see the verb charts in Appendix 4C.)

Words beginning with an **h** are preceded by a bullet (•) if the **h** is aspirate; that is, if the word is treated as if it begins with a consonant sound.

A

a, an un, une **5, 18**
  a few quelques **17**
  a little (bit) un peu **15**
  a lot beaucoup **15**
about whom? de qui? **16**
according to après: d'après; selon
address l'adresse *f.*
  e-mail address l'adresse électronique
afternoon: in the afternoon de l'après-midi **4**
to **agree** *être d'accord **14**
all tout
  all right d'accord **13**
  all the time tout le temps
  all year round en toute saison
also aussi **2, 15**
always toujours **15**
  not always pas toujours **13**
a.m. du matin **4**
am (*see* to be)
  I am + nationality . . . je suis + *nationality* **2**
American américain **2, 19**
  I'm American je suis américain(e) **2**
amusing amusant **19**

an un, une **5, 18**
and et **2, 14**
  and you? et toi? **1**
annoying pénible **20**
another un(e) autre
to **answer** répondre
answering machine un répondeur
any des; du, de la, de l', de
  not any pas de **18**
apple une pomme
  apple juice le jus de pomme **10**
April avril *m.* **8**
are (*see* to be)
  are there . . .? est-ce qu'il y a...? **17**
  are you . . .? tu es...? **2**
  are you acquainted with...? tu connais...? **6**
  there are il y a **17**
  these/those/they are ce sont **20**
at à **14**
  at . . . o'clock à... heure(s) **14**
  at home à la maison **14**
  at the restaurant au restaurant **14**
  at what time (is) . . .? à quelle heure (est)...? **4**

  I have an appointment at . . . j'ai un rendez-vous à... **4**
athletic sportif (sportive) **19**
attention: to pay attention *faire attention **16**
August août *m.* **8**
aunt une tante **7**
automobile une auto, une voiture **17**
autumn l'automne *m.*
  in (the) autumn en automne **12**
average: on the average en moyenne

B

back: in back of derrière **17**
bad mauvais **20**
  I'm/everything's (very) bad ça va (très) mal **3**
  it's bad (weather) il fait mauvais **12**
  that's bad c'est mal **20**
  too bad! dommage! **15**
badly mal **3**
  things are going (very) badly ça va (très) mal **3**
bag un sac **17**

to be *être **14**

    to be . . . years old
      *avoir... ans **18**

    to be careful *faire attention
      16

    to be cold out (weather) il
      fait froid **12**

    to be hungry *avoir faim **18**

    to be thirsty *avoir soif **18**

beautiful beau (bel, belle; *m.pl.*
  beaux) **17**

    it's beautiful (nice) weather
      il fait beau **12**

because parce que (qu') **16**

bed un lit **17**

bedroom une chambre **17**

behind derrière **17**

between entre

beverage une boisson **10**

bicycle un vélo, une bicyclette
  17

big grand **17, 20**

birthday un anniversaire **8**

    my birthday is (March 2)
      mon anniversaire est (le 2
      mars) **8**

    when is your birthday?
      c'est quand, ton
      anniversaire? **8**

bit: a little bit un peu **15**

black noir **20**

blond blond **17**

blue bleu **20**

book un livre **B, 17**

boom box une radiocassette **17**

bothersome pénible **20**

boy le garçon **5, 6**

boyfriend un petit copain

brother un frère **7**

brown brun **17**; marron (*inv.*)
  20

bus un bus; l'autobus *m.*

but mais **13**

C

café un café **14**

    at (to) the café au café **14**

calculator une calculatrice **17**

to call téléphoner **15**

camera un appareil-photo (*pl.*
  appareils-photo) **17**

can pouvoir

    can you . . .? est-ce que tu
      peux...? **13**

    I can't je ne peux pas **13**

Canada le Canada

Canadian canadien
  (canadienne) **2, 19**

    he's/she's (Canadian)
      il/elle est (canadien/
      canadienne) **6**

cannot: I cannot je ne peux pas
  13

    I'm sorry, but I cannot je
      regrette, mais je ne peux pas
      13

car une auto, une voiture **17**

card une carte

careful: to be careful *faire
  attention **16**

cassette tape une cassette **B,**
  17

    cassette recorder un
      magnétophone **17**

cat un chat **7**

CD (audio) un CD, un (disque)
  compact **B**

CD player un lecteur de CD
  (compact, (disque) compact)

CD-ROM un disque optique, un
  CD-ROM **B**

    internal CD-ROM drive un
      lecteur optique interne

chair une chaise **B, 17**

chalk la craie **B**

    piece of chalk un morceau
      de craie **B**

    chalkboard un tableau (*pl.*
      tableaux) **B**

child un(e) enfant

Chinese chinois **19**

chocolate: hot chocolate un
  chocolat **10**

cinema le cinéma **14**

    to the cinema au cinéma
      14

city: in the city en ville **14**

class une classe **14**

    in class en classe **14**

    classmate un (une)
      camarade **17**

coffee le café **10**

cold le froid

    it's cold (weather) il fait
      froid **12**

college student un étudiant,
  une étudiante **17**

color une couleur **20**

    what color? de quelle
      couleur? **20**

come: here comes . . . voici...
  5

compact disc un (disque) compact
  (un CD, un compact) **17**

    compact disc player un
      lecteur de compact disque

computer un ordinateur **B, 17**

    **computer games (on
    CD-ROM)** les jeux *m.*
    électroniques (sur CD-ROM)

cool: it's cool (weather) il fait
  frais **12**

cordially (in friendship)
  amicalement

to cost coûter

    how much does . . . cost?
      combien coûte...? **11**

    it costs . . . il/elle coûte...
      11

course: of course! bien sûr!
  13; mais oui! **14**

    of course not! mais non! **14**

cousin un cousin, une cousine **7**

crepe une crêpe **9**

croissant un croissant **9**

cute mignon (mignonne) **19**

D

to dance danser **13, 15**

dark-haired brun **17**

darn! zut! **3**

date la date **8**

    I have a date at . . . j'ai un
      rendez-vous à... **4**

    what's the date? quelle est la
      date? **8**

day un jour **8**

    per day par jour

    what day is it? quel jour
      est-ce? **8**

    whole day une journée

December décembre *m.* **8**

depend: it depends (on)
  dépend: ça dépend (des)

desk un bureau **B, 17**

differently différemment

difficult difficile **20**

dinner le dîner

    to have (eat) dinner dîner
      15

    **to have dinner at a
    restaurant** dîner au
    restaurant **13**

director une directrice (un
  directeur)

disc (computer) une disquette **B**

to **discuss** discuter

to **do** *faire **16**

dog un chien **7**

door une porte **B, 17**

downtown en ville **14**

drink une boisson **10**

dumb bête **19**

during pendant

E

e-mail, electronic mail e-mail, le courrier électronique

e-mail address l'adresse *f.* électronique

easy facile **20**

to **eat** manger **15**

I like to eat j'aime manger **13**

to eat dinner dîner **15**

eight •huit **1**

eighteen dix-huit **2**

eighty quatre-vingts **6**

eleven onze **2, 11**

eleventh onzième

engineer un ingénieur

England l'Angleterre *f.*

English anglais(e) **2, 19**

especially, above all surtout

evening: in the evening du soir **4**

everything tout

everything's going (very) well ça va (très) bien **3**

everything's (going) so-so ça va comme ci, comme ça **3**

how's everything? ça va? **3**

exam un examen

F

fall l'automne *m.* **12**

in (the) fall en automne **12**

false faux (fausse) **20**

family une famille **7**

fashion la mode

father un père

this is my father voici mon père **7**

to **fax** faxer

fax machine un fax-modem, télécopieur

February février *m.* **8**

few: a few quelques **17**

fifteen quinze **2**

fifty cinquante **3**

filmmaker un(e) cinéaste

fine ça va **3**

fine! d'accord! **13**

everything's fine ça va bien **3**

that's fine c'est bien **20**

first le premier (la première)

it's (June) first c'est le premier (juin) **8**

five cinq **1**

floppy disc une disquette **B**

following suivant(es)

for pour **14**

for whom? pour qui? **16**

forty quarante **3**

four quatre **1**

fourteen quatorze **2**

franc un franc **11**

that's (it's) . . . francs ça fait... francs **11**

France la France **14**

in France en France **14**

French français(e) **2, 19**

how do you say . . . in French? comment dit-on... en français? **B**

French fries les frites

steak and French fries un steak-frites **9**

Friday vendredi *m.* **8**

friend un ami, une amie **5**; un copain, une copine **5**

boyfriend, girlfriend un petit copain, une petite copine

school friend un (une) camarade **17**

friendship l'amitié *f.*

from de **14**

are you from . . . ? tu es de...? **2**

I'm from . . . je suis de... **2**

front: in front of devant **17**

funny amusant **19**; drôle **20**

G

game un match **16**

computer games les jeux électroniques

to play a game (match) *faire un match **16**

gentleman un monsieur (*pl.* messieurs) **5**

German allemand

girl une fille **15**

girlfriend une petite copine

to **give** donner

give me . . . donne-moi, donnez-moi... **9, 10**

please give me . . . s'il te plaît, donne-moi... **10**

good bon (bonne) **20**

good morning (afternoon) bonjour **1**

that's good c'est bien **20**

the weather's good (pleasant) il fait bon **12**

good-bye! au revoir!, salut! **3**

good-looking beau (bel, belle; *m.pl.* beaux) **17, 20**

grandfather un grand-père **7**

grandmother une grand-mère **7**

grape juice le jus de raisin **10**

gray gris **20**

great chouette, super **20**

green vert **20**

guitar une guitare **17**

H

hair les cheveux *m.* **E3**

he/she has dark hair il/elle est brun(e) **17**

half demi(e)

half past . . . ...heure(s) et demie **4**

half past midnight minuit et demi **4**

half past noon midi et demi **4**

hamburger un hamburger **9**

handbag un sac **17**

handsome beau (bel, belle; *m.pl.* beaux) **17, 20**

hard difficile **20**

hard drive (computer) le disque dur

to **have** *avoir **18**

do you have . . . ? est-ce que tu as...? **17**

I have j'ai **17**

I have to (must) je dois **13**

to have dinner at a restaurant dîner au restaurant **13**

he il **11, 14, 18**

he/she is . . . il/elle est + *nationality* **6**

headphones un casque
hello bonjour **1, 3**
help: may I help you? vous désirez? **10**
her: her name is . . . elle s'appelle... **6**
   what's her name? comment s'appelle-t-elle? **17**
here ici **14**
   here comes, here is voici **5**
   here's my mother/father voici ma mère/mon père **7**
hey! dis! **20**; tiens! **5, 18**
   hey there! dis donc! **20**
hi! salut! **3**
high school student un (une) élève **17**
his: his name is . . . il s'appelle... **6**
   what's his name? comment s'appelle-t-il? **17**
home, at home à la maison **14**; chez (moi, toi...)
homework assignment un devoir **B**
hot chaud **12**
   it's hot (weather) il fait chaud **12**
hot chocolate un chocolat **10**
hot dog un •hot dog **9**
how? comment? **16**
   how are you? comment allez-vous?, comment vas-tu?, ça va? **3**
   how do you say . . . in French? comment dit-on... en français? **B**
   how many hours . . .? combien d'heures...?
   how much does . . . cost? combien coûte...? **11**
   how much is that/this/it? c'est combien?, ça fait combien? **11**
   how old are you? quel âge as-tu? **7**
   how old is he/she? quel âge a-t-il/elle? **17**
   how old is your father/mother? quel âge a ton père/ta mère? **7**
   how's everything? ça va? **3**
   how's the weather? quel temps fait-il? **12**
hundred cent **6**

hungry avoir faim **9**
   are you hungry? tu as faim? **9**
   I'm hungry j'ai faim **9**
   to be hungry *avoir faim **18**

I

I je **14**
   I don't know je ne sais pas **B, 17**
   I have a date/appointment at . . . j'ai un rendez-vous à... **4**
   I know je sais **B, 17**
   I'm fine/okay ça va **3**
   I'm (very) well/so-so/(very) bad ça va (très) bien/comme ci, comme ça/(très) mal **3**
ice la glace **9**
   ice cream une glace **9**
in à **14**; dans **17**
   in (Boston) à (Boston) **14**
   in class en classe **14**
   in front of devant **17**
   in the afternoon de l'après-midi **4**
   in the morning/evening du matin/soir **4**
   in town en ville **14**
information highway l'autoroute de l'information, l'Inforoute, le Cyberespace
interactive interactif (interactive)
interesting intéressant **19**
internal CD-ROM drive un lecteur optique interne **B**
Internet Internet, le Net
to invite inviter **15**
is (*see* **to be**)
   is there? est-ce qu'il y a? **17**
   isn't it (so)? n'est-ce pas? **14**
   there is il y a **17**
it il, elle **14, 18**
   what time is it? quelle heure est-il? **4**
   who is it? qui est-ce? **5, 17**
it's . . . c'est... **5**
   it's . . . (o'clock) il est... heure(s) **4**
   it's . . . francs ça fait... francs **11**
   it's fine/nice/hot/cool/ cold/bad (weather) il fait

beau/bon/chaud/frais/froid/ mauvais **12**
   it's (June) first c'est le premier (juin) **8**
   it's not . . . ce n'est pas... **20**
   it's raining il pleut **12**
   it's snowing il neige **12**
Italian italien, italienne **19**

J

January janvier *m.* **8**
Japanese japonais(e) **19**
juice le jus
   apple juice le jus de pomme **10**
   grape juice le jus de raisin **10**
   orange juice le jus d'orange **10**
   tomato juice le jus de tomate **10**
July juillet *m.* **8**
June juin *m.* **8**

K

keyboard le clavier
kind gentil (gentille) **19**
know connaître *(people)*; savoir *(facts)*
   do you know . . .? tu connais...? **6**
   I (don't) know je (ne) sais (pas) **B, 17**

L

lady une dame **5**
large grand **17, 20**
laserdisc un CD vidéo, un vidéodisque **B**
   laserdisc player un lecteur de CD vidéo
left gauche
lemon soda la limonade **10**
to lend prêter à
   lend me prête-moi **11**
less : less than moins de
let's talk parlons
to like aimer **15**
   do you like? est-ce que tu aimes? **13**

I (also) like j'aime (aussi) **13**

I don't (always) like je n'aime pas (toujours) **13**

I like . . ., but I prefer . . . j'aime..., mais je préfère... **13**

I'd like je voudrais **9, 10, 13**

what does he/she look like? comment est-il/elle? **17**

what's he/she like? comment est-il/elle? **17**

what would you like? vous désirez? **10**

to **listen** écouter **15**

to listen to the radio écouter la radio **13**

little petit **17, 20**

a little (bit) un peu **15**

to **live** habiter **15**

living room (formal) un salon

to **look (at)** regarder **15**

look! tiens! **5, 18**

look at that regarde ça **17**

what does he/she look like? comment est-il/elle? **17**

lot: a lot beaucoup **15**

love: I'd love to je veux bien **13**

M ▬▬▬▬▬▬▬▬▬▬

to **make** *faire **16**

man un homme **17;** un monsieur *(polite term)* **5**

many beaucoup (de) **15**

map une carte **B**

March mars *m.* **8**

to **match** faire correspondre

match (sports) un match **16**

to play a match *faire un match **16**

May mai *m.* **8**

maybe peut-être **14**

me moi **1**

mean méchant **19**

mean: what does . . . mean? que veut dire...? **B**

Mexican mexicain(e) **19**

midnight minuit *m.* **4**

Miss Mademoiselle (Mlle) **3**

Monday lundi *m.* **8**

money l'argent *m.*

month un mois **8**

moped une mob (mobylette) **17**

more than plus: plus de

morning le matin

good morning bonjour **1**

in the morning du matin **4**

mother une mère **7**

this is my mother voici ma mère **7**

motorbike une mob (mobylette) **17**

motorcycle une moto **17**

motorscooter un scooter **17**

mouse (computer) une souris **B**

mousepad un tapis de souris

movie theater un cinéma **14**

at (to) the movies au cinéma **14**

Mr. Monsieur (M.) **3**

Mrs. Madame (Mme) **3**

multimedia le multimédia

much: very much beaucoup **15**

how much does . . . cost? combien coûte...? **11**

how much is it? ça fait combien?, c'est combien? **11**

I must je dois **13**

my mon, ma; mes **7**

my birthday is (March 2) mon anniversaire est (le 2 mars) **8**

my name is . . . je m'appelle... **1**

N ▬▬▬▬▬▬▬▬▬▬

name: his/her name is . . . il/elle s'appelle... **6**

my name is . . . je m'appelle... **1**

what's . . .'s name? comment s'appelle...? **6**

what's his/her name? comment s'appelle-t-il/elle? **17**

what's your name? comment t'appelles-tu? **1**

nasty méchant **19**

nationality la nationalité **2**

to **navigate** naviguer

neighbor un voisin, une voisine **17**

network (computer) un réseau

nice gentil (gentille), sympathique **19**

it's nice (beautiful) weather il fait beau **12**

night: tomorrow night demain soir **4**

nine neuf **1**

nineteen dix-neuf **2**

ninety quatre-vingt-dix **6**

ninth: ninth grade troisième: en troisième

no non **2, 14**

no . . . pas de... **18**

no? n'est-ce pas? **14**

noon midi *m.* **4**

not ne... pas **14**

not a, not any pas de **18**

not always pas toujours **13**

it's (that's) not ce n'est pas **20**

of course not! mais non! **14**

notebook un cahier **B**

November novembre *m.* **8**

now maintenant **15**

O ▬▬▬▬▬▬▬▬▬▬

o'clock heure(s)

at . . . o'clock à... heures **4**

it's . . . o'clock il est... heure(s) **4**

object un objet **17**

October octobre *m.* **8**

of de **14**

of course not! mais non! **14**

of course! bien sûr **13**

of whom de qui **16**

office: tourist office office *m.* de tourisme

often souvent **15**

oh: oh, really? ah bon? **16**

okay d'accord **13**

I'm okay ça va **3**

old: he/she is . . . (years old) il/elle a... ans **7**

how old are you? quel âge as-tu? **7**

how old is he/she? quel âge a-t-il/elle? **17**

how old is your father/mother? quel âge a ton père/ta mère? **7**

I'm . . . (years old) j'ai... ans **7**

to be . . . (years old) *avoir... ans **18**

omelet une omelette **9**

on sur **17**

on Mondays le lundi **18**

on the average en moyenne

on vacation en vacances **14**

one un, une **1**

open *ouvrir

    open . . . ouvre... (ouvrez...) **B**

or ou **2, 14**

orange (color) orange (*inv.*) **20**

    orange juice le jus d'orange **10**

to **organize** organiser **15**

over there là-bas **14**

    that (one), over there ça, là-bas **17**

to **own** *avoir **18**

P ▬▬▬▬▬▬▬▬▬

p.m. du soir **4**

pain: a pain pénible **20**

paper le papier **B**

    sheet of paper une feuille de papier **B**

party une boum, une fête, une soirée

past: half past . . . ...heure(s) et demie **4**

    quarter past . . . ...heure(s) et quart **4**

to **pay: pay attention** *faire attention **16**

pen un stylo **B, 17**

pencil un crayon **B, 17**

people des gens *m.* **18**; on

    people who like to use the Internet les internautes, les cybernautes

per: per day par jour

perhaps peut-être **14**

person une personne **5, 17**

pet un animal (*pl.* animaux) domestique **7**

to **phone** téléphoner **15**

piece: piece of chalk un morceau de craie **B**

pink rose **20**

pizza une pizza **9**

to **play** jouer **15**

    to play a game (match) *faire un match **16**

    to play basketball (soccer, tennis, volleyball) jouer au basket (au foot, au tennis, au volley) **13**

pleasant sympathique **19**

it's pleasant (good) weather il fait bon **12**

please s'il vous plaît (formal) **10**; s'il te plaît (informal) **9**

    please give me . . . s'il te plaît, donne-moi... **10**

poorly mal **3**

poster une affiche **17**

to **prefer** préférer

    I prefer je préfère **13**

    I like . . ., but I prefer . . . j'aime..., mais je préfère... **13**

pretty joli **17**

printer une imprimante

pupil un (une) élève **17**

Q ▬▬▬▬▬▬▬▬▬

quarter un quart

    quarter of . . . ... heure(s) moins le quart **4**

    quarter past . . . ... heure(s) et quart **4**

quickly vite

R ▬▬▬▬▬▬▬▬▬

racket une raquette **17**

radio une radio **17**

    to listen to the radio écouter la radio **13**

rain: it's raining il pleut **12**

rarely rarement **15**

rather assez **19**

to **read** lire

really: oh, really? ah bon? **16**

record un disque **17**

red rouge **20**

restaurant: at (to) the restaurant au restaurant **14**

    to have dinner at a restaurant dîner au restaurant **13**

right vrai **20**; droite

    right? n'est-ce pas? **14**

    all right d'accord **13**

room une chambre **17**; une salle

to **run** (referring to objects) marcher **17**

S ▬▬▬▬▬▬▬▬▬

salad une salade **9**

same: the same things les mêmes choses

sandwich un sandwich **9**

Saturday samedi *m.* **8**

    see you Saturday! à samedi! **8**

to **say** *dire

    say! dis (donc)! **20**

    how do you say . . . in French? comment dit-on... en français? **B**

school friend un (une) camarade **17**

screen (computer, TV) un écran

season une saison **12**

    in every season en toute saison

see: see you tomorrow! à demain! **8**

seldom rarement **15**

to **send** envoyer

    to send an e-mail message envoyer un message par e-mail

    to send a voice mail message envoyer un message par messagerie vocale

September septembre *m.* **8**

seven sept **1**

seventeen dix-sept **2**

seventy soixante-dix **5**

she elle **14, 18**

sheet of paper une feuille de papier **B**

shoe une chaussure

short court; petit **17, 20**

    he/she is short il/elle est petit(e) **17**

to **shut** fermer **B**

shy timide **19**

silly bête **19**

to **sing** chanter **13, 15**

sir Monsieur (M.) **3**

sister une soeur **7**

six six **1**

sixteen seize **2**

sixty soixante **3, 5**

small petit **17, 20**

snow: it's snowing il neige **12**

so alors **19**

so-so comme ci, comme ça **3**

    everything's (going) so-so ça va comme ci, comme ça **3**

soda un soda **10**

    lemon soda une limonade **10**

software un logiciel

some des 18; quelques 17; du, de la, de l'

sorry: to be sorry regretter
  I'm sorry, but (I cannot) je regrette, mais (je ne peux pas) 13

Spanish espagnol(e) 19

to **speak** parler 15
  to speak French (English, Spanish) parler français (anglais, espagnol) 13

spring le printemps 12
  in the spring au printemps 12

steak un steak 9
  steak and French fries un steak-frites 9

stereo set une chaîne stéréo 17

student (high school) un (une) élève 17; **(college)** un étudiant, une étudiante 17

studies les études f.

to **study** étudier 13, 15

stupid bête 19

summer l'été m. 12
  in the summer en été 12

Sunday dimanche m. 8

supper: to have (eat) supper dîner 15

sure bien sûr 13
  sure! mais oui! 14

to **swim** nager 15
  I like to swim j'aime nager 13

Swiss suisse 19

T ▬▬▬▬▬▬▬

table une table B, 17

to **take** *prendre B
  to take a trip *faire un voyage 16

to **talk** parler 15
  let's talk parlons

tall grand 17, 20

tape: tape recorder un magnétophone 17
  cassette tape une cassette B, 17

tea le thé 10

teacher un (une) prof 5, 17; un professeur 17

telephone un téléphone 17

to **telephone** téléphoner 15

television la télé B, 17
  to watch television regarder la télé 13

ten dix 1, 2

tennis le tennis
  to play tennis jouer au tennis 13

tenth dixième

terrific chouette 20; extra 20; super 20

test un examen
  to pass a test réussir à un examen 27

than que

thank you merci 3

that que; ce, cet, cette
  that is . . . c'est... 17, 20
  that (one), over there ça, là-bas 17
  that which, what ce que
  what's that? qu'est-ce que c'est? 17

that's . . . c'est... 5, 17, 20; voilà 5
  that's . . . francs ça fait... francs 11
  that's bad c'est mal 20
  that's a good idea! c'est une bonne idée!
  that's good (fine) c'est bien 20
  that's not . . . ce n'est pas... 20

the le, la, l' 6, 18; les 18

theater un théâtre
  movie theater un cinéma

their leur, leurs

them eux, elles; les
  (to) them leur
  themselves eux-mêmes

then alors 19; ensuite

there là 14
  there is (are) il y a 17
  there is (here comes someone) voilà 5
  there is (some) il y a + du, de la; voilà + du, de la *(partitive)*
  over there là-bas 14
  that (one), over there ça, là-bas 17; ce...-là
  what is there? qu'est-ce qu'il y a? 17

these ces
  these are ce sont 20

they ils, elles 14; eux; on
  they are ce sont 20

thin: to get thin maigrir

thing une chose
  things are going (very) badly ça va (très) mal 3
  the same things les mêmes choses

to **think** penser
  to think of penser de, trouver
  to think that penser que
  what do you think of . . .? comment trouves-tu...?, qu'est-ce que tu penses de...?

third troisième

thirsty: to be thirsty *avoir soif
  are you thirsty? tu as soif? 10
  I'm thirsty j'ai soif 10

thirteen treize 2

thirty trente 3

trois three 1
  trois heures et demie 4

this ce, cet, cette
  this is . . . voici... 5

those ces

those are ce sont 20

thousand mille

Thursday jeudi m. 8

tie une cravate

tights des collants m.

time: at what time is . . .? à quelle heure est...? 4
  at what time? à quelle heure? 4
  what time is it? quelle heure est-il? 4

title un titre

to à 14; chez
  to (the) au, à la, à l', aux
  in order to pour
  to class en classe 14
  to someone's house chez + person
  to whom à qui 16

today aujourd'hui 8
  today is (Wednesday) aujourd'hui, c'est (mercredi) 8

toilet les toilettes f.

tomato une tomate
  tomato juice le jus de tomate 10

tomorrow demain **8**
    tomorrow afternoon demain après-midi
    tomorrow is (Thursday) demain, c'est (jeudi) **8**
    tomorrow morning demain matin
    tomorrow night (evening) demain soir
    see you tomorrow! à demain! **8**
tonight ce soir
too aussi **2, 15**; trop
    too bad! dommage! **15**
touring bus un autocar, un car
tourist: tourist office office *(m.)* de tourisme
town un village
    in town en ville **14**
track suit un survêtement
train un train
    by train en train
to **travel** voyager **13, 15**
    trip: to take a trip *faire un voyage **16**
trousers un pantalon
true vrai **20**
T-shirt un tee-shirt
Tuesday mardi *m.* **8**
tuna le thon
to **turn** tourner
    to turn on *mettre
TV la télé **B, 17**
    to watch TV regarder la télé **13**
twelfth douzième
twelve douze **2**
twenty vingt **2, 3**
two deux **1**

U

ugly moche
uncle un oncle **7**
under sous **17**
to **understand** *comprendre
    I (don't) understand je (ne) comprends (pas) **B**
understanding compréhensif (compréhensive)
unfashionable démodé
United States les États-Unis *m.*
upstairs en •haut

---

us nous
    (to) us nous
to **use** utiliser

V

vacation les vacances *f.*
    on vacation en vacances **14**
    summer vacation les grandes vacances
VCR (videocassette recorder) un magnétoscope **B**
veal le veau
vegetable un légume
very très **19**
    very well très bien **15**
    very much beaucoup **15**
videocassette une vidéocassette **B**
videodisc un CD vidéo **B**
    videodisc player un lecteur de CD/vidéo
violin un violon
to **visit (place)** visiter **15**; (people) rendre visite à
voicemail la messagerie vocale
volleyball le volley (volleyball)

W

to **wait (for)** attendre
walk une promenade
to **take (go for) a walk** *faire une promenade à pied **16**
to **walk** *aller à pied; marcher **17**
walkman un walkman **17**
to **want** *avoir envie de; *vouloir
    do you want . . .? tu veux...? **9**
    do you want to . . .? est-ce que tu veux...? **13**
    I don't want . . . je ne veux pas... **13**
    I want . . . je veux... **13**
    I want to je veux bien
    what do you want? qu'est-ce que tu veux? **9**; vous désirez? **10**
wanted voulu *(p.p. of* *vouloir)*
warm chaud **12**
    to be warm (people) *avoir chaud
    it's warm (weather) il fait chaud **12**
was été *(p.p. of* *être)*

---

to **wash** laver
to **waste** perdre
watch une montre **17**
to **watch** regarder **15**
    to watch TV regarder la télé **13**
water l'eau *f.*
    mineral water l'eau minérale
to **waterski** *faire du ski nautique
waterskiing le ski nautique
we nous **14**; on
to **wear** *mettre; porter
    weather: how's (what's) the weather? quel temps fait-il? **12**
    it's . . . weather il fait... **12**
Wednesday mercredi *m.* **8**
week une semaine **8**
    last week la semaine dernière
    next week la semaine prochaine
    this week cette semaine
weekend un weekend
    last weekend le weekend dernier
    next weekend le weekend prochain
    this weekend ce weekend
weight: to gain weight grossir
well bien **15**
    everything's going (very) well ça va (très) bien **3**
well! eh bien!
    well then alors **19**
went allé (p.p. of *aller)
what comment? quoi? **17**; qu'est-ce que **16**
    what color? de quelle couleur? **20**
    what day is it? quel jour est-ce? **8**
    what do you think of . . .? comment trouves-tu...?, qu'est-ce que tu penses de...?
    what do you want? qu'est-ce que tu veux? **9**; vous désirez? **10**
    what does . . . mean? que veut dire...? **B**
    what does he/she look like? comment est-il/elle? **17**
    what is it? qu'est-ce que c'est? **17**

what is there? qu'est-ce qu'il y a? **17**

what time is it? quelle heure est-il? **4**

what would you like? vous désirez? **10**

what's . . .'s name? comment s'appelle...? **6**

what's he/she like? comment est-il/elle? **17**

what's his/her name? comment s'appelle-t-il/elle? **17**

what's that? qu'est-ce que c'est? **17**

what's the date? quelle est la date? **8**

what's the price? quel est le prix?

what's the weather? quel temps fait-il? **12**

what's your address? quelle est ton adresse? **21**

what's your name? comment t'appelles-tu? **1**

at what time is . . .? à quelle heure est...? **4**

at what time? à quelle heure? **4, 16**

when quand **16**

when is your birthday? c'est quand, ton anniversaire? **8**

where où **14, 16**

where is . . .? où est...? **14**

where is it? où est-ce?

from where? d'où?

whether si

which quel (quelle)

that which, what ce que

white blanc (blanche) **20**

who qui **16**

who's that/this? qui est-ce? **5, 17**

whom: about whom? de qui? **16**

for whom? pour qui? **16**

of whom? de qui? **16**

to whom? à qui? **16**

with whom? avec qui? **16**

why pourquoi **16**

wife une femme

to win gagner

window une fenêtre **B, 17**

to windsurf *faire de la planche à voile

windsurfing la planche à voile

winter l'hiver *m.* **12**

in the winter en hiver **12**

with avec **14**

with me avec moi **13**

with you avec toi **13**

with whom? avec qui? **16**

"with it" dans le coup

woman une dame (polite term) **5**; une femme **17**

to work travailler **13, 15**; *(referring to objects)* marcher **17**

does the radio work? est-ce que la radio marche? **17**

it (doesn't) work(s) well il/elle (ne) marche (pas) bien **17**

world le monde

World Wide Web le Web ("la toile d'araignée")

would: I'd like je voudrais **9, 10, 13**; j'aimerais

to write *écrire

wrong faux (fausse) **20**

to be wrong *avoir tort

Y ▬▬▬▬▬▬▬▬

year un an, une année **8**

he/she is . . . (years old) il/elle a... ans **7**

I'm . . . (years old) j'ai... ans **7**

to be . . . (years old) *avoir... ans **18**

yellow jaune **20**

yes oui **2, 14**; *(to a negative question)* si! **18**

yes, of course oui, bien sûr **13**

yes, okay (all right) oui, d'accord **13**

yes, thank you oui, merci **13**

yesterday hier

yesterday afternoon hier après-midi

yesterday morning hier matin

yogurt le yaourt

you tu, vous **14**; on

you are . . . tu es + *nationality* **2**

and you? et toi? **1**

(to) you te, vous

your ton, ta; tes **7**; votre; vos

what's your name? comment t'appelles-tu? **1**

young jeune **17**

Z ▬▬▬▬▬▬▬▬

zero zéro **1**

Photo Credits

Cover: photo: Owen Franken © D. C. Heath; cover design, Elliot Kreloff.
All text photos by Owen Franken, © D. C. Heath, except the following: 2: *mr*, Palmer-Brilliant © D.C. Heath; 2: *bl*, Jack Elness/Miller-Comstock; 3: *tl*, P.W. Holzgraf/ Monkmeyer Press; 3: *tr*, Kennon Cooke/Valan Photos; 3: *ml*, VPG/Woods; 3: *mr*, Susan Doheny; 3: *bl*, Jack Mitchell/ Boston Ballet Co.; 3: *br*, Andrew Brilliant; 6: *b* David Ball/The Picture Cube; 7: *m*, Brian Robb; 7: *b*, G. Barone /Monkmeyer Press; 12, 13 Adine Sagalyn; 16: *t*, Yves Levy; 19: *t*, Ann Purcell; 19: *b*, Carl Purcell; 20: *l*, Mark Antman/The Image Works; 23: *bl*, 24: br, Patrick Pipard, Adine Sagalyn; 26: VPG/Woods; 28: *b*, Yves Levy; 30: *br*, Palmer-Brilliant © D.C. Heath; 32: Peter Menzel/Stock Boston; 34: Yves Levy; 36: *t*, VPG/Woods; 37: *t*, Patrick Pipard; 38: *tm*, Nancy Sheehan; 38: *bm*, Patrick Pipard; 41: *m*, Ken Kaminsky/Nawrocki Stock Photo; 41: *b*, G. Zimbel/Monkmeyer Press; 45: *t*, Adine Sagalyn; 47: Patrick Pipard; 52: *m*, Palmer-Brilliant © D.C. Heath; 53: *tl, tm*, Patrick Pipard; 53: *tr*, Palmer-Brilliant © D.C. Heath; 53: *bl*, Adine Sagalyn; 53: *bm*, Henebry Photography © D.C. Heath; 54: *tl*, J. A. Wilkinson/Valan Photos; 54: *tm*, Kevin Galvin/Stock Boston; 54: *tr*, H. Mark Weidman; 54: *ml*, © Horii/-International Stock Photo; 54: *mm*, Ed Carlin/The Picture Cube; 54: *mr*, Mike Malyszko/Stock Boston; 54: *b*, Lynn McLaren/The Picture Cube; 57: *t*, J. Charlas; 57: *b*, Sophie Reiter; 58: J. Charlas; 61: Yves Levy; 63: *t*, 64b, 65 Adine Sagalyn; 66: *b*, 67 m, *b* Susan Doheny; 69, 71: *t*, 72: *b*, 73: br, Adine Sagalyn; 76–77: Sophie Reiter; 77: *t, mr, br*, 78: *tl, bl, br*, Patrick Pipard; 78: *mr*, Sophie Reiter; 78: *tr, ml, ml*, Yves Levy; 78: *tm*, VPG/Woods; 79: Yves Levy; 80: *tl,* "The Bridge at Mantes," Musée du Louvre; 80: *tr*, Scala Art Resource; 80: *b,* Yves Levy; 84–85: Patrick Pipard; 86: Yves Levy; 86–87: Adine Sagalyn; 87: *t*, Patrick Pipard; 87, 89: *mr*, 90: Yves Levy; 92: Adine Sagalyn; 83: Yves Levy; 94: Sophie Reiter; 96, 97 *t, mr* Patrick Pipard; 97: *ml*, Yves Levy; 101, 104: *tr, bm, br*, Patrick Pipard; 110: Yves Levy; 118: *t, b*, Carl Purcell; 118: *m*, J. Pavlovsky/ Sygma; 119: *t*, Yves Levy; 119: *b*, UNESCO/Français-Hamell/Interphot; 130: *b*, Richard Lucas/The Image Works; 133: #4, Carl Purcell; 134: *l*, Yves Levy; 135: *t*, © D.C. Heath; 134–135: Yves Levy; 138: Adine Sagalyn; 139: *t*, D. Logan/H. Armstrong Roberts; 139: *l-r* Richard Pasley/Stock Boston, Jocelyn Boutin/The Picture Cube, Ann Purcell, Bob Daemmrich/Stock Boston, Carl Purcell, Fujihara-Ivamur/Monkmeyer Press; 140, 143: Patrick Pipard; 144: Adine Sagalyn; 146: Palmer-Brilliant © D.C. Heath; 147: Adine Sagalyn; 148: *l*, Mike Mazzaschi/Stock Boston; 148: *r*, Robert Fried/Stock Boston; 149: *t*, Dallas & John Heaton/Stock Boston; 149: *b*, © Tabuteau/The Image Works; 154: Patrick Pipard; 160: *r*, Yves Levy; 162: *l*, Adine Sagalyn; 162: *r*, Patrick Pipard; 163: *l*, Yves Levy; 163: *r*, Sophie Reiter; 167: Patrick Pipard; 169: *tl*, Sipa Press; 169: *tr*, Paul J. Sutton/Duomo; 169: *bl*, Claude Gassian; 169: *br*, Pool Passation de Pouvoir/Mitterand-Chirac/Gamma; 170: Patrick Pipard; 171: *t*, Philippe Gontier/The Image Works; 171: *b*, Palmer-Brilliant © D.C. Heath; 175: Patrick Pipard; 176: Adine Sagalyn; 177: Andrew Brilliant; 181: Sophie Reiter; 182: *b*, Meauxsoone/Sygma.